Leading Primary
Geography

The essential handbook for all teachers

Edited by Tessa Willy

Geographical Association

To access your online support see page 164

Acknowledgements

I would like to thank the exceptional writers and all those who have supported them; it has been a privilege and a pleasure to work with them on this book. Many thanks are also due to the wider community of primary geographers, teachers, teacher educators and past students, as well as my patient and encouraging partner, Justine, my family and friends. I would also like to convey my sincere thanks to Steve Rawlinson who was supported me throughout the editing as well as writing the introduction with me and finally, and most importantly, to Anna Grandfield who has been a constant 24/7 support, guide and inspiration, and an absolute joy to work alongside.

Dedication

This book is dedicated to Roger Carter (1938-2017). The very epitome of a gentleman, a geographer and an educator, Roger forged a new path for primary publishing at the GA as Editor of the first *Handbook of Primary Geography* in 1998, and laid the foundations on which this book is built. It is befitting to reflect Roger's spirit in the passionate enthusiasm and support offered here.

© Geographical Association, 2019

This book is copyright under the Berne Convention. All rights are reserved. Apart from any fair dealing for the purpose of private study, research, criticism or review, as permitted under the Copyright, Designs and Patents Act 1988, no part of this publication may be reproduced, stored in a retrieval system, or transmitted in any form or by any means, electronic, electrical, chemical, mechanical, optical, photocopying, recording or otherwise, without the prior written permission of the copyright owner. To request copyright permission for any of the material held by the Geographical Association, please follow the link at: www.geography.org.uk/Contact-Us. The views expressed in this publication are those of the authors and do not necessarily represent those of the Geographical Association.

ISBN 978-1-84377-450-1 (print)
ISBN 978-1-84377-451-8 (eBook)
First published 2019
Impression number 10 9 8 7 6 5 4 3 2 1

Published by the Geographical Association, 160 Solly Street, Sheffield S1 4BF
Company number 07139068
Website: www.geography.org.uk
E-mail: info@geography.org.uk
The Geographical Association is a registered charity: no 1135148

Copy edited by Fran Royle
Designed and typeset by Ledgard Jepson Ltd
Printed and bound in the UK by Severn

The Geographical Association is the leading subject association for all teachers of geography. Our charitable mission is to further geographical knowledge and understanding through education. Our journals, publications, professional events, website, and local and online networks support teachers and share their ideas and practice. The GA represents the views of geography teachers and plays a leading role in public debate relating to geography and education.

Section opener images

1: Ash tree © Artorn Thongtukit/Shutterstock.com. 2: Road to Superstition Mountain, Arizona, USA © Joe Belanger/Shutterstock.com. 3: Lighthouse at Fanad Head, Co. Donegal, Northern Ireland © Greg Fellman/Shutterstock.com. 4: Wind turbines in Khao Kho Park, Thailand © strucuresxx/Shutterstock.com. 5: Orange tree grove in Andalucia, Spain © Sopatnicki/Shutterstock.com. 6: Tributaries in the Everglades National Park, Florida, USA © Jon Chica/Shutterstock.com. 7: Wheat field © djgis/Shutterstock.com.

Foreword

Why do we have schools and what is education for? As we move into a new decade of the twenty first century, this is a question that seems even more important now than it did in the past. There are many possible responses. Some people see education as equipping young people for the world of work; others focus on the transmission of knowledge and cultural heritage. Pupils' needs and personal fulfilment form another enduring thread.

Of course, these different perspectives overlap, but whether you focus on employment, socialisation or personal development, geography has a part to play. For example, geography graduates are highly successful in a wide range of jobs and careers; geographical perspectives are essential in understanding the modern, multi-cultural world. The way that geography helps build a sense of personal identify and belonging makes a vital contribution to human well-being.

Geography also contributes to human endeavour at an even deeper level. Whether we are willing to acknowledge it or not, we now know that humanity is experiencing the foreshocks of a crisis that could threaten the very foundations of our civilization. Climate change, the loss of biodiversity and soil degradation are already well-advanced; poverty, inequality, conflict and migration are indicators of social and cultural stress. The concepts that geographers use – place, space, scale, interconnections, environment, cultural diversity and sustainability – illuminate our understanding of current issues at a deep and lasting level. As a curriculum subject, geography is part of a basic toolkit that young people need at their disposal if they are to play their part in the world as events unfold and evolve.

Helping pupils to understand geographical perspectives is no easy matter. The pedagogical skill of the teacher sits alongside subject knowledge as key elements of successful practice. A creative geography curriculum blends personal and transmitted knowledge, recognises affective as well as cognitive aspects of learning, addresses controversial issues and respects the integrity of pupils' voice. Sometimes the impact that teachers have on their pupils is not immediately apparent, but those who affirm they are interested in geography as adults often say they were inspired by a teacher in their childhood. Quite simply, geography educators, and that means every teacher in a primary school today, have the potential to light a fire in young people that can last a lifetime.

This book is an invitation – it is an invitation to introduce pupils to geography not as a set of tasks to be completed but as a range of experiences that they can savour and enjoy. Written by a team of leading practitioners, it encapsulates the advice and wisdom that is deeply rooted across the primary geography education community. It aims to provide you with guidance and ideas to address the perils and the promises that lie ahead. The focus is on solutions rather than problems – on hope rather than despair. There may never have been a time when a geography education has been more urgent or had so much to offer. As Nelson Mandela said in his speech at Madison Park High School, Boston, in 1990, 'Education is the most powerful weapon you can use to change the world'.

Dr Stephen Scoffham
Geographical Association President 2018–19

Contents

Foreword	3
■ **Section 1:** Introduction	6
Steve Rawlinson and Tessa Willy	
Navigating primary geography	8
Geography in the primary school	9
The value of geography	10
Geography's place	11
Supporting primary geography professionals	12
Nurturing young geographers	14
■ **Section 2:** Key concepts	16
Simon Catling	
Geography's significance	18
Understanding geographical knowledge	20
Propositional geographical knowledge	21
Substantive geographical knowledge	21
Procedural geographical knowledge	22
Thinking geographically	22
Connecting through environmental geography	25
■ **Section 3:** Key skills	28
Stephen Pickering	
Geographical skills	30
Making use of maps	30
Maps for a purpose	31
Maps and stories	33
Maps and technology	34
Making meaning with vocabulary	34
Making sense through graphicacy	35
Making learning real through fieldwork and the outdoors	36
Learning outdoors around the school	38
Learning outdoors further afield	40
Developing skills	40
■ **Section 4:** Teaching approaches	42
Richard Hatwood	
Different teaching approaches	44
Start local, go global	44
New and topical content	44
Questioning	45
Enquiry	46
Planning for enquiry	47
Critical thinking	47
Debate	48
Teaching for a sustainable world	51
Planning for sustainability	52
■ **Section 5:** Geography in your curriculum	54
Richard Greenwood	
Geography in the whole-school curriculum	56
The curriculum 'big picture'	56
Geography's place in the curriculum	56
Adapting to changes in national curricula	56
Curriculum making	57
Fundamentals of planning	58
Everyday geography	58
Powerful knowledge	59
Teachers' subject knowledge	60
Personalising your geography teaching	61
Local geography	61
Topical geography	61
Enquiry geography	62
Cross-curricularity	63
Pupil voice	63

Section 6: Integrating geography — 66

Introduction to teaching geography in a cross-curricular way — 68
Leszek Iwaskow

- Subject knowledge — 68
- Powerful ideas — 69
- Keeping in touch with the curriculum — 69
- Geographical themes for a cross-curricular approach — 72
- Support for a cross-curricular approach — 75

Integrating geography with the core subjects — 77
Julia Tanner

- Integrating with English — 77
- Speaking, listening, reading, writing and drama — 77
- Start with a story — 78
- Non-fiction genres — 79
- Drama and role play — 79
- Integrating with mathematics — 80
- Mathematics and geographical enquiries — 83
- Integrating with science — 83

Integrating with the foundation subjects —
Ben Ballin

- Finding meaningful overlaps — 88
- Integrating with the humanities — 88
- Religious education — 88
- PSHE — 89
- Citizenship — 89
- History — 91
- Integrating with the arts — 94
- Art and design — 94
- Music — 96
- Drama — 96

Integrating geography through topics —
Susan Pike

- Why teach geography through topics? — 98
- Benefits to pupils of topic-based learning — 98
- Advantages to teachers of topic-based teaching — 99
- Drawbacks of topic-based teaching — 100
- How can we plan for topics? — 100
- Topics based on everyday geography — 102
- Topics about distant places — 105
- Topics based on physical, human and environmental geography — 107

Section 7: Effective subject leadership — 112
Paula Owens

- Leading geography in your classroom — 114
- Informal conversations — 114
- Formal conversations — 115
- Indirect channels — 118
- Essential geography resources — 119
- Leading geography in your school — 122
- Developing a vision — 123
- Creating a school geography policy — 125
- Planning a curriculum — 126
- Managing change — 128
- Creating an action plan — 135
- Celebrating geography — 135
- Assessment and progression — 135
- Transition — 147
- Professional development — 149
- The Primary Geography Quality Mark — 150
- Evidence-informed teaching — 151
- Action research — 151
- Subject association support — 152
- CPD — 153
- Quality assurance — 155
- Subject leader impact and inspection — 156

Index — 158

Online support — 164

Your Geographical Association — 165

Contributors — 166

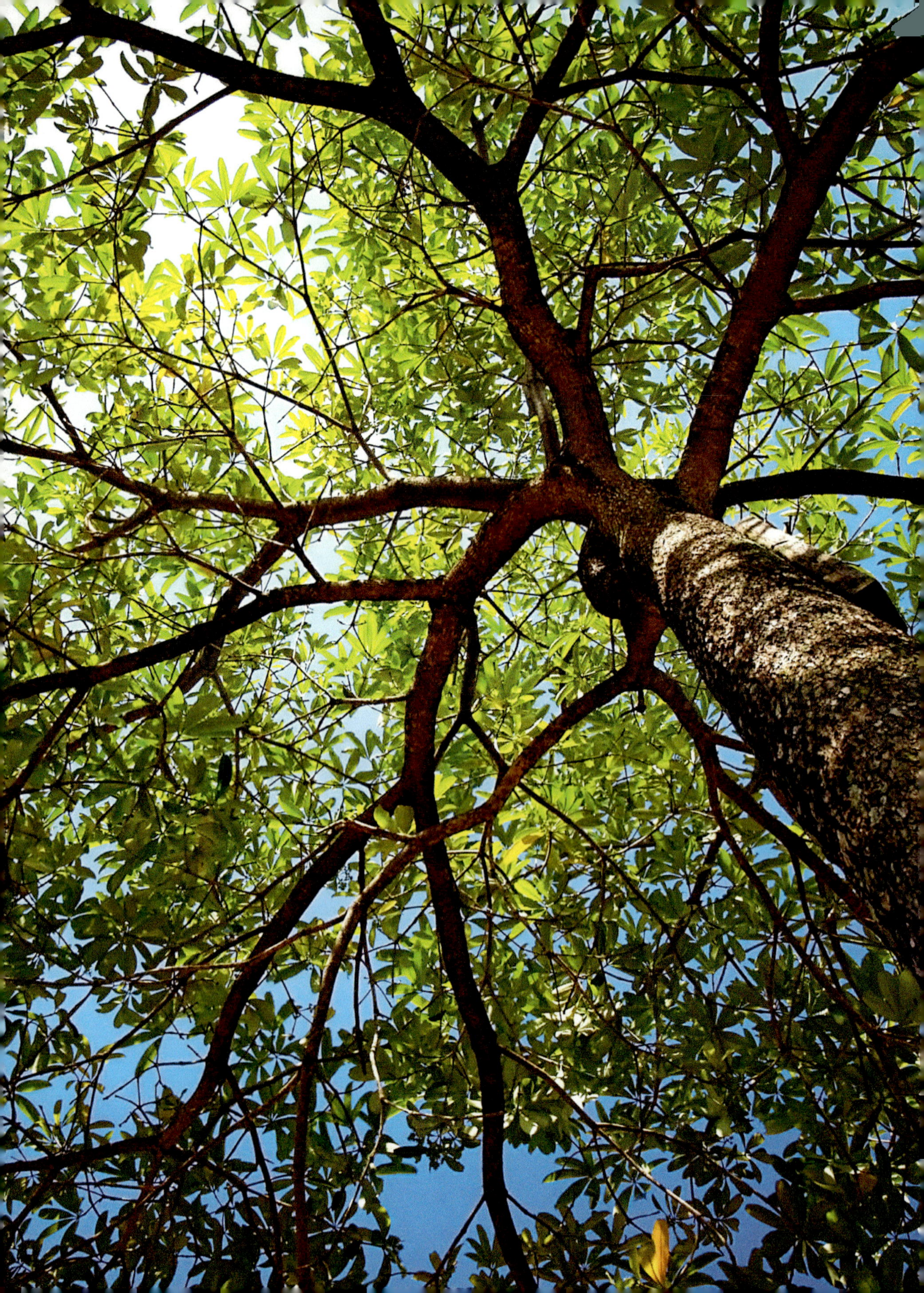

SECTION 1

Introduction

Tessa Willy and
Steve Rawlinson

This section outlines the purpose and layout of the book and its online support, and the main themes developed in subsequent sections. It introduces ideas about the nature and value of primary geography and how you can develop and invigorate the subject in your school and local community whether you are a student, class teacher, or a new or experienced subject leader. It encourages you to nurture young geographers through engaging and empowering learning, to develop their curiosity and understanding of the world around them and instil in them the desire to find out more. We hope it will also help you to develop your own inner geographer and enthusiasm for the subject.

Navigating primary geography

Designed to be the definitive guide for all primary geography leaders, class teachers and trainee teachers, this book offers:

- a carefully considered approach to planning for, and delivering, outstanding geography across the full primary age range, in and outside the classroom
- a clear statement of what constitutes outstanding primary geography and a rationale for geography's place in the primary curriculum.

It has been written by experienced leaders in the field of primary geography who understand the pressures facing teachers. They identify the techniques and pedagogies you need to meet the everyday demands of the classroom, and suggest approaches that are flexible and adaptable to changing local and national curriculum requirements (Figure 1). Whether you are a subject leader, classroom teacher, student teacher or student educator, reference to, and familiarity with, this handbook will support these aspects of your role:

- your subject and pedagogical knowledge
- your understanding of geography's importance and potential as a pivotal subject in the primary curriculum.

The book is supported by online resources, including links to keep you up to date on the constant changes and developments in primary education and beyond. For details on how to access your online material see page 164.

For Early Years practitioners the book offers perspectives on an integrated and inclusive curriculum as is routinely found in Early Years pedagogies. Indeed, Section 6 explores the kind of holistic learning taking place so effectively with the youngest pupils, and the ideas and exemplars can be adapted to earlier age phases and your particular pupils. Further reading on approaches to geography in the Early Years can be found via the online resources (see page 164).

Figure 1: A happy geography subject leader feels that...
Pupil's work by the Happy Geography Club, Swanmore CE (Aided) Primary School.

> I understand how I am connected to other people and places in the world.

> I take an active part in all my learning.

> I think about my future and want to help shape it with optimism and hope.

> My learning is exciting, playful and FUN!

> I understand more about where I live and the world around me so I can help look after it.

> My ideas are valued.

> I believe in myself and what I can achieve.

> I ask questions and find out about things.

> I enjoy learning with all my different classmates.

> I learn everywhere, inside and outside the classroom.

Figure 2: In great geography lessons, pupils feel that...
Pupil's work by the Happy Geography Club, Swanmore CE (Aided) Primary School.

Similarly, the exemplars and case studies throughout the book can be developed and extended for older pupils. It is the pedagogy and the approach that is important; the content can be adapted. We have not prescribed how you should teach but rather offer guidance to inspire adaptation and foster your own curriculum-making skills.

Geography in the primary school

At the heart of your role as a teacher or leader of geography is what your pupils need from you and their geography education (Figure 2).

This book offers guidance on how to help your pupils to fulfil these aspirations. They will learn to explore their world geographically by:

- asking geographical questions
- assessing and critically evaluating potential answers to those questions
- making reasoned judgements on the evidence
- understanding and empathising with the views of others
- considering possible actions/reactions and their consequences.

Exploring the world in this way will develop the instinctive geographer in every child and enable them to view, and plan for, the future – not as a set of problems to be overcome, but as a series of challenging but comprehensible opportunities, to which they can respond from a position of knowledge and understanding. They can explore their aspirations, offer explanations and propose solutions that are realistic and achievable.

The value of geography

Geography is all around us, and even in the simplest of daily activities pupils can learn geography and act as geographers (Figure 3). In addition, the quotations in Figure 4, from a range of different sources, demonstrate the wide range of primary geography's reach and ambition, in terms not just of children's education but their lives.

Too often, geography has been undervalued in the primary context. Activities that are geographical in nature are often not recognised as such by other teachers, Head teachers, parents or even the pupils themselves. This book aims to reposition geography on the curriculum map by asking you to consider some fundamental questions about the subject in your class, school and community.

In your classroom
- Do you consider geographical perspectives in other lessons?
- Does your classroom offer opportunities to develop geographical thinking and talking, e.g. by the nature and variety of the reference books that are available?
- Are geographical issues discussed and developed in other subject lessons?
- Do you think about geography as an umbrella subject for topic work?
- Do you consider how an aspect of geography can be used as a context for learning in a core subject such as maths or English?
- Are you able to provide a rich menu of nourishing geographical learning that satisfies the growing environmental appetites of the pupils in your class?
- Do you plan opportunities for pupils to learn outside the classroom and use the outdoor environment and natural world as a medium for meaningful teaching and learning?

In your school
- How does your school perceive geography?
- What does 'geography' mean in your school?
- Is geography supported by the SLT?
- Are trips out encouraged and made easy to plan and manage?
- Does anyone ever ask how geography could support other lessons or how it may be integrated into a particular topic?
- Are you encouraged to share geographical pedagogy, such as enquiry, with history or science?

Figure 3: In all aspects of their lives pupils show that they are natural geographers... Pupil's work by the Happy Geography Club, Swanmore CE (Aided) Primary School.

> 'A high-quality geography education should inspire in pupils a curiosity and fascination about the world and its people that will remain with them for the rest of their lives. Teaching should equip pupils with knowledge about diverse places, people, resources and natural and human environments, together with a deep understanding of Earth's key physical and human processes. As pupils progress, their growing knowledge about the world should help them to deepen their understanding of the interaction between physical and human processes, and of the formation and use of landscapes and environments. Geographical knowledge, understanding and skills provide the framework and approaches that explain how Earth's features at different scales are shaped, interconnected and change over time' (DfE, 2013, p. 184).
>
> 'Geography is a living, breathing subject, constantly adapting itself to change. It is dynamic and relevant. For me geography is a great adventure with a purpose. Geography is a subject which holds the key to our future' (Michael Palin)
>
> 'The study of geography is about more than just memorizing places on a map. It's about understanding the complexity of our world, appreciating the diversity of cultures that exists across continents. And in the end, it's about using all that knowledge to help bridge divides and bring people together' (US President, Barack Obama).
>
> 'Geography is the subject that knits together people and the planet and at a time when we see how intrinsic that link is and why sustainability matters, it's never been clearer cut. My message to [all primary teachers] is 'go for it'. Your subject matters... give your children a curiosity, a love of finding out how and why our planet is as it is, a love of their bit of the world they see every day when they step outside home. And your subject matters because we need a generation of children who are going to take care of this amazing planet of ours' (Greening, 2016, p. 19).

Figure 4: Views on the scope of geography in the primary years and for life.

- Do you have the opportunity to participate in specific professional development for geography?
- Is planning a collaborative activity across different subjects utilising the strengths of individual teachers and drawing on geographical knowledge and skills?

In your school community

- How is geography represented within your school community?
- Do you have a governor responsible for geography?
- Do you offer events for parents with a geographical focus?
- Do you utilise the knowledge and skills of parents and carers who have careers with a geographical aspect?
- Have you invited those who have lived in, or travelled to, other places to share their first-hand experiences, photos and artefacts with the pupils?
- How do your pupils connect with the local area and community, e.g. does your gardening club have regular inputs from local gardeners?
- Do your debates about topical issues include contributions from members of the local council or your MP?

Geography's place

These questions should inspire you to think about geography's place in, and contribution to, the lives of your pupils and their community both in and outside the school. Geography is the repository of the knowledge and skills that the children of today will need, both to realise their own potential and to solve the problems that will confront them in the future. Studying geography will equip them to take an active and informed part in shaping their place in their world (see Section 3). Geography is the only subject that has multiple ways of empowering children to re-imagine the future of the world.

From an early age, children are curious about and aware of the environment around them, and as teachers we should both harness this enthusiasm and ensure it is based upon sound geographical understanding and reasoning. By giving geography its central place in the curriculum, and the pupils the opportunity to engage with it, you will find that ALL the pupils will begin to participate in lessons in a positive and interested way, revealing skills, understanding and values that might otherwise remain latent. Geography is an inclusive subject that both values and encourages differing viewpoints and ideas. Fostering their geographical knowledge and understanding will enable pupils to appreciate how thinking geographically can have a positive impact on their lives and those of others.

Exploring, enquiring, explaining and **empowering** are the key words that underpin sound geographical teaching and learning, and this book will help you promote the resulting high-quality geography teaching inside and outside your classroom and school.

Figure 5: Creative and exploratory geographers learning through playful imagination. Pupil's work by the Happy Geography Club, Swanmore CE (Aided) Primary School.

The ideas and approaches discussed are based on experience and research, are tried and tested, and will inform and empower future generations of geographers. A further word, **enjoying**, should be added to this list. Though geography addresses serious and significant issues about the world, by its very nature it also invites pupils to play and experiment in and with their surroundings. Taking a creative and exploratory approach – Forest Schools sessions, den building, creating small-world scenarios and inviting gnomes to explore the world with us (Witt and Clarke, 2018) – will encourage pupils to engage with multiple environments and learn through play (Figure 5).

Supporting primary geography professionals

Different parts of the book will be particularly relevant to geography educators at different stages of their careers.

Starting out

If you are a trainee or early career teacher, this book will develop your understanding of the role, value and potential of geography in the primary curriculum and introduce you to key pedagogical approaches. We also provide, through exemplification, sources and methods to organise the complex and interconnected content of the geography curriculum, enabling you to both understand and teach the subject, as covered in Section 6. Learning about effective geography teaching in a supportive and developmental way will give you the confidence to take some risks, and exposure to innovative geographical thinking will enable you to take a playful approach to your lessons, ensuring that you have as fulfilling a time as your pupils. A playful approach to geography can be rigorous, offering possibilities to reinvigorate geographical thinking and practices through 'immersing, engaging and connecting… pupils with geography in lively, fun and spirited ways' (Witt and Clarke, 2018). This helps pupils to tune into primary geography experiences.

Leading in the classroom

As an experienced teacher you will have taught geography for some time, but you may not regard yourself as a geographer (Figure 6). Indeed, you may be concerned that you do not have any qualifications in what is often perceived as a content-heavy subject. We aim to reassure you that much of your current practice will in fact constitute 'good geography', and help you identify it as such and take it further. Section 4 outlines the value and purpose of specific pedagogical approaches that will motivate and enthuse pupils and stimulate their curiosity about their world; adapting the ideas to your particular context and pupils will develop your confidence and enhance your effectiveness in teaching excellent geography. You will gain as much from the process as the pupils; geography is about a way of thinking, not just a matter of qualifications. After all, learning together has long been seen as a positive and effective strategy – especially with regard to using rapidly-developing and sometimes, for the teacher, overwhelming new technology: pupils have no fear of buttons on a device and sharing their discovery of 'what it does' with you is very empowering. The 'flipped classroom' approach can be fun and productive for everyone: 'it is the quality of human relationships in the classroom that is the measure of 'good' geography teaching' (Smith, 2002).

Leading the subject

We aim to support new and existing subject leaders by considering the nature of the subject lead role, including phase or subject cluster leads, the essential responsibilities of the post and the opportunities it offers you. This guidance applies equally to humanities subject leaders: additional support through joint associations such as Humanities 2020 can help you integrate geography with history, citizenship and RE in particular.

In Section 7 Paula Owens explores ways you can develop your leadership role to raise geography's status with colleagues and enhance the quality of geography teaching across the school. The key here is to give you confidence in your geographical understanding and skills. This will enable you to encourage and lead pupils and colleagues to take risks, to be challenged and challenge others, and to explore in geography lessons the difficult and controversial issues we can be reluctant to tackle. We hope that this will also result in you, and your colleagues, nurturing a passion for the subject, which will in turn have a positive impact on all the pupils in your school.

Figure 6: The image of a modern geography teacher or subject leader is a far cry from the stereotype! Pupil's work by the Happy Geography Club, Swanmore CE (Aided) Primary School.

Further detailed advice on planning a high-quality geography curriculum and curriculum making for both EYFS and the primary phase may be found in Sections 4 and 5 of this book and on the web page.

Beyond the school environment

The combination of the authors' experience of both classroom practice and higher education, alongside current research, provides a holistic and comprehensive coverage of the subject and its value for teacher educators and researchers. Exemplars of best practice in the classroom are underpinned by robust theoretical knowledge and understanding of the subject. Teacher educators can use the high-quality exemplars and corresponding explanation and exemplification when teaching and supervising student teachers and engaging with mentors in school.

Researchers are provided with a range of examples of primary geography teaching and can identify areas that they might be interested in pursuing further through their own research in schools. We would welcome any of the possible outcomes from this research to add to the online presence, to keep it current and topical.

Nurturing young geographers

Geography is a dynamic subject that engages pupils' natural curiosity and enables them to connect with and make informed decisions about the world from a position of evolving knowledge and understanding. As teachers you need to consider what motivates the pupils in your class, what they want to know more about and how you can offer them the means to satisfy this curiosity. Providing them with 'geographical glasses' and showing them how to use them will encourage your pupils to become ever more curious and hungrier for new knowledge – a positive, virtuous spiral of curiosity. It will also help them, as well as you, to 'think geographically'. As Simon Catling suggests in Section 2, geography has a number of real positive outcomes for pupils. It:

- extends pupils' experience and awareness beyond the personal to the wider world
- encourages pupils to think in new ways about their own contexts and the world
- enables pupils to describe, analyse, explain, understand and appreciate the world
- gives pupils access to discussions and debates about local, national and global events, concerns and issues, and develop their own values
- empowers pupils through their application of geographical thinking.

It is always revealing to ask (and keep on asking!) a class 'what is geography?' Can they name a geographer (apart from you!)? What does a geographer do? Do they know what they might be able to do, know and understand if they become geographers? You may be surprised by their answers, which will offer a valuable context for your geography planning; keep reminding yourself of what is meaningful to the pupils, what their aspirations, hopes and dreams are and how the geography experiences you offer can help them to realise these.

From this position of knowledge of your class you can begin planning those exciting, engaging and fun lessons that will help equip them for the future and their place in the world. Working collaboratively on a shared issue/problem, understanding different viewpoints, identifying patterns and processes, and recognising complexity and connectivity in decision making, will all become normal and regular components of the activities in your lessons. Although your lessons will often deal with sensitive, controversial and complex issues, they will increasingly develop an optimistic approach (Figure 7).

Figure 7: An optimistic approach and a geographical mind can help learners realise their aspirations. After: Freire, 1998, p. 45.

Too often in the past educators have focused on the extent of the problems rather than the range of solutions. Education in the 21st century should be about teaching and learning in a spirit of hope and optimism, which recognises the rights and responsibilities of both present and future generations, on a global scale (Hicks, 2018). Learning to live in a sustainable way is a key concept of primary geography, not just because we have to, but because we want to, because we care about our environment, on whatever scale. We want to not just hand our world on in the same state that we found it but to improve it; pupils need to know how they might begin to do that (Figure 8).

Such an approach will result in you and your pupils learning together about the world and preparing together for an unknown and unpredictable future with realism, hope and enthusiasm. A different way of structuring learning about the world offers a more rewarding and lasting experience for everyone involved, including you, their teacher. We hope that using this book will enable you to drop a geographical pebble into the curriculum pool and that the ripples will spread throughout the school community and have a positive impact on the pupils and their future lives. It is our privilege as primary teachers to light the spark of pupils' curiosity; inspired by their enthusiasm we can also fulfil our responsibility to keep the flame burning throughout their primary learning journey.

Figure 8: Happy geographers learn about the world through different viewpoints and perspectives. Pupil's work by the Happy Geography Club, Swanmore CE (Aided) Primary School.

> To access further support and resources from the *Leading Primary Geography* web page, see page 164

References

DfE (2013) The *national curriculum in England Key stages 1 and 2: Framework document*. Available at: https://assets.publishing.service.gov.uk/government/uploads/system/uploads/attachment_data/file/425601/PRIMARY_national_curriculum.pdf (last accessed 12/6/2019).

Freire, P. (1998) *Pedagogy of Hope: Reliving Pedagogy of the Oppressed*. New York, NY: Continuum.

Greening, J. (2016) 'The Primary Geography Interview', *Primary Geography*, 90, p. 19.

Hicks, D. (2018) *A rationale for global education*. Available at: www.unesco.org/education/tlsf/mods/theme_c/popups/mod18t05s02.html (last accessed 12/6/2019).

Obama, B. (2012) National Geographic Bee (US TV Quiz Show)

Palin, M. (2011) *Geography students hold the key to the world's problems*. Available at: https://www.theguardian.com/education/2011/aug/18/geography-top-10-alevel-subjects (last accessed 12/6/2019)

Smith, M. (2002) *Teaching Geography in Secondary Schools: A Reader*. Abingdon: Routledge.

Witt, S. and Clarke, H. (2018) 'There's no play like gnome', *Primary Geography*, 95, pp. 10-14.

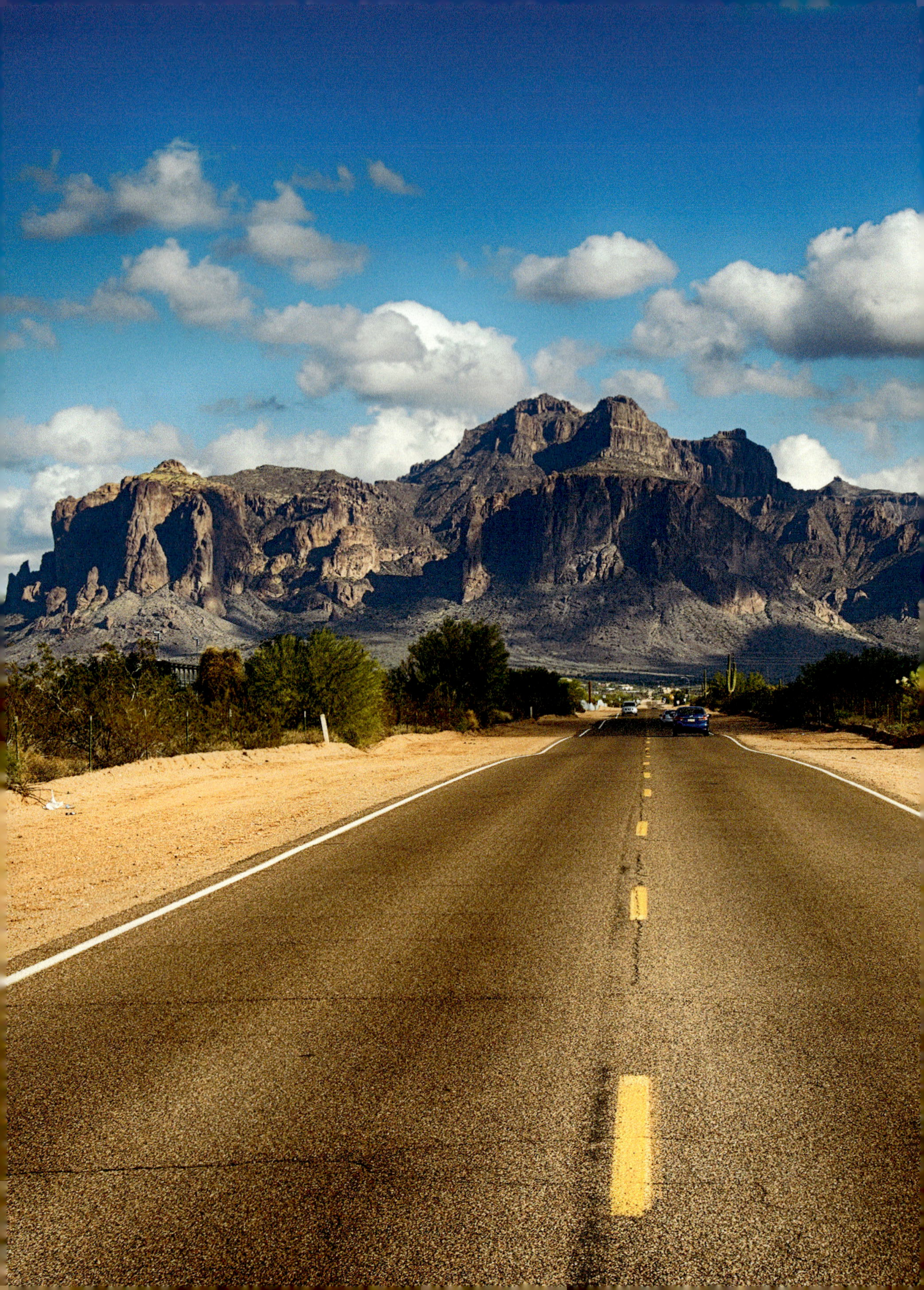

SECTION 2

Key concepts

Simon Catling

This section outlines what geography is about, its significance and place in the curriculum, and what pupils need to know in order to be able to think geographically, become familiar with the key concepts or 'big ideas' of the subject, and understand that all aspects of the world are inter-related and interdependent. It considers the physical and human aspects of geography and the interface where they meet, impacting on one another to provide this very rich, diverse and holistic subject that inspires and enthuses young geographers.

Geography's significance

As inhabitants of Earth, we are all involved in geography; it is part of our make-up. Geography explores and explains many aspects of the world, including:

- our familiar places and journey-making
- producing, trading and consuming food, water and energy
- what happens where, how and why
- people's responses to human and environmental events and disasters
- decision-making and its effect on our own and others' places and lives.

Geography has meaning for us all, during and beyond childhood, because we are curious about our world and want to explore it – an instinct exhibited by our earliest explorations of home. We constantly revisit familiar places: seeing them afresh in different weathers and seasons, noticing what we have 'missed', recognising and responding to subtle or dramatic changes, gradually updating our local mental maps. The understanding geography can impart is increasingly essential for us all in today's complex, globally inter-related world: *geography matters* (Murphy, 2018).

Geography's scope is global. Exploring new places invites us into new experiences, both directly and through stories and non-fiction, news media and the internet, gradually extending our wider-world mental maps. New worlds open up: knowledge and images from the humdrum to the awesome, from the impacts of migration to volcanic eruptions. Geography helps us understand the *what* and *where* of these aspects of our world. It investigates *how* and *why* they come about and their *effects* on the environment and people's lives. It considers what might occur next and later, naturally or anthropogenically, intentionally or inadvertently (Figure 1) (Dorling and Lee, 2016; Crane, 2018).

Geography is an active and enquiring discipline and school subject: 'one of humanity's big ideas' (Bonnett, 2008, p. 1). Its disciplinary roots lie in classical times, since when geographers have sought to teach about the world and have developed systematic studies and insights into human and physical geography. Over time, geography's scope has broadened and deepened through key concepts such as interconnections, space and scale. Geography's value in the Early Years and right through primary education is that it enables pupils to make greater sense of, and act more thoughtfully about, both where they live and the wider world. This is important because what happens in their own localities and across the globe affects them, directly and indirectly. Figure 2 summarises the importance of geography in primary education.

In developing their geographical knowledge and understanding, primary pupils should learn about a wide range of information, the major themes that geography studies, and its underpinning key concepts or 'big ideas'. These are the basis for thinking geographically and are strongly drawn together by a holistic and relational approach through environmental geography. The development of pupils' geographical thinking from the earliest school years enables them to build their geographical awareness and understanding throughout their primary schooling. It is the initial part of their journey in geographical education. Its disciplinary perspective gradually extends their capability to make more sense of their world, as they become increasingly better informed.

Figure 1: Geography examines environmental events, such as the melting of Arctic ice, and likely outcomes and impacts. Photo © Denis Burdin/Shutterstock.com.

Geography:

- develops pupils' knowledge and understanding of the world, from their local everyday experience to the global picture. It helps them gain deeper and more extensive insights into both natural processes and human actions and influences at different scales.

- builds pupils' sense of what is where in the world and the ways in which things are connected – and why.

- engages pupils with the wondrous and hazardous nature of the world, from looking afresh at the familiar to being amazed or concerned by new encounters with places, environments, lives and events.

- helps pupils become better informed, so they recognise and appreciate the variety of their own and distant surroundings.

- enables pupils to realise that the spatial connections, networks and patterns they see and map, locally and globally, result from natural and human actions.

- helps pupils realise that local and global interconnections mean that people, places and environments are interdependent, and that their own activities can affect them, often unwittingly.

- enables pupils to reflect on and sometimes act to mitigate the ways we impact on other lives, environments and places, and consider sustainable approaches to living.

- develops pupils' sense of responsibility for Earth's environments, places and people – and to act in accordance with what they value as far as possible.

- helps pupils to make sense of their own place in the world.

- enables pupils to identify, describe and communicate about places and environments.

Figure 2: Geography's significance in primary education. Image © koya979/Shutterstock.com.

Developing pupils' geographical understanding draws on studies of places and regions and systematic studies of human, physical and environmental geography. Human geography includes studies of settlements, trade and agriculture, while physical geography covers, for example, the processes causing volcanoes and earthquakes, rivers and lakes and weather and climate. These can be studied at all scales from the local to the global.

Environmental geography draws physical and human geography together to understand, for instance, the impact of river floods and the effects of deforestation. To investigate these and other areas of geographical interest and enquiry, geographers ask many questions. Figure 3 illustrates a variety of such questions about different geographical topics at a range of scales, for different primary age phases, which can be adapted for different topics.

Topic	Seeking initial information	Wanting to know more	Considering what if and what next?
A local play area *An Early Years focus*	Where is it? What is there? When is it available? Who uses it? Who looks after it?	How do children play there or otherwise use it? How well is it looked after? What happens when damage occurs? Is it an inviting place?	How has it been or might it be improved? What other local play space amenities would adults and children prefer to have, and why? How might these be provided?
The impact of floods [in Bangladesh] *A middle primary years focus*	Where is Bangladesh? What are the main rivers of Bangladesh? Where do the floods occur and when in the year? At what scale do they happen? What types of weather lead to the flooding? Who and what is affected by the floods?	Why does flooding occur? How are the causes of flooding related to the regional climate and weather patterns? What is the impact of the floods, on whom and why? How does flooding affect the land? How do people respond?	What actions have been, are being, or could be taken to lessen the impact of flooding? How are they or might they be effective, and what might undermine their effectiveness? Who or what are they designed to help and why? What further action to mitigate flooding can be recommended?
A matter of pollution *An upper primary years focus*	Why are household waste, litter and poor air quality labelled as 'pollution'? What variety of pollution occurs in the local area, and where? What appears to cause this pollution? Does pollution occur elsewhere, and is it in similar or different ways? How is pollution tackled locally and in other places?	Which are visible and invisible forms of pollution, and why? How do people react to different forms of pollution? How does pollution affect people and the physical environment? Is pollution increasing, static or declining, and why? Who is responsible for tackling pollution? How do they go about this task? What do people think about what is done to tackle pollution?	What actions have been, are being, or are intended to be taken to tackle pollution? How do people wish to have their environments improved to limit or reduce pollution? Why might there be different priorities for tackling (different forms of) pollution in different places? What should be the priorities for reducing pollution?

Figure 3: Examples of questions for primary geography topics.

Understanding geographical knowledge

Exploring questions such as those in Figure 3 involves pupils in geographical thinking: applying geographical knowledge and understanding to the world. It requires thinking about places and environments and what happens at different scales in order to explain, understand and, perhaps, consider actions and make appropriate decisions. It draws on the different threads of knowledge that are essential to all geographical learning. These three interplaying

Threads of knowledge   **Threads of geographical knowlege**

Propositional

Substantive — GEOGRAPHY

Procedural

Facts Information

Place and systematic/ thematic studies

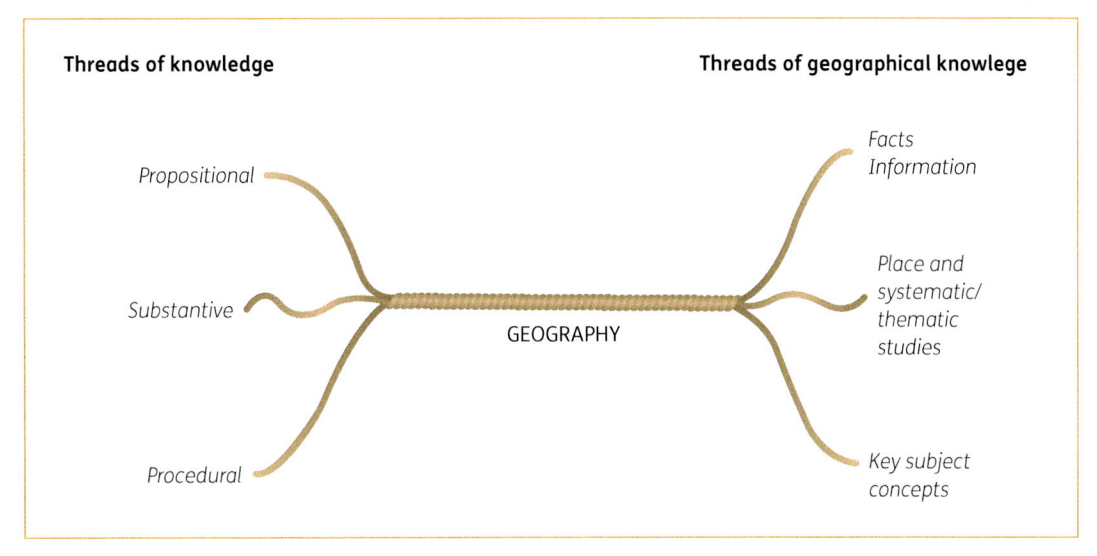

Key subject concepts

Figure 4: The three threads of geographical knowledge.

threads – propositional, substantive and procedural knowledge – articulate how we understand and use knowledge in geographical thinking (Figure 4).

Propositional geographical knowledge

Knowledge in the sense usually associated with geography is *propositional* knowledge – true factual and informational knowledge, such as knowing what a road or a lake is, where and what are the local shops, names of places, countries and capitals, and what some places are known for, such as tourism or manufacturing. Propositional knowledge is a core thread for geographical thinking. Knowing information is helpful in everyday dealings and discussions. It concerns knowing *what* and *where*, locally and globally, and provides the vocabulary to name, for example, features, goods, routes and places.

However, such facts and information are not in themselves geography. They must be set in a disciplinary, or subject, context to be coherent and have meaning (Counsell, 2018); otherwise they are little more than lists of what we know: they do not help us appreciate geography other than very superficially. For geographical insight we need another knowledge thread.

Substantive geographical knowledge

Substantive knowledge helps us to group, classify, connect, explain and make sense of facts and information about the environment and places. It leads us to the *how* and *why* of the world. It is essential for disciplinary or subject geographical knowledge. When we refer to biomes, settlements, trade, agriculture, energy and climate, we order and make sense of what is happening in the world by cohesively categorising aspects of our environment and places. Substantive knowledge provides a deeper level of understanding and forms the basis for investigating and explaining the geographical range and vitality of the world. It ensures a systematic perspective on places and environments.

Substantive knowledge gives us the thematic studies that are the explicit content in geography's investigations, such as urbanisation and its consequences and the meanings of coasts. Much geographical learning in primary schools focuses on the themes of substantive geographical knowledge. However, geography is underpinned by a further thread of knowledge, which connects its themes to provide the consistency and coherence essential in geographical thinking.

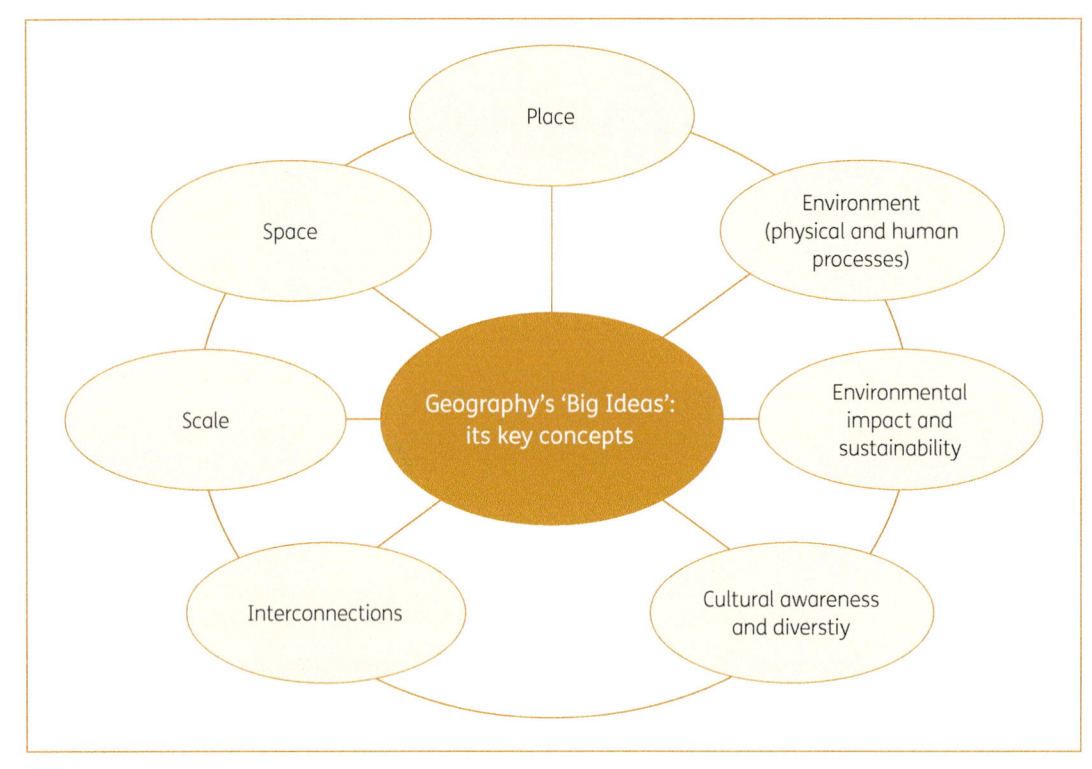

Figure 5: Geography's 'big ideas' or key concepts (after Catling and Willy, 2018, p. 35).

Procedural geographical knowledge

Procedural knowledge enables us to apply our propositional and substantive knowledge appropriately and usefully: to think geographically. Procedural knowledge runs within and across geography's themes. It provides the subject's sense of itself through its 'big ideas' or key concepts, such as place, scale and interconnections. Their application to and across geography's substantive knowledge lies at the heart of geographical thinking and gives substance to the subject. They are listed in Figure 5 and briefly summarised in Figure 6 (see also Catling and Willy, 2018). As with propositional and substantive knowledge, these are essential to geography teaching and learning at all ages.

Thinking geographically

Geographical thinking is explicit or implicit in the many decisions we make, be these where to play or which environmental charity to support. Geographical knowledge and thinking empowers us to be considered and effective in our choices.

Learning to think geographically requires employing the three threads of geographical knowledge together, not discretely. Pupils need (*propositional*) factual knowledge about places, environments and lives to be aware of them. They take in a range of information about other places, environments and lives from their everyday, familiar encounters – much, but not all of it, accurate. By examining a wide range of information about the world in the context of geography's (*substantive*) place and thematic studies, they are able to develop their understanding of places and environments systematically, beginning to see links and explanations, enabling them to focus their thinking in geography. Through encouragement to see and note interconnections, scale and

Geography's 'big ideas'	The key concepts briefly summarised
Place	…encompasses real as well as perceived and imagined places and refers to: what is in places and what happens there, ways places change and develop, their character and what they are like, how we conceive of and respond to places, whether we prefer them to stay the same or evolve. Place is multifaceted, involving cognitive and affective understandings of places.
Environment (physical and human processes)	…relates to the land and oceanic surface of Earth, its geology and its atmosphere. It includes the range of Earth's natural and people-created features, and the natural and human actions affecting the world. It explains the processes that create and change natural, built, modified and social environments. This concept helps us predict and plan what might happen.
Space	…refers to where features and places are located, their distribution, the patterns they form and the networks connecting them. *Space* describes the formal layout of the natural and human environment and their fluidity and change. It enables us to recognise and explain the processes affecting them.
Scale	…provides the lens to look at the world, from very small sites to local, regional, national, continental and oceanic areas, to the whole world. Scale enables many relationships to be identified and particular and wide-ranging patterns and connections to be recognised. Scale supports understanding environmental and place processes and making predictions.
Interconnections	…refers to the nature and significance of links between features, places, events and people. It enables recognition and appreciation of interdependence, locally, regionally or globally, whether ecological or socially generated. It examines the importance and impact of maintaining, modifying or breaking interconnections.
Environmental impact and sustainability	…concerns the interactions between the natural and human environments and their effects on each other, particularly of change and its consequences. It examines the quality, management and care of environments, places and lives. It considers the responsible and exploitative uses of Earth's resources alongside responses to the degrading of natural and modified environments and damage to people's lives. It considers ways to improve people's futures and Earth, and the ethics of doing so.
Cultural awareness and diversity	…encompasses local and global diversity and the disparities in and of people's lives and communities and their connections to the natural world. It encompasses social and cultural interests and the dynamics in shared, common and different ways in which people use environmental resources, adapt places, interact and value and modify or conserve their local and national cultures, places and identities.

Figure 6: Geography's procedural knowledge 'big ideas' summarised.

place, for instance, pupils begin to apply the (*procedural*) key concepts of geography. In doing so, they internalise a geographical way of thinking.

Developing primary pupils' thinking through geographical information, themes and 'big ideas' fosters their understanding of the world, from their own to the global context, and it identifies approaches through which they can apply it. This empowers them as geographical thinkers. Maude's (2018) deliberations on how geographical knowledge is powerful for pupils is helpful here. What makes knowledge of a subject *empowering* is that it enables pupils to begin to understand and apply a subject's substantive and procedural thinking, to recognise and appreciate what is happening in the world and to realise that this impacts on them, as they affect it in various ways. Adapting Maude's analysis, learning to think with geography's propositional, substantive and procedural knowledge provides several ways in which pupils begin to become empowered as geographical thinkers.

- **Geography extends pupils' experience and awareness beyond the personal to the wider world.** Primary pupils informally develop personal geographical awareness and knowledge. This tends to be information about their familiar places, others they have visited, and places and environments they have encountered through secondary sources. It builds across their primary years. Through their geographical studies pupils can broaden and deepen their knowledge of the world, relating this to new geographical information, themes, contexts and ideas. This stimulates their curiosity about the world and enables them to look at the familiar anew. Pupils become increasingly knowledgeable about the world, are more widely informed and can reflect more deeply.

- **Geography encourages pupils to think in new ways about their own contexts and the world.** Through geography studies pupils can draw on, address, challenge and think beyond their current experience and views of the world. They can develop their understanding through case studies from around the world, using geographical themes to learn more widely and fully about places, for instance about weather and climate, land use, resources and settlements, and what is similar and different between them. In doing this, pupils encounter big geographical ideas such as place, scale and environment. This helps them to consider afresh what seems familiar. Thus, pupils build understanding they can apply to places and environments that they encounter in new studies and sources. They begin to think geographically about the world.

- **Geography enables pupils to describe, analyse, explain, understand and appreciate the world.** Geography asks wide-ranging and detailed questions about places, environments, events and lives, focused through its themes and applying its 'big ideas'. This helps pupils to learn to ask pertinent geographical questions, to seek relevant information and to provide explanations in order to understand the world. By inter-relating information about the environment, looking at locations and patterns at different scales and considering the underlying processes, whether about shopping areas or flooding, pupils can begin to recognise and apply geographical generalisations and learn when it is appropriate to generalise. They begin to apply learning from one context to another and ask more incisive and critically thoughtful questions.

- **Geography gives pupils access to discussions and debates about local, national and global events, concerns and issues.** Developing pupils' knowledge of geography's information, themes and 'big ideas' helps them to become more aware of local and global geography and engages them in what may be topical or long-standing matters of significance to their own and other people's lives and places. Such topics might include shifting climatic patterns and their impacts, the causes and effects of people's migration and the ways in which wealth and poverty enhance or inhibit life chances. Enabling pupils to learn about and debate such concerns, including examining the facts critically and offering their views, engages them in constructing fuller and increasingly deeper senses of the world. Equally, it helps them begin to recognise the limits of their knowledge and understanding. It can foster their involvement and potential contribution as citizens.

- **Geography empowers pupils through their application of geographical thinking.** Pupils extend their information about the world, build their understanding of the range of geography's themes, and recognise how geography's key concepts provide insight. They gain a deepening perspective about the ways in which the natural and human aspects of the world intermesh to change places and environments. This interweaving of geographical learning and the understanding gained empowers pupils through their growing sense of the world. This enables them to apply their own perspectives to understand more fully what is happening in the world alongside promoting and supporting actions to create a better world for all.

Connecting through environmental geography

Thinking geographically involves considering the inter-relationships and interactions in the world about us. Jackson (2006) refers to this as 'relational' geographical thinking. It enables us to examine and reflect on, for instance, the effects of the interconnections between places and the scales and spatial networks between physical and human environmental processes and impacts. It helps us to understand the extent and effect of sustainable actions and intercultural dynamics in responding to earthquake disasters. This relational perspective identifies geography as a subject or discipline that considers aspects of the world holistically, as multiple facets interacting with each other, not as composed simply of separate and discrete areas of interest and study (Rawding, 2013; Holt-Jensen, 2018).

Though we might concentrate on specific aspects in geographical studies, it is essential that pupils explore and appreciate the multiple inter-relationships involved. Primary pupils might investigate rivers as a curriculum focus. While they examine and gain information about several named rivers, their locations, features and uses, they develop their understanding of **physical and human processes** and their effects, **environmental impact and sustainability** in the ways rivers can be degraded and improved, **place** in terms of what they are like and how they are used, the human and physical **interconnections** involved, **space** through their catchment areas and networks, and apply **cultural awareness and diversity** in examining various contexts in people's lives, doing so at range of **scales**. This holistic, relational approach is that of *environmental geography*; it demonstrates how geography's propositional (factual), substantive (thematic) and procedural (big ideas) knowledge is integrated.

A focus for primary geography

The term *environmental geography* not only provides a link between physical and human geography but also explores and examines the multiple interactions between people and the natural environment to provide a fuller and deeper meaning (Castree *et al.*, 2009; Rawding, 2013). It identifies primary geography's ability to lead pupils towards understanding that the world is complex, that we are implicitly involved, and that what happens elsewhere affects us, whether directly or indirectly (Murphy, 2018). For instance, climate change can lead to drought or unexpectedly wet weather, inhibiting the growth of crops and leading to a shortage of raw materials for breakfast cereal. This may mean that workers have to be laid off; it may also increase the price to the consumer, resulting in fewer purchases or the choice of a cheaper, less healthy option. A damaging weather event can have far-reaching repercussions.

In this example, what has occurred is that a dramatic variation in nature's environmental cycle has had direct consequences for many people in many places. What happens in one place affects other places and this can occur at different scales with many social effects, yet it may not be this straightforward to explain. The research into global climatic change indicates that there is human influence affecting the atmosphere, leading to more extreme and more frequent weather events and impacts, some in places that are not well-prepared (IPCC, 2018). This can have far-reaching effects, not just for the individual producer or consumer; it can include longer-term impacts, such as migration to cities from rural areas and changing access to basic foodstuffs. National governments and non-governmental agencies

Criteria	Example
People-physical environment relationships: Examine and inter-relate aspects of the physical and human environment.	In a local study consider: - its landscape (including water resources) - land and water uses by local people, and their views about this - people's responses to local weather - the nature of and access to residential and commercial areas.
People's meaning-making about environments: Investigate and discuss the meaning, purpose and management of physical and human aspects.	In a school play area study examine: - where different play areas are and what they are like - reasons why they are there and when they are used - the effect of different types of weather on when they are used and pupils' views on the effect of the weather on their playtime - what pupils would change about play times, areas and activities and why.
Impacts on natural and human environments: Examine concerns and issues that affect the physical environment and people's lives and activities.	In a study of energy investigate: - energy use in homes and other places - generating energy from ground, water, wind and sun sources - causes of and concerns arising from growing demand for energy - actions to reduce waste of energy - controversial types of energy use and generation.
Be topical and of interest: Investigate matters that are current and pertinent.	In a study of flooding locally and further afield examine: - the causes and consequences - the effects floods have on the land and people's lives - ways flood defences are and might be undertaken - the long-term impacts of flooding.
Engage geographical knowledge: Find out relevant (propositional) facts and information; investigate appropriate (substantive) geographical themes; and apply some of geography's (procedural) key concepts.	In a study of quarry reclamation include: - information about one or more quarries being reclaimed, their location and why they are there - the processes and effects of quarrying - some uses to which ex-quarry sites can be put - the purposes and methods of reclamation: benefits and limitations - the impacts of reclamation on natural and human environments - the benefits and limitations of improving a landscape.
Take personal geographies into new territories: Draw on pupils' personal knowledge about the relationship between physical environments and people's activities to extend and deepen their understanding.	In a study of coasts consider: - what and where coasts are, using known and new examples - the images people have of coasts and why - examples of how coastal landscapes form - various uses of coastal environments - impact of changing coasts on people and nature - why coasts tend to fascinate and draw people to them.

Figure 7: Criteria to use in planning an environmental geography topic.

may attempt to mitigate these effects, some more effectively than others; their efforts can sometimes exacerbate problems. Such developments affect many people's lives, places and environments. This is the 'stuff' of environmental geography, and should be a major focus for primary geography.

Pupils can be introduced to environmental geography through many topics and contexts. Some examples have been given in this section and there are others throughout this book. Figure 7 suggests criteria for an environmental geography topic, with examples to promote a focus on geographical thinking. You can apply them in planning both individual topics and your geography curriculum.

Conclusion

Primary geography must emphasise the subject's holistic elements. This involves building pupils' propositional, substantive and procedural geographical knowledge so they can think geographically. Such an approach empowers primary pupils to build their knowledge of the world, appreciate their own and others' contexts and challenges, debate the matters that will affect their lives, and learn to analyse critically and contribute creatively to their world. This empowerment can be developed through a balanced focus on places and themes that emphasise the inter-relationships that are explored through environmental geography's integration of geographical knowledge and its use of key concepts.

While geographical experience permeates pupils' lives, their primary school geography studies should enable them to be more effective agents in both their own lives and those of others, as well as in the places and environments that are important to them and others and for Earth as a whole. The power of geographical education is that it deepens pupils' growing understanding of the world today through enhancing their potential and power to apply their knowledge and thinking tomorrow and in the future.

> To access further support and resources from the *Leading Primary Geography* web page, see page 164

References

Bonnett, A. (2008) *What is Geography?* London: Sage.

Castree, N., Demeritt, D., Liverman, D. and Rhoads, B. (eds) (2009) *A Companion to Environmental Geography*. Chichester: Wiley-Blackwell.

Catling, S. and Willy, T. (2018) *Understanding and Teaching Primary Geography*. London: Sage.

Counsell, C. (2018) 'Taking curriculum seriously', *Impact*, 4, Autumn, pp. 6–9.

Crane, N. (2018) *You Are Here: A brief guide to the world*. London: Weidenfeld & Nicholson.

Dorling, D. and Lee, K. (2016) *Ideas in Profile: Geography*. London: Profile Books.

Holt-Jensen, A. (2018) *Geography: History and Concepts* (5th edition). London: Sage.

IPCC (Intergovernmental Panel on Climate Change) (2018) *Global Warming of 1.5°C: Summary for Policy Makers*. Geneva: IPCC. Available at: www.ipcc.ch/reports/sr15 (last accessed 12/6/2019).

Jackson, P. (2006) 'Thinking geographically', *Geography*, 91, 3, pp. 199–204.

Maude, A. (2018) 'Geography and powerful knowledge: A contribution to the debate', *International Research in Geographical and Environmental Education*, 27, 2, pp. 179–90.

Murphy, A. (2018) *Geography: Why it matters*. Cambridge: Polity Press.

Rawding, C. (2013) *Effective Innovation in the Secondary Geography Curriculum*. Abingdon: Routledge.

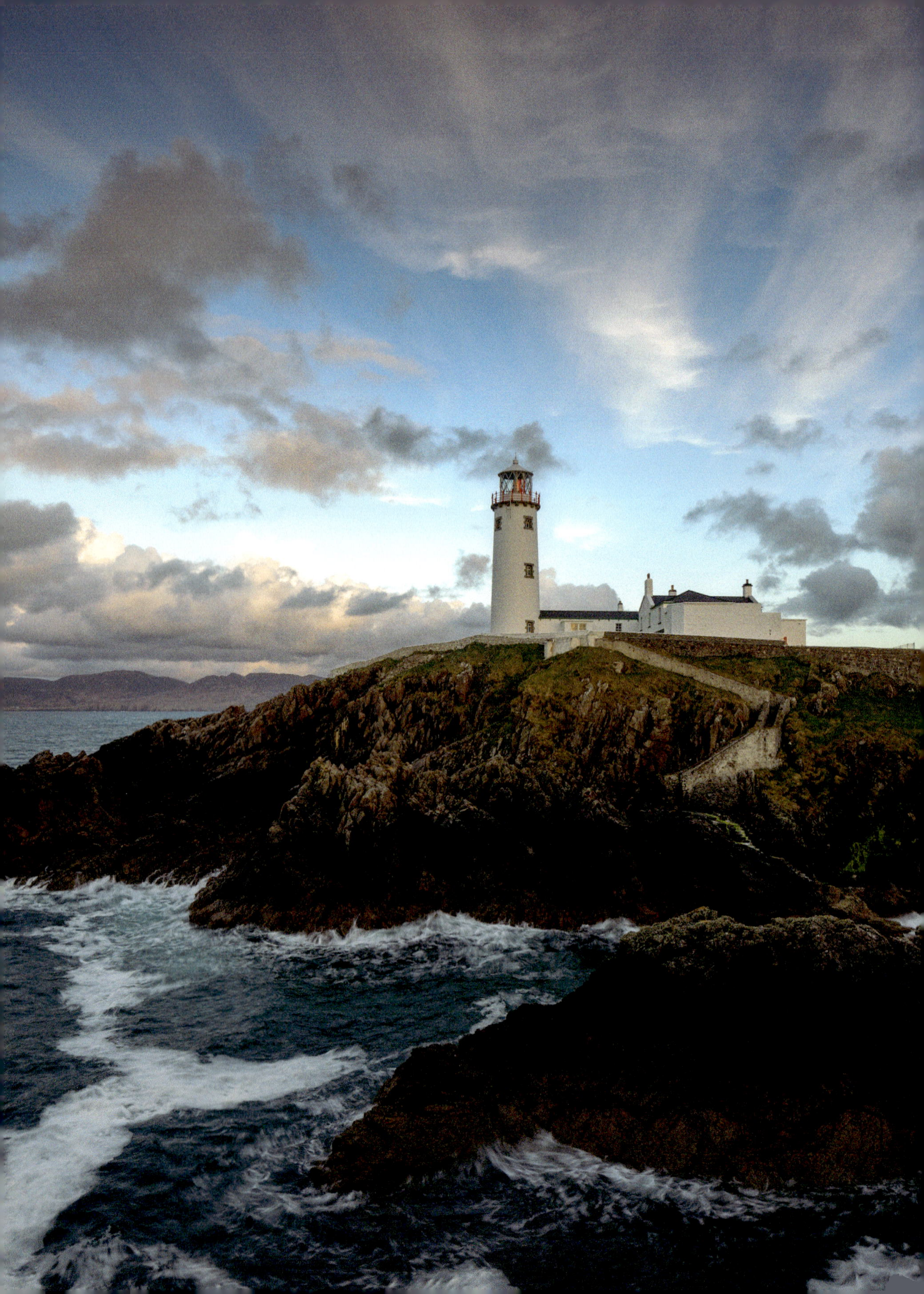

SECTION 3

Key skills

Stephen Pickering

This section is all about the key skills or 'tools' of geography and outlines how the subject is communicated through a variety of traditional ways, such as maps and fieldwork, as well as through less conventional methods, such as graphicacy, vocabulary and stories. These supportive tools allow pupils to access and learn about the subject while bringing it alive and making it both engaging and challenging. They are also essential in demonstrating pupils' developing geographical learning and thinking, making them invaluable assessment as well as learning tools.

Geographical skills

Geographical skills are the means by which we decipher the complexities of the world around us. If you think of geography as a house then the **patterns** are the layout of the rooms, the shape of the garden and the layering of the floors. The **processes** are the movements and interactions of the people in the house, for example playing in the garden or producing food in the kitchen, and also the movement of water, gas and electricity through the pipes, drainage systems and cables.

Geographical **skills** enable us to plot, measure and record these patterns and processes; they are also the tools we need to make sense of them. Geographical skills help pupils develop an understanding and appreciation of geographical patterns and processes, solve problems, and develop and present new learning from the very earliest stages of their education and throughout their lives.

The four key skills examined in this section are:

- making use of maps
- making meaning with vocabulary
- making sense through graphicacy
- making learning real through fieldwork and the outdoors.

Developing these key geographical skills enables pupils to become effective and independent geographical learners.

Making use of maps

Maps are the means by which pupils make sense of their expanding world, in scales increasing from the area of a school desk to the entire globe. Once pupils have developed the skills needed to make sense of a simple map, they are well-placed to start exploring and making sense of the world.

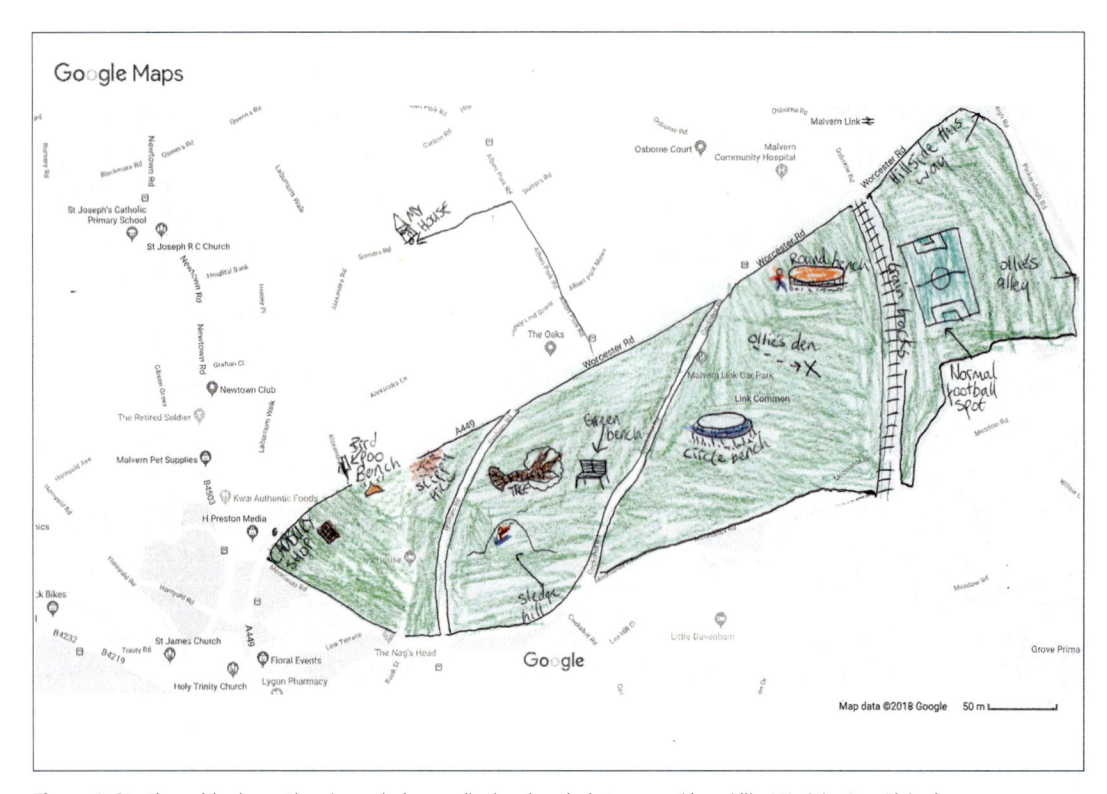

Figure 1: Starting with places they know helps pupils develop their map-making skills. Work by Ben Pickering.

As an abstract representation of reality, maps can be quite challenging for pupils to understand. It takes a leap of faith to grasp that the coloured squiggles and shadings on the paper are actually a 'drawing' of a real place. Although there is evidence that in recent years safety fears have restricted pupils' spatial movement, it has long been demonstrated that even very young pupils can use maps and plans to locate objects (Wiegand, 1999).

From an early age, map skills can be developed incrementally, from simple map directions (up/down/behind/in front) with simple symbols and maps in EY settings through to compass points, positional language and world maps at ages 5–7. Older pupils can tackle increasingly complex maps with grid references, distances, keys, bearings and symbols. You can download and use a comprehensive table of age-appropriate map skills (see web page). The key to helping pupils perceive maps as an accurate and useful picture of what is on the ground is to start with pupils creating their own maps of places they know (Figure 1). Completing a sound map is one way that pupils can develop an understanding of maps as a representation of a place (Figure 2).

Maps for a purpose

An exercise that works particularly well in age 7–11 settings, but could easily be adapted to challenge younger pupils, is to create maps for a set purpose. This involves writing a route for pupils to follow (see Figure 3). Ideally, the route should link to a part of the curriculum currently being studied, or to their home environment, as map skills are best taught in context rather than in isolation (Mackintosh, 2017). Groups of 3-4 pupils are challenged to draw the same map, but for a range of different purposes; for example, one group could be drawing maps specifically for young pupils, another for an illustration in a book. The class can then compare the various maps, and if the route is

Sound maps

Much of learning is visual, and none more so than map-making! So why not mix things up a little with a musical map? Schools tend to be busy, noisy places, but most schools also have quiet spots outdoors. Take your class to a quiet area and tell them that they are going to make maps, but not the usual types of maps of things you see; this time they will make maps of things you hear. Ask the pupils for complete silence as they spread out, clipboard and paper in hand, to stand and listen for a few minutes. Ask them to draw a sign or symbol to represent themselves in the middle of the page and as they hear noises around them to map them on their paper. They will need to decide what signs and symbols (no words) to use for the sounds they hear, and how they represent distance and volume.

The beauty of this exercise is that, whereas with a visual map pupils tend to draw the object they see, they naturally use signs and symbols to represent sounds, so you are likely to get much more creative use of symbols, e.g. waves and circles for windy spots, musical notes for birdsong. Back in the classroom pupils can use their new skills to develop the maps, adding grid lines and a key, scale and compass points. This is an excellent way to demonstrate to the pupils that something that might look quite abstract is actually a representation of a place. You could then compare their maps to a printed map of their school, or even to a range of different types of maps. Through questioning, pupils can learn that different maps are created for different uses and that maps tend to show physical features rather than the transient sounds that they have drawn (Pickering, 2017a).

Figure 2: Mapping sounds in familiar places.

Description of route
Start with a steep slope to the west of you.
Head 40m north to a staggered crossroads. One road goes north, one north east and one south east. Take the right fork to head 60m in a NE direction. There are a few old houses to the left of you and a field on your right.
Take a sharp right turn onto a new road to head S for 60m to the end of the road.
Then join the main road SSW for 160m. You will pass a school to the E of you and trees to the W.
Take a sharp left turn to head along a road that starts off heading N but gently curves so that after 500m you are heading E. There is a range of houses to your right and open land on your left.

Different purposes		
You work for a **theme park** and have found that many families get lost on their way to your park. Draw a map that shows the route to take and the things to look out for very clearly. It needs to be able to be understood by **young pupils**.	You work as an **architect** and your customer needs a very precise map in order to plan for some new buildings.	You work for a **tourist office** that specialises in the weird and wonderful, spooky and fantastical.
You work for a **travel agent** and your clients do not understand English. Your map has to be clear and include no words, only signs and symbols that are easy to understand without needing an explanatory key.	Your challenge is a tough one for mathematicians. You work for a **travel company** that needs to know how long a journey takes, so your map should show the time it takes to travel rather than the actual distance. The first 100m is to be travelled on foot at a speed of 100m/minute, the second 100m by bicycle at 200m/minute, and the rest by car at 500m/minute. Can you draw a map to show distance in minutes taken rather than metres travelled?	You are an **artist** for a publishing house and the map needs to represent the journey travelled in the **story**. You can make up the theme of the story.

Figure 3: Maps for a purpose exercise. Work by Y6 pupils at Wyche CE Primary School, Malvern.

based on an actual map you can compare the pupils' maps to the original one. Following the route on Google Earth may help pupils who struggle without concrete examples.

Pupils could be given a list of things to include in their map – a scale, compass points, a key and grid lines – or they could be challenged to discuss and decide which key elements of a map they should include, bearing in mind the purpose of their particular map. They start to see the benefits of symbols over diagrams, and grid references as a good means to navigate around a map. Such activities help pupils to realise the range of applications that maps can support and provide critical opportunities for the development and assessment of map skills.

Maps and stories

In many primary schools there is a focus on developing core skills in literacy and numeracy. There are, however, numerous ways in which such core skills can be developed through geography, and similarly geographical skills through the core subjects (see also Section 6). A large number of children's books, throughout all key stages and within Early Years settings, involve journeys and adventures. Many books contain maps, too, or provide the potential for pupils to create maps based on the story (Figure 4). The *Narnia Chronicles* (Lewis, 1950–56), for example, contain beautiful adventure maps, while *Meerkat Mail* (Gravett, 2007) provides clear detail for pupils to draw their own maps as the Meerkat mail travels across the Kalahari Desert. Many outdoor learning activities make use of stories like *We're Going on a Bear Hunt* (Rosen, 1989) and traditional tales such as the Three Little Pigs to create maps from natural objects in the woods. *Journey Sticks* (Whittle, 2006) describes a well-documented way to help young pupils develop the idea of mapping a journey. Maths skills can also be developed by pacing out and measuring the routes taken in such settings and then recording these, as far as possible to scale, when creating maps of the routes taken or read (see web page).

His Dark Materials

Philip Pullman's *His Dark Materials* trilogy superbly blends the real city of Oxford into a fantastical fictional backdrop. You can use the accompanying *Lyra's Oxford* (Pullman, 2003) as the starting point for map work. It contains a pull-out map of Lyra's Oxford – a mixture of the real and the imaginary. Comparing Lyra's map to an OS map or, more readily available, a Google Earth map, is a good starting point to identify buildings, streets, areas and landmarks. Groups of pupils can be given a series of features to identify using 'real' maps, if possible. It is worth including some of the fictional places from the story and discussing why they had been added – or indeed, if the pupils were to create a fantasy based on the reality of their home town, what fictional landmarks they might include and why.

Figure 4: The *His Dark Materials* trilogy (Pullman, 1995–2000) contains beautiful descriptions of local and distant places and journeys, from Oxford to Svalbard.

If you explore your local maps you may find a wealth of interesting names: Lovers Lane, Hangman Hill, Goldmine Valley or Stock's Corner. Can the pupils create their own stories based on the names that they find on their local maps? Or indeed, can the pupils re-name their own local area to better represent it through their own sense of place – Big-swing Park, Creaky Fence Road or Dodgeball Lane (see also Figure 1) – and overlay these on existing maps? This builds connections between the pupil and the place. The act of adding your own names to a place that is familiar supports your engagement with the area where you live, helping pupils to view maps as dynamic, and also providing resources that they can work with. This can fuel imagination and deep questioning about places. Who decided on the original names? What stories lie behind the names on the maps?

Maps and technology

GIS stands for **Geographic Information System** and is a way of displaying, recording, manipulating and making use of digital maps and other spatial data. Many software packages are suitable for primary school use, such as mapping annotation websites and programmes that enable pupils to manipulate existing maps, and even to create their own. Some online programmes include learning and teaching support and activities to enable pupils to explore a wide variety of maps at different scales. Additionally, Google Earth and Google Maps, probably the best known and most widely used of GIS tools, have the capacity to toggle between maps and aerial photographs, measure routes and compare current and historical maps. Many pupils are already familiar with them and find them accessible and easy to navigate.

Maps are no longer static in the way they once were; like a Harry Potter Marauders' Map, Google Earth can imbue maps with movement and reality by dragging the little yellow person icon onto the map (Figure 5). This tool is a fascinating way to bring maps and places to life; pupils feel as if they are zooming from the map down to land in the actual place. The task for teachers is to harness these wonderful visual resources to create engaging lessons and deep learning, equipping the pupils with skills to investigate geographical patterns and processes. The activity is not an end-point in itself: the ability to start with a map and zoom down to photographic images of the actual place translates the map into a real place in pupils' minds.

Follow-up activities can be based, for example, on emotive learning – discussing the things the people in the images might see, do and think as well as describing places and routes from a map and then from the images of the place. Google Earth maps of their local area can be printed for pupils to add their own names, symbols, scale, compass points and grid references, and activities can be developed further in mathematics by making use of co-ordinates.

Making meaning with vocabulary

Pupils love new words – the longer and weirder the better – and in geography we have many of the best, from pollution and migration to evapotranspiration. How many words ending with the sound 'shon' can pupils think of? The suffix 'tion' can be used as a way to identify processes. Geographical literacy games can be played, e.g. recognising verbs, nouns and gerunds from the terminology, and switching from one mode to another (e.g. erosion – erode). On a river valley diagram, pupils can be encouraged to write the names of patterns in one colour and processes in another. When pupils start talking like geographers it helps them to feel more confident as geographers, and to think like geographers. Using geographical language helps pupils to explore, demonstrate and develop geographical understanding.

There are also many ridiculous geographical words for pupils to discover, from a 'nunatak', which conjures up images of pitchfork-wielding

Figure 5: Putting yourself into the map is an excellent feature that brings maps to life.

nuns charging at an enemy, to a 'slip-off-slope' that isn't even slippery! Correct terminology actually influences thinking and learning processes. Many pupils love learning long and interesting words and although they do not always use them entirely accurately this is simply part of the learning process. Games can test pupils' knowledge of terminology and give them an opportunity to demonstrate their understanding of patterns and processes.

There is a more serious side to developing vocabulary. Dawes describes how 'talk precipitates thought' (2018, p. 204), highlighting the importance of terminology, not just to demonstrate learning, but to question, deepen and share learning. In talking about their work pupils need to make choices about the words they use dependent on their developing understanding (Carter, 2003). Spoken text often employs different grammatical processes from written text, so it is important for pupils to discuss as well as write, and to listen as well as read. Knowledge of, and opportunities to use and make sense of, terminology helps pupils to develop confidence in their understanding, thinking and work and, through talk, provides opportunities for pupils to work as experts by researching and giving presentations. This is a motivational process, and can quickly lead to deeper learning.

When pupils label diagrams or draw field sketches, they can be encouraged to be creative with their calligraphy skills. Wordyglyphs (Pickering, 2017b) are the onomatopoeic world of writing. Pupils can use adjectives as well as nouns to describe and label their diagrams. For example, 'hot bubbling lava' rather than just 'lava' will help with memory and understanding; and when the words are written to look as if they are hot and bubbling pupils do more than just record a geographical process, they breathe life and understanding into it. Creating word glossaries with pupils and having them available can reinforce understanding and encourage pupils to use appropriate geographical vocabulary and talk as geographers.
(See web page for a sample glossary.)

Making sense through graphicacy

Graphicacy is the visual representation of geographical information. Graphs, tables, sketches and plans can all provide information and detail clearly. Pupils develop skills in creating such graphs and plans, as well as in interpreting them. This is a vital skill for problem solving, enquiry-based work and collecting and presenting important information. By creating their own graphs and diagrams pupils deepen their understanding of them. Pupils need to decide on the most effective graphical skills to employ, the most relevant geographical information to include, and how to present it.

Graphs and tables, charts and even maps can appear quite bland and abstract, so it is important to seek ways to enliven and bring meaning to them. Learning has greater resonance if some form of emotional attachment enables pupils to visualise the geographical stories behind the figures, and living graphs and map activities can bring meaning and a personal touch to information. In its simplest form this could mean providing the means for pupils to annotate tables and graphs with questions and thoughts as well as factual detail. Setting questions that allow progression of ideas also helps: it can lead the pupils towards a constructed understanding.

Another idea is for pupils to imagine the lives and events taking place behind the figures and charts on display. You can personalise a chart by adding speech bubbles that pupils have to place by the relevant statistic (see Figure 7) or ask the pupils to create the imagined stories and phrases behind the statistics, maps and pictures. This is a great way for them to demonstrate their understanding in a creative and easily assessed manner. Almost anything can have a story attached to it, from weather charts to waves on the ocean, and this helps to develop literacy and thinking skills, demonstrate understanding and provide a creative approach to deciphering charts and graphs. Further examples can be found via the web page.

Vehicle	Number
Foot	🚶 🚶 🚶
Bicycle	🚲
Motorbike	🛵 🛵
Car	🚗 🚗 🚗 🚗 🚗 🚗 🚗 🚗 🚗 🚗
Van	🚚 🚚
Lorry	🚛
Bus	🚌 🚌

Figure 6: Local traffic data recorded in a tally chart.

Figure 6 is a typical tally chart showing the range of vehicles travelling past school on a Monday morning that a road survey might reveal. Figure 7 shows a set of conversations and thoughts that the drivers might be having. In placing the statements next to the vehicle from which they thought they might have originated, the pupils can immediately see the part that the vehicles have to play, not just outside their school, but beyond. They can start to imagine – and then investigate – the lived geographies of the people in the vehicles. A much deeper understanding of human geography can be developed than just by looking at a set of statistics.

Making learning real through fieldwork and the outdoors

Fieldwork means using first-hand observation and geographical skills to gain knowledge and practical experience in both physical and human outdoor environments. One of the aims of the primary geography National Curriculum for England is 'to collect, analyse and

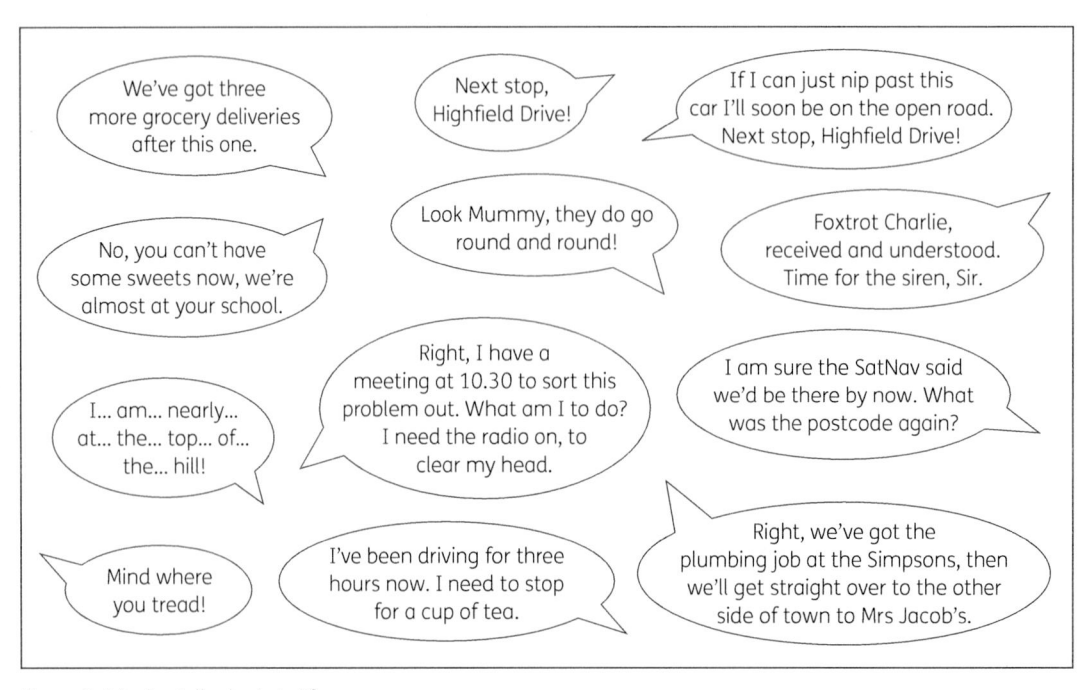

- We've got three more grocery deliveries after this one.
- Next stop, Highfield Drive!
- If I can just nip past this car I'll soon be on the open road. Next stop, Highfield Drive!
- No, you can't have some sweets now, we're almost at your school.
- Look Mummy, they do go round and round!
- Foxtrot Charlie, received and understood. Time for the siren, Sir.
- I... am... nearly... at... the... top... of... the... hill!
- Right, I have a meeting at 10.30 to sort this problem out. What am I to do? I need the radio on, to clear my head.
- I am sure the SatNav said we'd be there by now. What was the postcode again?
- Mind where you tread!
- I've been driving for three hours now. I need to stop for a cup of tea.
- Right, we've got the plumbing job at the Simpsons, then we'll get straight over to the other side of town to Mrs Jacob's.

Figure 7: Bringing tally charts to life.

communicate with a range of data gathered through experiences of fieldwork that deepen their understanding of geographical processes' (DfE, 2013). Similar statements exist in the Welsh Primary Curriculum (DCELLS, 2018) and in Scotland, where the curriculum is created around 'experiences and outcomes' (Education Scotland, 2010).

The word 'experience' is important. Fieldwork is not simply about collecting data that can be used to learn about geography; it is a whole system of pedagogies and skills in its own right. The experiential aspect of learning taps into different aspects of cognition, emotional intelligence and sensory learning that can impact deeply and positively on a pupil's holistic development. The key values added through learning and teaching outdoors are summarised in Figure 8.

Fieldwork provides practical, sensory and experiential learning that fits the hand-heart-head pedagogy originally proposed by Pestalozzi at the end of the eighteenth century (Martin and Martin, 2010). Pupils complete work using their hands, they have an emotional response to such work and the learning becomes embedded once they think about and make sense of it. Key geographical skills that can be developed by fieldwork include observing, noting and sketching, asking questions, measuring and collecting data. Pupils can use a variety of tools and equipment to measure and collect data, manually as well as electronically, using tablets/iPads, for example, to collect quantitative as well as qualitative data. This data can be easily stored for further work later.

Values added	Learning and teaching outdoors
Cognition	Opportunities for collaborative work help development of questioning and problem-solving skills. The 'messy' nature of learning outdoors requires creative thinking to see the way through a problem (Catling and Pickering, 2010). Metacognition is promoted by asking the pupils to apply the principles they arrived at when learning outdoors to learning in the classroom.
Health and well-being	A range of research into biophilia (Jordan, 2015), attention restoration therapy (Reese and Myers, 2012) and nature deficit disorder (Louv, 2005) highlights the importance of providing time for pupils to operate in natural settings. Waite et al. (2016) conducted large-scale research into the benefits for both pupils and teachers in terms of health and quality of work-life balance.
Motivation and aspiration	Pupils learn by doing, and learning outdoors is both experiential and highly interactive, with the surroundings and with other pupils. As pupils work with natural objects, building, measuring and engaging with their environment, the satisfaction achieved, particularly when working as a team, motivates pupils to do more and to learn more. The success of real-life investigations and fieldwork, coupled with the additional freedoms associated with learning outdoors, is a motivating force.
Responsibility and independence	Outdoor pedagogies depend to a certain extent on pupils taking responsibility for their learning, as tasks tend to take place with less overt supervision and direction than in a classroom. This, coupled with the motivational aspects of learning, tends to instil a sense of responsibility and independence that the pupils rise to.
Collaboration and communication	Problem solving, exploring, measuring and recording demand teamwork and clear communication.

Figure 8: Value added through outdoor learning (adapted from Pickering, 2018).

There is a danger, however, of compartmentalising fieldwork as something that is done off-site and remotely, that it is something special that takes a lot of planning, time and resources and as a result happens infrequently. Not all outdoor learning is fieldwork, just as not all fieldwork has to be completed outside. Many fieldwork skill experiences can be developed as part of a classroom lesson with learning taking place inside and outside. Short bursts of productive outdoor work, such as regular measuring of the weather or completing part of a video presentation, make effective links between the classroom and outdoor areas. These transitions can be planned or spontaneous, to form a rich combination of learning skills in different spaces and environments. In other words, fieldwork is to be viewed as just one of many pedagogies that can be used to help develop creative, inquisitive learners. Perhaps the most important consideration is that to teach geography outdoors and conduct fieldwork, there needs to be a clear purpose. The purpose can be linked to any of the values of outdoor learning listed above, but also to clear geographical objectives.

Articles in *Primary Geography* (see link on web page) detail purposeful and valuable outdoor learning and fieldwork activities.

Learning outdoors around the school

Orienteering is the process of navigating from one location to another using geographical skills like compass points and bearings. Pupils love orienteering and it is easy to develop these skills as part of a broader geography topic at any age. It can be an interactive way to learn about direction, compass points and directional language, develop spatial awareness and read maps. With pupils aged 5–7, simple games such as retrieving objects from the north, south, east and west of an area, or attaching a compass rose to a Beebot, can develop with increasing complexity to include NE, SSW and so on and then progress to bearings. Such activities can also support learning in both mathematics and PE. Compasses can be bought quite cheaply and used, both outdoors and inside, with maps. It is relatively easy for pupils to grasp how they work, particularly if they have already worked on degrees of a circle in mathematics. Figure 9 outlines the golden rules for compass work.

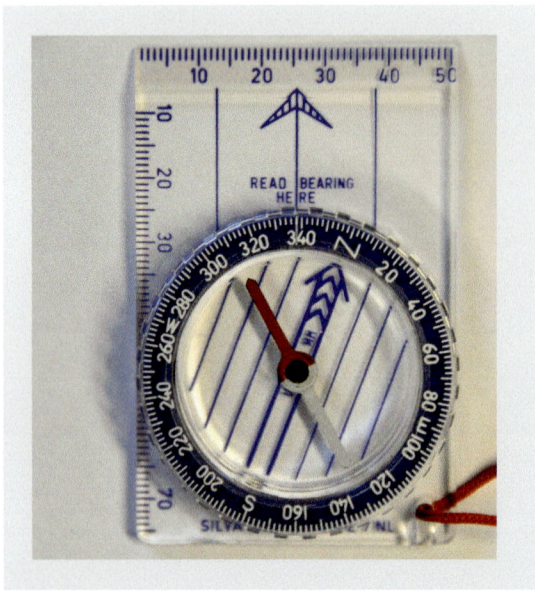

1. The red arrow on a compass always points north.

2. Underneath the red arrow, on the circular dial there is a hashed arrow that looks a bit like a thin garden shed (with a little imagination). Tell the pupils that when they 'put the red in the shed' (i.e. turn the compass until the red north arrow covers the hashed area) this shows north.

3. The arrow on the rectangular base points in the direction that you want the bearing for. When the 'red is in the shed' the base arrow will show you the correct reading.

4. Remember to hold the compass flat and keep it away from metal objects.

Figure 9: The golden rules for compass work. Photo © Sally Jones.

Once pupils have practised and feel secure with using a compass in the classroom you can set them off on a treasure trail. This requires basic compass and map skills; further skills and learning can be developed with the use of questions found round the trail. (See web page for more ideas.)

Part of the educational value, and also the joy, for pupils working outside is the feeling of freedom that it affords. To develop pupils' responsibility for learning and independent thinking, problem-solving tasks work particularly well. Making mistakes is part of the learning process! Figure 10 is an example that blends indoor and outdoor investigative fieldwork and can take place in the school grounds.

The aim of this enquiry, which can be adapted for different age groups, is to develop an understanding of the ways in which the natural environment influences the human one, as well as providing a focus on weather and micro-climates. To help pupils develop as independent learners when conducting an enquiry, a model like the 4 Ds of enquiry (Pickering, 2017c) can help pupils to structure their work.

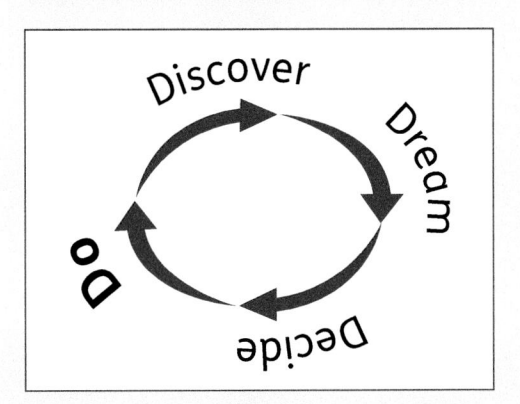

In groups of four or five, pupils are assigned a task to research the best place to put a bench in the school grounds. They will need to conduct a survey and complete questionnaires, asking geographical questions to find out who is likely to use the bench and what their requirements are (view, shade, and distance from school building) before proposing four potential sites. Once the pupils recognise that the weather is an influencing factor, and that the weather can vary over the course of a day owing to the movement of the sun, the teacher introduces the notion of micro-climates, and asks the pupils to measure the weather in each of their four locations. They have to build their own weather station, researching how to measure temperature, wind speed, even – with simple resources found around the school or home – air pressure, in the four locations before presenting the best one to the class and giving geographical reasons. These reasons include the human perspective, people's different viewpoints, the type of material with which to make the bench, the outlook from the bench and the micro-climate.

1) Pupils **discover** everything they can about the topic by research and exploration
2) Pupils **dream** of all the ways to explore the topic and improve or resolve any issues. This allows opportunities for creative thinking
3) Pupils discuss their dreams carefully and **decide** on the best options to explore.
4) Pupils convert their plans into **action** and present their enquiry.

A simple geographical enquiry like this, making use of the school grounds as well as the classroom, requires proficiency in a range of geographical (and design) skills as well as all the social skills needed to work effectively as a group, manage disappointments if it isn't successful and present to an audience.

Figure 10: Where is the best place for a school bench?

Figure 11: Using fieldwork skills further afield. Photo © Jane Whittle.

Learning outdoors further afield

Clearly, if you can travel away from the local area and work on a geographical theme for a day, or better still over a residential field trip, then the opportunities for creative, engaging and motivating fieldwork ideas are even greater (Figure 11). The same philosophy applies, however, in that good geography fieldwork and learning outdoors must have a clear focus, a solid structure, and a means to evaluate the work. Any evaluation of work completed, be it in class or outdoors, should focus not just on the task completed and the pupils' understanding, but also on the learning processes. Ask the pupils how they learned, how they managed to overcome barriers to learning, how they feel about their work, and how they intend to apply new learning to subsequent tasks.

If travel further afield is not possible, there is the option of virtual fieldwork, using software that can be enhanced further with 3D virtual reality hardware.

Teachers planning a field trip must undertake a risk assessment to ensure that pupils learn safely. Encouraging pupils to carry out their own risk assessment, by annotating a photograph of the location that they will be visiting, helps to raise their awareness of possible risks. This can help pupils to feel part of the preparation for a trip and take responsibility for managing the risks themselves. (See web page for further information.)

Developing skills

Providing opportunities for pupils to develop map work, graphicacy, geographical literacy and fieldwork skills helps them to understand geographical patterns and processes and enriches their learning. These skills can transfer across to other subject areas, too. More than this, however, they provide the means for pupils to take responsibility for their work and developing geographical understanding and for them to become better independent learners. These skills do not have to be complex. The activities in this section and online demonstrate that the foundation for the development of a good range of skills can be acquired through activities that are straightforward to plan and, importantly, work best when tackled as part of a lesson rather than separately or out of context. Developing geographical skills can introduce pupils to a new way of looking at the world that goes far beyond schoolwork. In navigation and exploration, discovery and explanation, geographical skills help pupils to learn to live in, understand and make the most of their world.

To access further support and resources from the *Leading Primary Geography* web page, see page 164

References

Carter, R. (2003) 'The grammar of talk: spoken English, grammar and the classroom' in *New perspectives on spoken English in the classroom: Discussion papers*. London: QCA.

Catling, S. and Pickering, S. (2010) 'Mess, mess, glorious mess', *Primary Geographer*, 73, pp. 16–17.

Catling, S. and Willy, T. (2018) *Understanding and Teaching Primary Geography*. London: Sage.

Dawes, L. (2018) 'Organising Effective Classroom Talk' in Cremin, T. and Burnett, C. (eds) (4th edn) *Learning to Teach in the Primary School*. Abingdon: Routledge. pp. 203–15.

DCELLS (Yr Adran Plant, Addysg, Dysgu Gydol Oes a Sgiliau/Department for Children, Education, Lifelong Learning and Skills) (2018) *Geography in the National Curriculum for Wales*. Available at: http://learning.gov.wales/docs/learningwales/publications/130424-geography-in-the-national-curriculum-en.pdf (last accessed 12/6/2019).

DfE (2013) *Geography programmes of study: key stages 1 and 2. National curriculum in England*. Available at: https://assets.publishing.service.gov.uk/government/uploads/system/uploads/attachment_data/file/239044/PRIMARY_national_curriculum_-_Geography.pdf (last accessed 12/6/2019).

Education Scotland (2010) Scottish Government/Riaghaltas na h-Alba (2010) *Curriculum for Excellence*. Available at: https://education.gov.scot/parentzone/learning-in-scotland/curriculum-areas (last accessed 12/6/2019).

Gravett, E. (2007) *Meerkat Mail*. Basingstoke and Oxford: Macmillan Children's Books.

Jordan, M. (2015) *Nature and therapy: Understanding counselling and psychotherapy in outdoor spaces*. Abingdon: Routledge.

Lewis, C.S. (1950) *The Narnia Chronicles*. London: HarperCollins.

Louv, R. (2005) *Last Child in the Woods*. London: Atlantic Books.

Martin, J. and Martin, N. (2010) 'Rousseau's "Émilie" and educational legacy' in Bailey, R., Barrow, R., Carr, D. and McCarthy, C. (eds) *The Sage Handbook of Philosophy of Education*. London: Sage. pp. 85–98.

Mackintosh, M. (2017) 'Representing Places in Maps and Art' in Scoffham, S. (ed) *Teaching Geography Creatively* (2nd edition). Abingdon: Routledge. pp.76–87.

Pickering, S. (2017a) 'Everyday Places and Spaces' in Pickering, S. (ed) *Teaching Outdoors Creatively*. Abingdon: Routledge. pp. 1–11.

Pickering, S. (2017b) 'The Start Gallery: Wordyglyphs', *Primary Geography*, 83, p. 5.

Pickering, S. (2017c) 'Keeping geography messy' in Scoffham, S. (ed) *Teaching Geography Creatively* (2nd edition). Abingdon: Routledge. pp. 192–205.

Pickering, S. (2018) 'The Value of Outdoor Learning' in Cremin, T. and Burnett, C. (eds) (4th edn) *Learning to Teach in the Primary School*. Abingdon: Routledge. pp. 216–28.

Pullman, P. (1995–2000) *His Dark Materials Trilogy: Northern Lights, The Subtle Knife, The Amber Spyglass*. London: Scholastic UK.

Pullman, P. (2003) *Lyra's Oxford*. London: Scholastic UK.

Reese, R. and Myers, J. (2012) '"Eco-Wellness": the missing factor in holistic wellness models', *Journal of Counselling and Development*, 90(4), pp. 400–406.

Rosen, M. (1989) *We're Going on a Bear Hunt*. London: Aladdin Books.

Waite, S., Passy, R., Gilchrist, M., Hunt, A. and Blackwell, I. (2016) *Natural Connections Demonstration Project, 2012–2016: Final Report and Analysis of the Key Evaluation Questions (NECR215)*. Worcester: Natural England.

Whittle, J. (2006) 'Journey Sticks and Affective Mapping', *Primary Geographer*, 59, pp. 11–13.

Wiegand, P. (1999) 'Children's Understanding of Maps', *International Research in Geographical and Environmental Education*, 8, 1, pp. 66–8.

Acknowledgement

Stephen would like to acknowledge the help and support of Linzi McKerr with the *His Dark Materials* activities.

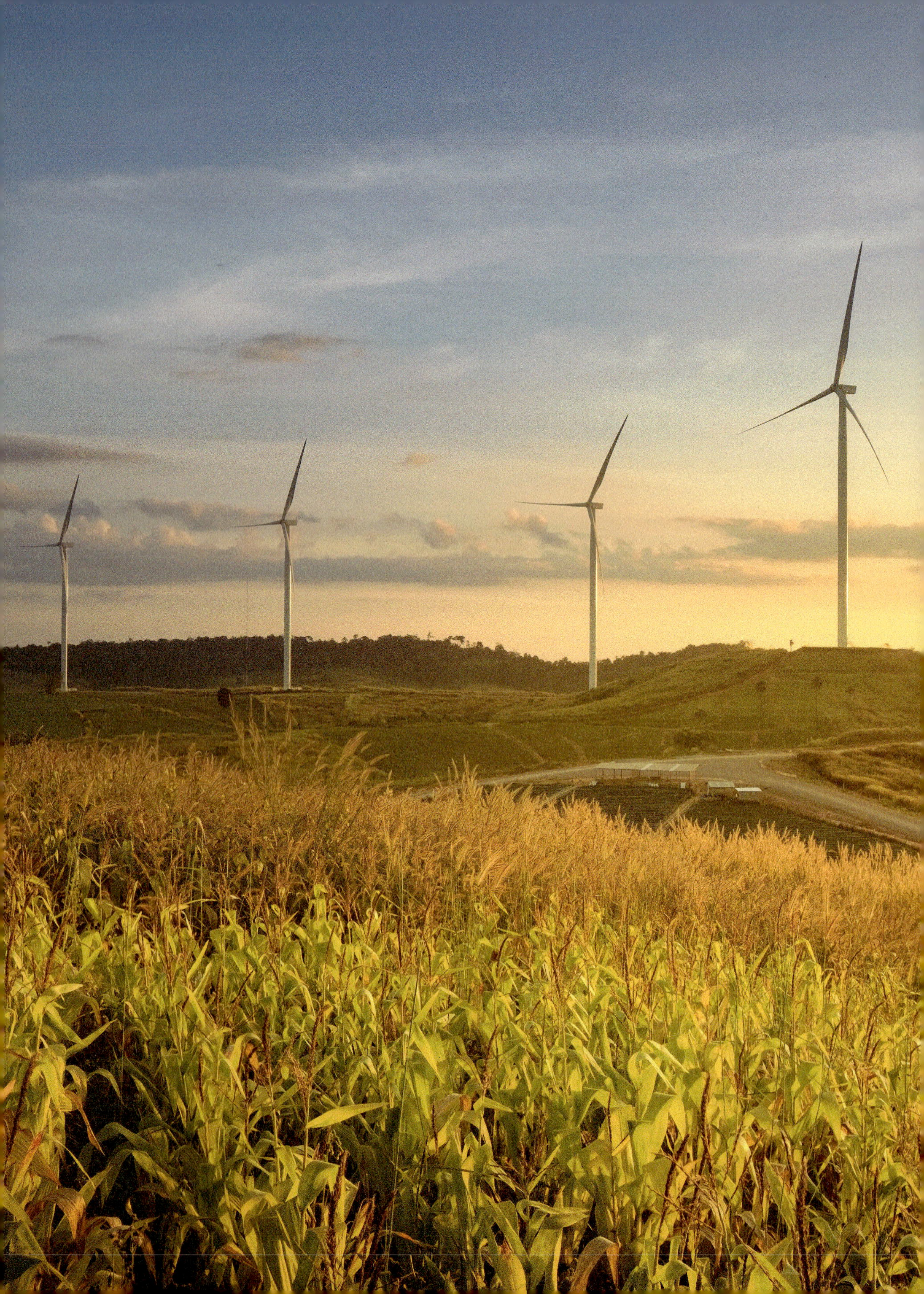

SECTION 4

Teaching approaches

Richard Hatwood

This section considers, explains and exemplifies the 'how to do' engaging and meaningful teaching that will support pupils in their learning of great geography. Key elements of what makes a really effective geography lesson through adopting teaching approaches such as enquiry and exploring pupils' curiosity are discussed and evaluated. Encouraging and equipping pupils to understand the need to be critical thinkers who make informed decisions about their future using their developing subject knowledge will help them to live not just in a sustainable world but an improved one.

Different teaching approaches

Being able to use a wide repertoire of different approaches to teaching geography, appropriate to the pupils and the context, is a crucial aspect of good primary geography teaching. This section deals with a number of different approaches, starting with how to handle the important question of connecting new content to pupils' prior knowledge, progressing through questioning techniques, the enquiry approach and debating, critical thinking and finally teaching for sustainability.

> *A good-quality geography lesson should be purposeful, problem-orientated, enquiry-based, undertaken co-operatively, involve active engagement and be stimulated by engagement with good-quality resources.* (Catling and Willy, 2018).

Each of these approaches can have a positive impact in isolation, but when combined really can drive forward the quality of teaching and learning.

Whichever approach is adopted, it needs to fit into a sound lesson structure, and teachers often structure their lessons following the 'plan, teach and reflect' cycle (Figure 1). This supports continuous development and improvement while allowing both teachers and pupils to evaluate learning and progress.

The reflect element is essential. Allowing time both for pupils to reflect on their learning and for the teacher to reflect on their planning, approach and delivery can foster a culture of improvement. Simple instant feedback can support pupils in improving their work; listening to pupils and looking at their work (books, photographs, videos, blogs, online activities) can tell teachers and subject leaders what has worked well and what needs developing.

Start local, go global

Teachers should look for ways to connect the geography they are teaching with pupils' prior knowledge and understanding. They should consider what the geography means to the pupils and enable them to apply the skills they have learnt. Curriculum making (see pages 57–58) has become a powerful tool to support pupils in learning about the world, from the local to the global. It can also help teachers to interpret the curriculum or scheme of work and turn it into a coherent and relevant sequence of teaching and learning activities that will challenge and engage pupils.

An initial focus on their own locality gives pupils an opportunity to develop fieldwork skills in a familiar environment. This can be applied further afield as the pupils progress through school; it will also inform their study of contrasting localities. Once pupils are familiar with their own local area, the focus can move on to improving their fieldwork skills, allowing more able pupils to be suitably challenged.

New and topical content

The world is constantly changing, and our geography teaching should reflect it. To teach good geography means sometimes venturing outside the established routine – exploring new content and different locality studies adds excitement and depth to geography lessons. It is also important to evaluate schemes of work regularly to ensure their continued relevance and ability to engage pupils; listening to pupils and holding pupil focus groups can help in this respect.

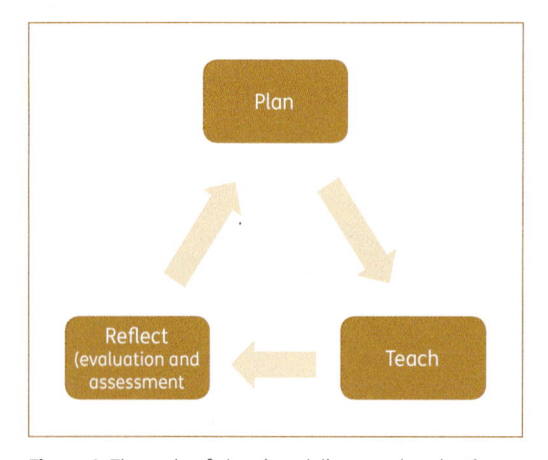

Figure 1: The cycle of planning, delivery and evaluation.

For an overseas locality study, international school links can really bring the study to life and can foster pupils' sense of connectedness. It is refreshing to see schools moving away from studying the more established localities to ones that are relevant to their school community – for example places twinned with their home town, or with which it has strong historical links. Developing the content of a place study around the first-hand experience of a member of staff is also a powerful way of engaging the whole staff in geographical learning and in raising the profile of the subject across the school.

Using current news items as a stimulus can be a really powerful and effective tool to deliver good geography lessons. It helps to ensure that the teaching is relevant to pupils' lives; it also provides a strong platform to develop links between home and school. Discussing the news as a follow-up activity at home can consolidate the learning from a geography lesson, encouraging pupils to develop as critical thinkers (see pages 47–50).

Questioning

When introducing new topics or areas of study, it is important to consider 'pupil voice' and how the pupils can have an input into the direction of the learning – not only what they are learning, but how. As a wide range of information, in a variety of media, becomes more freely accessible, many geography lessons are becoming joint learning opportunities for teachers and pupils. As topics and areas of study progress this can involve learning walls (Figure 2), which can also be virtual. Both teacher and pupils ask questions and find the answers together, and pupils are encouraged to become independent learners. As pupils' skills improve, teachers move from providing information towards fostering pupils' ability to acquire knowledge for themselves; they remain central to supporting pupils' learning.

Appropriate questioning can promote engagement and develop skills as well as help pupils mature into ethical and informed

Figure 2: Learning walls are an excellent method of recording collaborative development through questions or discussion during a topic or area of study. Photo © Jodie Martin.

citizens of their own locality and the wider world. When introducing new topics or areas of study, pausing and allowing the pupils to pose questions of their own, which the teacher then incorporates into the planning, is an effective way to develop excitement and interest in the topic. There are many approaches to questioning, and questions that teachers and pupils can use. Bloom's taxonomy is a graduated approach to developing questioning skills across all areas of learning (Figure 3).

For the questioning to result in real learning, pupils (and teachers) need time to reflect. Teachers should support pupils in considering the validity of their answers – how trustworthy are the resources they have consulted? Are there opposing views they have not considered? Is there, even, a right or wrong answer at all?

As an example, pupils could investigate whether the process of fracking is a 'good' or 'bad' thing. Deeply held local, environmental and economic arguments can all add to the complexity of the issue. Pupils should be encouraged to produce evidence to support their viewpoints and to bring ethical and moral values, as well as factual information, into the investigation. They will probably find convincing arguments for both sides and conclude that there is no clear-cut 'good' or 'bad', 'right' or 'wrong' outcome.

Enquiry

Enquiry skills are fundamental to primary geography, and the use of 'enquiry' is one of the most significant of all teaching approaches in geography. Enquiry is recognised as being

Create	▪ Write a detailed case study of the volcanic eruption in Montserrat ▪ Formulate a plan to investigate the features of the local river ▪ Write a letter explaining your view and reasoning on a local development
Evaluate	▪ Consider different opinions and facts to develop an argument for closing the high street to traffic ▪ Consider different opinions and facts to develop an argument for keeping the high street open to traffic ▪ How effective was our fieldwork in gathering the data needed for our enquiry?
Analyse	▪ Compare and contrast our town with the town that we are studying ▪ Can you distinguish between fact, opinion and belief in relation to this development? ▪ What does the data from our fieldwork investigation tell us?
Apply	▪ Demonstrate how tectonic plates move ▪ Explain how you would resolve a conflict in a National Park ▪ Annotate the features of a coastline and the processes that form them
Understand	▪ Classify the physical and human features of a locality ▪ Explain how a river gets to the coast ▪ Demonstrate how location in the world affects the types of plants and animals found there
Remember	▪ What is this place like? ▪ What does the flag look like? ▪ What are the features of a National Park?

Figure 3: This table explores the Bloom's taxonomy approach to questioning, with geographical examples.

important for three reasons: it influences 'what we learn, how we learn and how to develop skills and understandings that are essential for future societies' (Cooper *et al.*, 2006, p. 18).

The enquiry model has been described as 'the process of finding out answers to questions through actual knowledge and from other sources' (Blyth and Krause, 1999, p. 96). This is important: asking questions, processing information and finding answers, both for themselves and working with others, helps pupils make sense of their work. As well as finding answers, geographical enquiry encourages pupils to seek achievable solutions to any issues they identify (see pp. 39, 62–3). Questioning strategies employed by the teacher can enable pupils to influence the direction of the study, promoting their engagement and creating a real buzz and sense of excitement around school. Responding to the pupils' questions, and developing further questions, allows teachers to steer the direction of learning and tailor the teaching style to suit individual and collective interests in the class, promoting 'pupil voice' and the role of pupils in supporting their own study. Enquiries also give pupils the opportunity to get outside and explore and enjoy their local, and in some cases wider, environment. In contexts such as these, geography really does open doors.

Enquiry helps pupils to develop both questioning and investigative skills – it can be described as the space between what pupils can do on their own and what they can do with the support of others. It evolves from posing wide-ranging or broad questions that pupils can break into smaller, more meaningful questions that they can find answers to through research or fieldwork. Carrying out an enquiry develops pupils' geographical learning by providing opportunities for them to put into practice their geographical skills.

Planning for enquiry

The success of an enquiry depends on pupils having a clear understanding of the key questions (Dinkele, 2010). As pupils develop their geographical skills and understanding, enquiries allow teachers to pose questions that assess their understanding and progress.

The enquiry process can vary according to the needs of the pupils and the topic being studied. Access to the places pupils will need to visit must also be considered. The following case study (Figure 4) describes how one school used enquiry to effectively engage the pupils and develop their understanding and skills.

Critical thinking

Critical thinking was described by Lane (2007) as being a skill that is vital to effective teaching and learning in geography. As such, it has always had a clear role in geography lessons. Critical thinking and problem solving work hand-in-hand to equip pupils with the ability to reflect upon information gathered and to form their own opinions based on it. Essentially, critical thinking is the process of evaluating information, reflecting on it rather than accepting it unquestioningly, and using knowledge, experience and ethical judgement to form a view about it.

The proliferation of 'fake news' online and on social media has made the teaching of critical thinking even more important. It has been supported by schemes such as the British Council Connecting Classrooms Programme (see web page). Critical thinking helps pupils to pause and reflect on the content that they have found or are using and to analyse where it came from, who wrote it, how it was developed, the reliability of its source and how accurate it is.

Embedding critical thinking helps to prepare pupils for a future world in which ever-evolving skills and knowledge will be required. Being an adept critical thinker is a crucial skill for the 21st century and one that can be applied in all walks of life. The humanities in particular provide an excellent platform for the development of critical thinking; this is demonstrated by the nature and speed of the global events that feed into geography and history lessons.

Dog park

My idea is to build a dog park on some unused land on Rhyl promenade. A dog park is a safe area for dogs to play with other dogs and for the owners to be worry free and have a cuppa in our café. There is also going to be an indoor area for the winter months. At the dog park we will have lots of fun areas for a dog to exercise including tunnels and ramps also a digging area. There is a quiet area for dogs to chill and have a kip on a sofa or dog beds. There is a paddling pool for dogs to swim and have fun! There is a designated area for puppies to train.

In their geography and history studies, pupils can choose the theme and content that they would like to cover over the term or half term. The school uses open-ended questions and ensures pupils have time to think about the theme of the enquiry.

A class of 10-11-year-olds were given maps of their local area and were asked to identify a site that could be developed, and to discuss what should (or should not) be built there. Mixed ability groups worked on different ideas for different areas of Rhyl. They devised questionnaires, asked residents for their opinions and then came up with a proposal, which they delivered to the class. The class listened to the views put forward and then voted on their favourite idea.

This enquiry provided the opportunity to develop geographical skills and understanding such as:

- using maps, imagery and other tools including ICT to research and present information
- exploring and describing the causes and consequences of change and the impact these changes can have on environments
- identifying and describing natural and human features and exploring the links between them
- identifying and describing the distribution of places and people and how they are connected.

In addition, pupils were able to develop literacy and numeracy skills and practise using technology. All pupils were engaged and committed to their projects and the groups worked well together. The enquiry has demonstrated the positive impact of incorporating pupil voice into planning – not only on pupil engagement, but also on the quality and depth of their work, as well as on the transferrable questioning skills that they can apply in other subjects and projects. The entire school is now a keen proponent of such an approach.

Figure 4: A geographical enquiry to develop questioning skills at Ysgol Emmanuel, Rhyl. (A download of this case study is available from the web page.)

As an example, pupils could be asked to consider the photo in Figure 5, of a holiday resort on the Costa Brava. They could be asked to think about the views of the visiting tourists, the people who work in the resort and the local population. For instance, the local population may understand that the town needs the income generated by tourism but still feel overrun during the holiday season. Researching and sifting the evidence, and unpicking people's different, sometimes conflicting, views can add depth to your geography lessons and enable pupils to understand that there can be a number of different, and perhaps equally valid, perspectives on a given situation.

Debate

Providing opportunities to debate conflicting viewpoints, question the validity of evidence, embed deeper thinking and engage in meaningful and evidence-informed debate creates a learning environment conducive to teaching critical thinking.

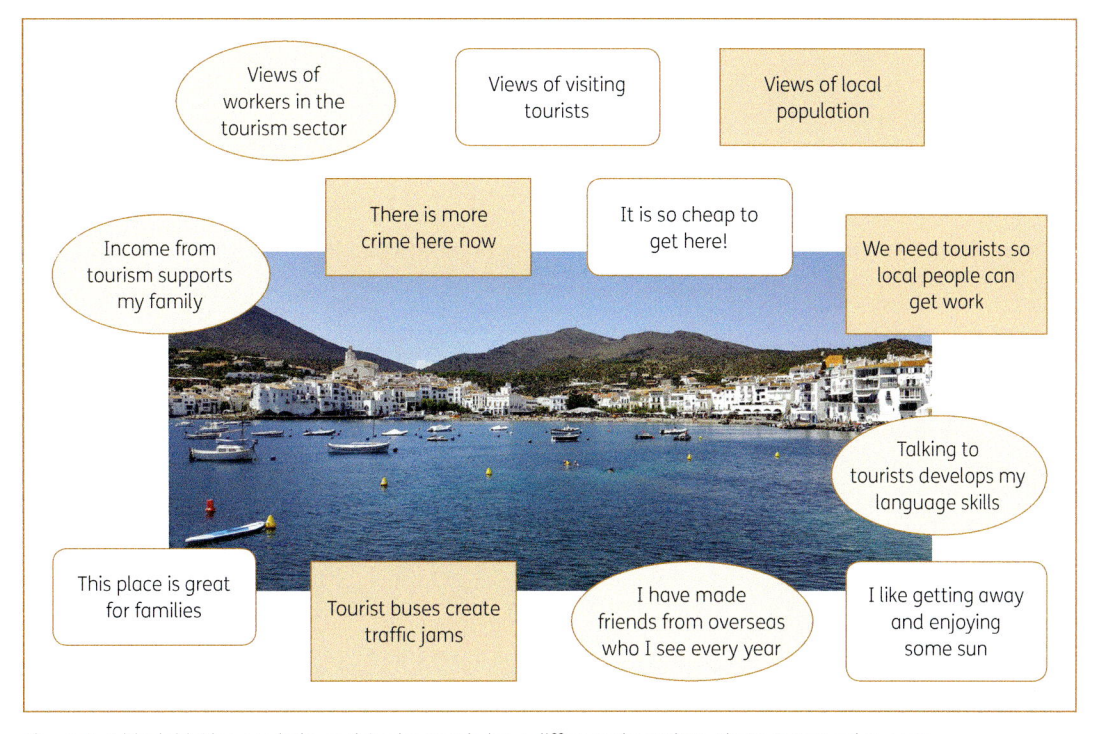

Figure 5: Critical thinking can help unpick why people have different viewpoints. Photo © Bernard Dupont.

Exploring local issues to develop critical thinking and problem solving allows pupils to develop their skills using relevant and familiar content. Over time, as the skills are embedded, the debates can move on to explore wider geographical issues. It is at this point that approaches such as Philosophy for Children, which aims for 'children and young people to experience rational and reasonable dialogue about things that matter to them' (Philosophy for Children, 2018) can come into play, empowering pupils and allowing them to drive the direction of study. Critical thinking and debate help pupils take their learning further and investigate issues at a much deeper level while respecting each other's viewpoints (Cooper *et al.*, 2006).

The contentious issue of fracking provides a relevant and meaningful platform for debate (Figure 6). Debating the issue enables pupils to consider varying viewpoints and the reasons behind them as well as how to move forward in a way that is acceptable to all parties.

In a 'silent debate' pupils respond in writing to given statements and to their peers' written responses. This work feeds into a general discussion afterwards. It is important that pupils give reasons for their views and have

Figure 6: An exemplar debate on the issue of fracking.

the opportunity to feed back their thoughts on the statements, as well as on the viewpoints of their peers. Teachers can adapt the statements being debated for their particular pupils and also enable pupil-led learning. Older pupils may be able to generate statements about a topic they have studied for their peers to debate, and younger pupils may access the activity by debating less detailed, more localised statements.

A silent debate provides a platform for all pupils to express their views, as well as begin to give reasons for them and explore how often issues in geography are interlinked, and for all their views to be heard (see web page for further information). It allows teachers to probe and focus on key geographical issues and to gather the pupils' perspectives on them. It develops core geographical concepts and helps to embed a deeper understanding.

The following is an example of a statement that could be debated with 7–11-year-old pupils:

A runway is to be built in Antarctica for aircraft to fly in researchers who are involved in conserving the whale population of the region.

This statement raises many issues and can help get the pupils thinking hard about how human activity can simultaneously have both positive and negative impacts on an environment.

This statement could stimulate a silent debate for 5-7-year-old pupils:

The council would like to close our local high street to cars and only allow people to walk along it

This statement could be adapted to make it more localised and relevant; it could also provide an interesting starting point for a topic on traffic, access, pollution and the local area.

Embedding critical thinking

To become effectively embedded, critical thinking should not happen in isolation. If possible, schools should aim for it to be embedded progressively, across year groups and the school. This enables pupils to build and develop their geographical knowledge, skills and understanding as they move through school and instils the confidence to transfer their understanding and skills into the world of work. This may not always be possible throughout the whole school, but it should be possible for individual teachers to create a classroom environment that promotes critical thinking and supports high-quality teaching and learning in geography.

Viewing the embedding of critical thinking skills as a progressive framework can help both individual teachers and the whole school understand where to start. Individual teachers can devise a progressive framework to show the development of critical thinking skills throughout a year group; key stage teams can develop similar frameworks across their key stage; whole-school staff can map the development across the school.

A good starting point would be for small groups of teachers to look in detail at where critical thinking is being developed in their current plans, where it could be easily developed and where there are gaps. Geography is ideal for developing critical thinking across the school as its content and values offer so many opportunities to develop the appropriate skills. Once any gaps have been identified professional development can be put in place. (See web page for further information.)

Preparing pupils for the future is an important, but often neglected, aspect of primary teaching. Developing critical thinking skills prepares them to be independent learners, able to reflect critically on what they read, make informed decisions and in turn contribute their own ideas in a clear and rational way (Figure 7). It avoids the danger of the 'single story', fostering instead an understanding of the complexity of our planet and the people who live on it. The link between geography and critical thinking is clear, and embracing it in the classroom will strengthen both the pupils' geographical understanding and their critical thinking skills.

As part of the British Council Connecting Classrooms project, staff and pupils at Thelwall Community School worked with their partner schools in South America to carry out a critical analysis of trends and anomalies in population data from a number of South American countries.

Asking 'why', 'what' and 'how' questions in an international context enabled pupils to develop a more robust understanding of the issues facing both their own and their partner schools. This ensured that they were not simply learning at a surface level but exploring in detail how their actions have an impact in the wider world, and also how we can we can all learn from each other, irrespective of the country we live in. With a focus on sustainable development and the challenges facing both their partner schools and their own community, pupils learnt about globally significant issues and developed empathy for the culture and arts of other countries.

The school found that embedding critical thinking across the school was a fairly seamless process, and that although it lends itself particularly well to geography, it can be applied with minimal alteration to a range of subjects. Pupils were observed to have gained a much deeper insight into geography's 'big ideas' (see pp. 22–3) and were able to not only answer questions with greater confidence and in greater depth but, more significantly, pose valid and thoughtful questions of their own.

Embedding critical thinking approaches has increased teachers' interest and engagement, and pupils have a greater appetite for and competence in problem solving and assessing sources of information. It has also helped the school to secure external recognition, including the Geographical Association PGQM (Primary Geography Quality Mark) and British Council ISA (International Schools Award).

Figure 7: Critical thinking and problem solving at Thelwall Community School. A download of this case study is available from the web page.

Teaching for a sustainable world

As educators, we are aiming to prepare pupils for a future world that is not yet known. Geography is a subject that considers not only the processes, but the beliefs and ethics behind the decision making that will go into shaping that future world. It is also the only subject that really addresses in a practical and informed manner the issues that will affect our future. The ever-increasing pressure that humans are putting on our planet and consequent changes to our climate, depletion of natural resources and globalisation all mean that teaching our pupils not only about sustainability, but how to live in a sustainable way, is more important than ever. By exploring and developing a deeper understanding of process and values, teachers are helping pupils learn how to make informed decisions.

Sustainability is a complex and challenging concept and one that is continually evolving as the environment changes and the science that explains how our world works develops. As its meaning in the primary school has evolved, sustainability has become a way of thinking about and seeing the world, rather than just a tick-box exercise in geography lessons, and has come to include the interconnections between economic, cultural and demographic sustainability. Although aspects of sustainability still need to be taught in geography lessons, the approach to understanding sustainability can span the whole curriculum and wider life in school, ensuring a deeper understanding by all involved as well as a reinforcement of geographical knowledge, skills and understanding.

Planning for sustainability

When planning and implementing pupil-led approaches, questioning strategies bring the focus back to sustainability, embedding it in the geography. As our understanding of sustainability has evolved and the scale of the challenge increased, teaching about sustainability from a standalone scheme of work is no longer enough. Although off-the-shelf schemes can be highly effective tools, the work must be contextualised in the curriculum, incorporating the needs of pupils and the wider environment, if primary geography is to have a powerful impact on the pupils in the school, their families and the wider community.

There are numerous ways to incorporate the teaching of sustainability into the curriculum. It is an effective platform to show the intrinsic links between human and physical geography and how each affects the other (see page 19). When developing a geography curriculum, it is important to ensure that pupils have opportunities to consider how the environmental impacts of human activities can be minimised. This can be achieved by linking pupils' learning to the wider sustainability agenda and allowing them to reflect on the physical impact of human actions at a local, national and international scale. This approach provides another link between geography and critical thinking, encouraging pupils to critically consider the evidence and then consider alternative viewpoints. This link is important to embed a deeper understanding of sustainability across the curriculum and wider school and demonstrates how important and interconnected the physical and human aspects of geography are.

Almost every aspect of study in geography can support the teaching of sustainability – transport, development, natural hazards, climate change, energy and coasts, to name a few. Each provides a unique avenue for pupils to learn about the underlying technical processes as well as consider its ethical dimension. For example, when studying natural hazards pupils can consider, at numerous different levels, how humans respond to living in a volcanically active region and whether the associated benefits are worth the risk.

Beginning with the local and familiar is an effective introduction to sustainability. Addressing local issues such as a new bypass, developments in National Parks, the construction of wind farms or fracking can all encourage your pupils and even the entire school community to engage in debate. It can also be a powerful method of taking key messages home to parents and carers or even out into the wider community. As pupils develop a deeper understanding of the concept of sustainability and reasons to promote sustainable living, they can begin to consider the wider global issues affecting sustainability.

The teaching of sustainability and its integration into the school curriculum and wider community allows us to teach and engage with our pupils and their families with a sense of optimism and hope for the future; something that is, perhaps, the responsibility of all primary teachers:

> *If we are not to overwhelm pupils with the world's problems, we should teach in a spirit of optimism. We should build environmental success stories into our curriculum and develop awareness of sources of hope in the world* (Huckle, 1990, p. 159).

Conclusion

The choices primary geography teachers make, and the quality of the teaching and learning in their classrooms, can have an impact on pupils for many years. They can influence pupils' decisions about future study and careers, as well as their personal beliefs and opinions.

Developing a meaningful curriculum that focuses on the pupils and gives them opportunities to develop their enquiry and questioning skills enhances the effectiveness of the subject, empowering pupils to participate in steering its course and making it relevant to their daily lives. This approach can increase pupils' engagement with the subject, as well as those teaching it, fostering a passion to learn about the world and how they can help to make it a better place.

In an ever-changing world, we must be able to make sense of the challenges that we face and suggest ways to resolve them, to create a sustainable future for us all. Geography provides a platform for understanding the moral and ethical reasoning behind decisions and choices made in the past and how those made in the future will be determined. As teachers we cannot shy away from challenging topics or themes; it is precisely these that can be the vehicle for efforts to create a more sustainable planet, that we are able to leave in a better condition than the one we inherited.

In essence, good-quality teaching in geography can be described as 'characterised by attitudes of open-mindedness, wholeheartedness and responsibility' (Cooper *et al.*, 2006, p. 175). When planned and delivered well, it really does take both the pupils and teachers far, both in terms of standards as well as beliefs and attitudes. Teaching the subject effectively is the springboard for driving pupils' understanding, their ambitions and their future. Ensuring that the teaching approach is appropriate and effective is paramount when planning for sustained and engaging learning.

> To access further support and resources from the *Leading Primary Geography* web page, see page 164

References

Blyth, A. and Krause, J. (1999) *Primary Geography: a developmental approach*. London: Hodder.

Catling, S. and Willy, T. (2018) *Understanding and Teaching Primary Geography*. London: Sage.

Cooper, H., Rowley, C. and Asquith, S. (2006) *Geography 3–11: A guide for teachers*. London: David Fulton Publishers.

Dinkele, G. (2010) 'Enquiries and investigations' in Scoffham, S. (ed) *Primary Geography Handbook* (Revised edition). Sheffield: The Geographical Association.

Huckle, J. (1990) 'Environmental Education: Teaching for a sustainable future' in Dufour, D. (ed) *The New Social Curriculum*. Cambridge: Cambridge University Press, pp. 150–65.

Lane, R. (2007) 'Improving the Critical Thinking Skills of Students in Geography', *The Social Educator*, 25, 1, pp. 29–37.

Philosophy for Children (2018) *Philosophy for Children*. Available at: https://p4c.com/about-p4c/ (last accessed 12/6/2019).

Roberts, M. (2011) *What makes a geography lesson good?* Available at: www.geography.org.uk/download/ga_prmghwhatmakesageographylessongood.pdf (last accessed 12/6/2019).

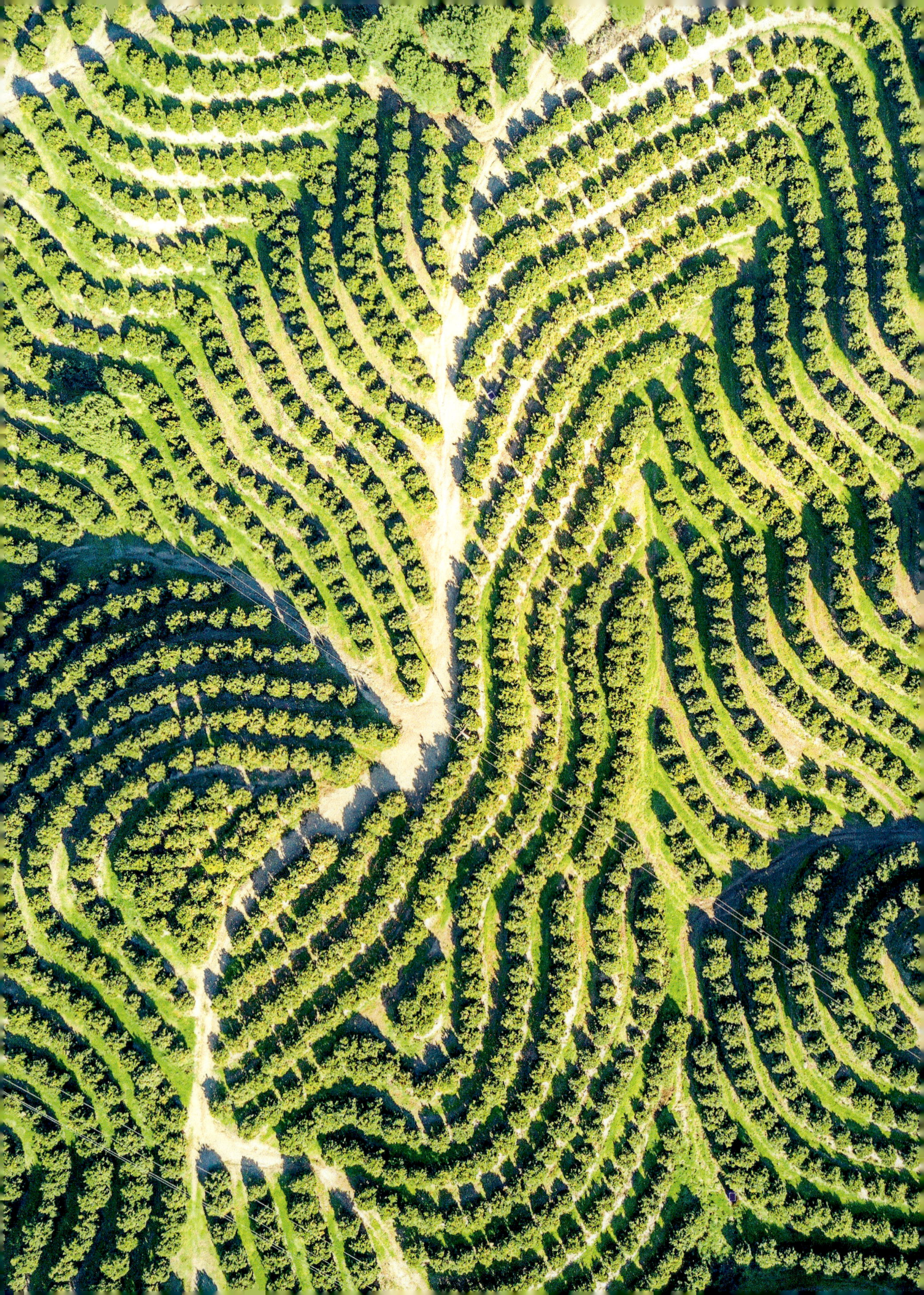

SECTION 5

Geography in your curriculum

Richard Greenwood

This section will help you to see where geography fits into your whole-school curriculum and gain a better understanding of why it is such an important, pivotal subject. The section considers how, as curriculum makers, you can formulate, shape, and develop the right curriculum for your school that has the flexibility to meet the needs of your pupils while conforming to the requirements of a general or national curriculum.

Geography in the whole-school curriculum

To be a good teacher of primary geography, you need to keep up to date with national and local curriculum requirements. It is equally important to make your geography curriculum as 'real' and relevant as possible, both for the pupils and yourself. This section discusses the aspects you should consider when planning your own primary geography curriculum.

The curriculum 'Big Picture'

Before planning your curriculum you need to think about what a 'curriculum' is. Definitions vary greatly in both breadth and scale – from the all-encompassing 'that which is taught in schools' to the more particular 'that which an individual experiences as a result of schooling' (see, e.g. Kelly, 2010). A number of authors have listed curriculum types, including 'curriculum as content' and 'curriculum as process' (Greenwood, 2013). Different ways of viewing the curriculum reflect fundamentally different philosophical orientations. According to Scott (2008), many governments have espoused the 'curriculum as content' approach: traditional subjects have clear boundaries, knowledge is efficiently transmitted from teachers to pupils, and there is an emphasis on targets and testing. In contrast, 'curriculum as process' emphasises what actually happens in classrooms – the interactions between teachers, learners and knowledge (Greenwood, 2013). Curriculum as process concentrates on the development of skills, concepts and understanding, rather than simply the transmission of knowledge. Its proponents argue that it breaks down potential subject barriers, emphasises pupil voice and empowers teachers to become curriculum makers.

Geography's place in the curriculum

Geography's distinctive role in the primary school is to develop pupils' curiosity, fascination and a sense of wonder about the world in which they live. In the Northern Ireland Curriculum (CCEA, 2007), geography, along with history, science and technology, is included in the 'World Around Us' (WAU) Area of Learning. This integration of geography with other relevant subjects is also found in the Early Years curriculum in England, and the Welsh curriculum for all primary pupils.

Most curricula include main themes or overarching concepts; in the case of geography these are the 'big ideas' (see page 22) plus map, enquiry and fieldwork skills (see pages 30–41). Place knowledge is usually a requirement, although the extent to which this is specified varies greatly. Underpinning all these aspects is 'understanding'; without understanding, pupil learning usually remains shallow.

Adapting to changes in national curricula

The influence of politics on education is rarely neutral. Organising the curriculum and deciding what should be included has inevitably been controversial. Agreement about ethos and purpose, as well as content, has been difficult to achieve between those in power, those who control the money and those at 'the chalk face'. Governments have varied in the degree to which they have wished to control curriculum content – what is to be taught – as well as how it is to be taught. Classroom teachers may feel that they are very far away from this level of debate and decision-making, but in the end, they are the people who have direct contact with pupils and implement the curriculum.

Catling (2015), in reviewing recent changes to the primary geography curriculum in England, argued that geography as a subject transcends any particular set of national curriculum requirements and that curriculum change allows teachers to consider ways in which geographical thinking (see pages 22–5) can be applied in the primary classroom. He also argued that the more succinctly curriculum content is defined, the more it is open to interpretation and (re)construction by teachers.

He concluded that curriculum change can be viewed optimistically, as an opportunity for schools and teachers to develop pupils' geographical thinking: that they should use all curricula simply as a starting point for planning. This process is called 'curriculum making'.

Curriculum making

Curriculum making can be defined as:

> '...interpreting a curriculum specification and turning it into a coherent scheme of work. The scheme of work then needs to be resourced and developed into lesson experiences... It is a creative act that lies at the heart of good teaching and heightens the enjoyment of teaching' (Owens, 2010, p. 8).

The GA identifies three main elements in the geography curriculum making process (Figure 1, see also web page) requiring teachers to draw on:

- different teaching approaches and specific teaching techniques
- their knowledge of their pupils and how they learn
- their own subject knowledge.

By balancing these three elements, teachers can create an engaging and challenging sequence of teaching and learning. Rather than simply setting out knowledge to be imparted, curriculum making is about bringing the given specification alive, giving it purpose and aiming for deep understanding. Teachers need to be able to 'fill in the gaps' in curriculum requirements, creating a curriculum that is suited to their pupils. In addition, for curriculum making to work well, teachers need to have a productive, ongoing relationship with the subject itself.

Trevor (2011) described how schools in England, working with the National Curriculum, showed real innovation by evolving local, child-initiated, enquiry-based, creative curricula. Similarly, Owens (2011) described schools who had amended and adapted National Curriculum statements to their context in what they referred to as 'our curriculum'; she suggested that a prerequisite is a climate in which teachers feel they have 'permission' to make appropriate changes to what they teach. However, they also need to acknowledge the unique properties of different subjects, choose relevant content, and apply their pedagogical understanding to decide how their pupils will learn.

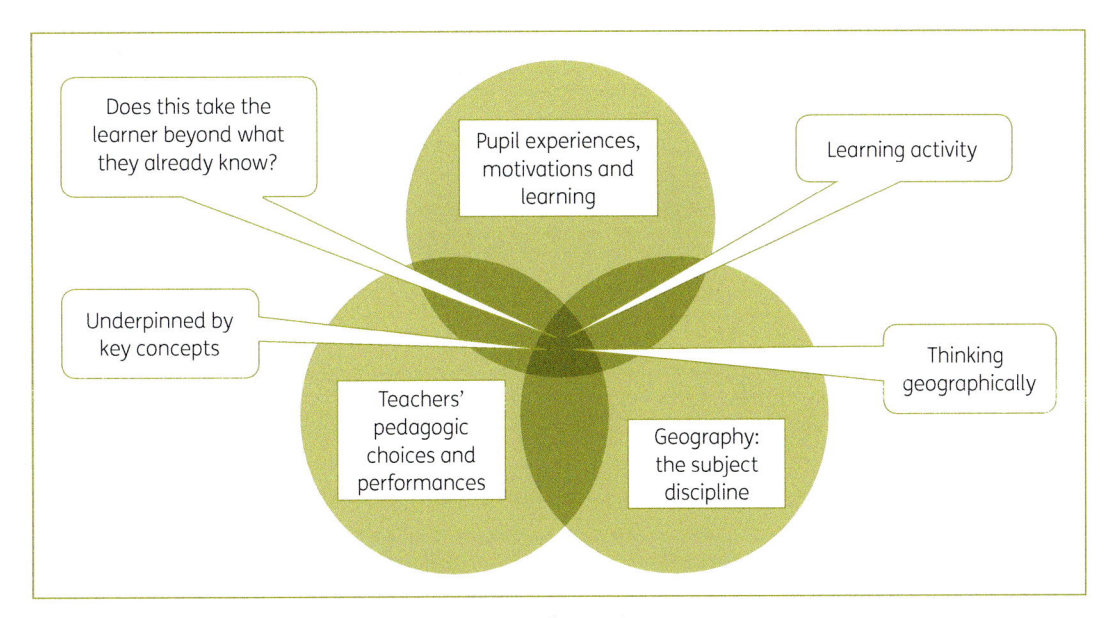

Figure 1: What is curriculum making? Source: www.geography.org.uk

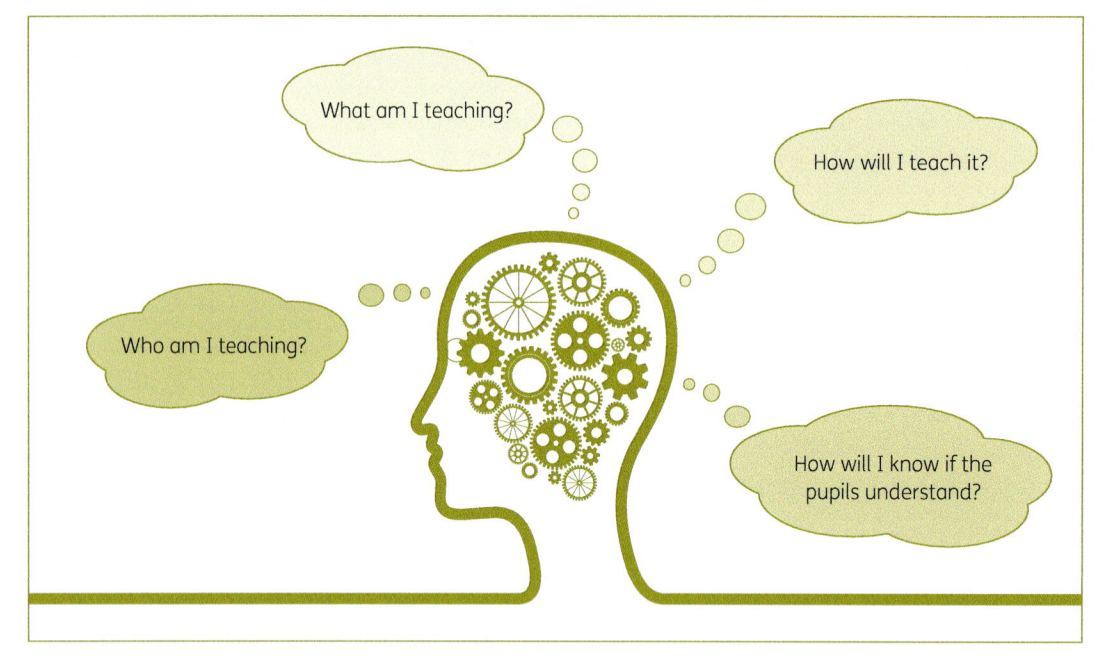

Figure 2: The essential questions you need to consider when planning. Image © Sky Motion/Shutterstock.com.

Catling's (2013) small-scale study of primary teachers' experiences of geography curriculum making reported that they expressed feelings of liberation – they felt they had regained control over decision making in their teaching. This re-energised their commitment, enthusiasm, aspirations and sense of agency. They spoke about 'retaking command' of their professional expertise and authority that, while daunting, was also emancipatory. Catling called on teachers to be confident in themselves as curriculum makers as they developed their knowledge of the various subject areas and the topics they taught.

Fundamentals of planning

Planning for the long-term and across the school is often done collaboratively and in conjunction with the subject co-ordinator or subject area lead (see pp. 126–34). Shorter term plans may also be completed with a parallel class teacher and often involve integrating geography with other subjects as discussed in Section 6. Such plans often follow a specified school format, to be completed on a template.

Figure 2 shows the essential questions you need to ask as you plan.

Figure 3 provides the features that should be included in shorter term plans but does not suggest a preferred format for presenting them. These are 'live' documents that should be annotated and adapted and need regular updating.

Everyday geography

Martin (2006a and 2006b) coined the word 'ethnogeography' to describe the everyday or personal geographical experiences that pupils bring to their geography learning. Ethnogeography focuses on pupils' interests, what is most relevant to them, their 'voice' and their concerns. 'Pupils do not feel connected to geography because it often appears to be about things "out there" rather than about their own lives, ideas and concerns about the world' (Martin, 2006a, p. 5). In the same way, many primary school teachers do not see themselves as geographers so may not feel a connection to a subject that is often perceived as mostly about 'knowing where places are'.

- Previous learning that is being developed
- Links to other subject areas
- Specific geographical learning objectives (what you want the pupils to understand by the end of the session, not just what they will be doing) in accordance with the school curriculum and considering geography's 'big ideas'
- Appropriate differentiation to enable inclusive learning
- Clear learning outcomes and regular, ongoing assessment opportunities (including self and peer assessment)
- Key questions
- Strategies for assessing the pupils and opportunities for feedback
- A sequence of teaching and learning activities following appropriate teaching approaches
- An outline of resources required
- An indication of timings, which may be adapted and tweaked as the need arises
- Opportunity for reflection and evaluation to inform next steps and where the learning may lead to

Figure 3: Features to include in planning.

Martin called for a reconnection between teachers, pupils and the subject to find 'ways in' to the subject, tapping into pupil experiences that they may not see as geographical, such as walking or driving around their local area, or playing in gardens or parks, while not diluting geographical understanding.

Geography is everywhere, and pupils, often unconsciously, bring its ways of understanding into the classroom as experiences, skills and knowledge that can inform their work and motivate them in their learning. It is up to teachers to exploit this resource, helping pupils make the right connections between their world and the wider subject. The skill for teachers is to recognise what is geographical about the everyday, and then structure the learning accordingly. The exciting thing about using the 'everyday' as a starting point is that it 'puts curriculum development, and the activities that follow, firmly back in the hands of teachers – the professionals who know pupils best' (Martin, 2006a, p. 7).

Powerful knowledge

Factual information is important; knowing the language, the vocabulary and the ways of thinking about what is being studied must go hand in hand with its understanding. Young (2008) described powerful knowledge in education as being systematic and specialised, often in the form of disciplinary knowledge, as found in school subjects. This kind of knowledge is defined according to what it can do – help pupils to a fuller understanding of the world, to explain, predict, envisage alternatives and think in new ways.

Everyday knowledge vs powerful knowledge

Among educationalists, particularly in the geography education community, a tension exists about the balance between powerful knowledge and everyday knowledge (Dolan, 2019). The proponents of powerful knowledge regard the everyday geography, or ethnogeography, approach as too limiting. However, Catling and Martin (2011) argued against the privileging in the primary geography curriculum of powerful knowledge over pupils' ethnogeography, disputing the assumption that academic disciplines and school subjects provide knowledge that is the key to allowing pupils to develop understanding of the world. They contested the idea that pupils' ethnogeography is poorly formed and therefore of limited use and value, arguing that it is 'powerful' in its own right, and needs to be seen alongside powerful knowledge as providing an important learning base.

Figure 4: Familiarity with the local site for fieldwork brings pupils' learning alive. Photo © Shaun Flannery.

Where governments or curriculum bodies seek to define the 'essential knowledge' that pupils should learn, a clear distinction needs to be made between propositional, substantive and procedural knowledge (see pages 20–3), allowing pupils to make sense of the world and understand it in new ways (Catling and Willy, 2018). The everyday geography approach should be seen as a starting point for, or a bridge to, the bigger world of the subject. It facilitates two of the most important linked ideas in primary geography: looking at similarity and difference and moving in understanding and knowledge from the local to the global.

Teachers' subject knowledge

Teachers' subject knowledge (see web page) and their professional judgement are at the heart of their ability to teach geography effectively. To become 'curriculum makers' demands high levels of skill in terms of subject knowledge and teaching methods, as well as a deep and sophisticated understanding of learning and a wide 'pedagogical repertoire' (Wood, 2011, p. 39). Teachers also need to develop a connection with their own ethnogeography. However, financial constraints mean teachers may lack opportunities to improve their geographical understanding by taking part in continuing professional development (Catling and Morley, 2013; Greenwood, 2013).

The elements of teacher knowledge, understanding, confidence and skill are all wrapped up in one word – 'pedagogy'. Divorcing curriculum content from pedagogy creates a false divide (Scoffham, 2013). Alexander (2010) suggests that how pupils learn is just as important as what they learn – even if a curriculum looks inspiring on paper, it will have little impact unless teachers are able to find ways to engage their pupils. Curriculum content must go hand in hand with creativity, emotional engagement, motivation and enjoyment in order for learning to be effective.

Personalising your geography teaching

So how can teachers carry out effective, high-quality curriculum making in their setting that:

- is based on the curriculum requirements that apply to them
- retains the integrity of geography as a subject
- takes account of the everyday geography that the pupils bring to school
- is interesting, challenging and 'real'?

Below are five ideas to keep in mind. Clearly, they are all very much inter-related and depend on teachers' flexibility and willingness to adapt.

1 Local geography

One of the most obvious and effective ways of personalising your geography curriculum is to include as much of the 'local' as possible in your planning and teaching. Incorporating pupils' everyday experience of their local community and environment can be a strong motivating factor and have a significant impact on their learning. Whether the work takes place within the school grounds, in the built-up areas surrounding the school, in 'natural' areas such as nearby parks and woodland (Figure 4) or further afield, for most pupils anchoring their geography work in a familiar place brings the learning alive; it also allows first-hand data to be gathered (Pickering, 2017). Planning for work to be done in a pattern of concentric circles around the school, at ever-increasing distances by younger to older pupils, can give staff a natural progression framework.

Local studies are almost by definition cross-curricular as they encourage the natural integration of a number of areas of the curriculum into the one study. For example, walks and trails around the local area involving surveys, map work and comparative photographs can lead to creative responses in the form of poetry, newspaper reports and paintings. Pupils can become very passionate, perhaps even defensive, about their local area (Catling and Willy, 2018), and a focus on their favourite and least favourite aspects of the area as well as their hopes and fears for its future can reap rich learning rewards.

It is important that pupils are not just learning about their local area but participating and collaborating in the research: it helps them make stronger links between their everyday experience and their school work, as well as develop their understanding of the local environment. This kind of involvement could also help them formulate and pursue their aspirations for themselves, others and even the wildlife in that environment. In doing this they would be developing as future local citizens with roles as consumers, residents, employees, stakeholders and voters.

Local studies can cause teachers anxiety, for the simple reason that they may be the least 'local' person in the class! Primary school teachers often commute to work whereas the pupils generally live nearby, so they are frequently the knowledgeable locals. Teachers should embrace this as an opportunity to engage the pupils in their learning by appealing to their expert knowledge of the local area.

2 Topical geography

Reports in the local and national news about people and places nearly always have a strong geographical component. It is the teacher's job to sift these stories for those related to the topic being taught that will be interesting and relevant to the pupils. As mentioned above, those with links to local studies are obvious candidates. Often local news media carry stories about changes in the local area, for example the building of a bypass, which may bring benefits for some and cause problems for others. It is important for primary school pupils to learn that change can be controversial and that it is usually impossible to 'please all of the people all of the time'. 'Geography gives us clarity and keeps us informed. It alerts us to our preferences, biases and prejudices, providing opportunities to reconsider' (Catling and Willy, 2018, p. 45).

Figure 5: The siting of wind farms, such as this one in South Wales, to meet our energy needs makes for a wide-ranging enquiry. Photo © Richard Whitcombe/Shutterstock.com.

Teachers should be willing to adapt their lessons to make best use of topical events in the media, using newsworthy events to bring a topic to life; for example, a recent volcanic eruption or tsunami would engage pupils in a natural hazards topic. It is also important to give pupils the opportunity to look at topical issues through a critical lens. In an era of so-called 'fake news', information sources need to be questioned and perhaps challenged (see pages 47–50). Pupils need to be taught to use more than one source of information and discuss possible error or bias in the reporting. A range of voices and points of view is better than a 'single story'.

3 Enquiry geography

Geographical enquiry (pp. 39, 46–7) occurs when: '...children are actively engaged in the creation of personal and shared meanings about the world, rather than being passive recipients of knowledge that has been created or selected by the teacher' (Martin, 2006b, p. 9).

One way of incorporating enquiry-based learning (EBL) into your planning is to devise a discrete unit of work using enquiry skills and first-hand data. For example, as part of a wider topic on renewable energy a number of lessons could be devoted to investigating whether it would be a good idea for a wind farm to be built on the edge of town (Figure 5). Ideally, first-hand information could be obtained from local people or invited experts who have differing opinions. This is an example of a 'philosophical' enquiry – one that does not necessarily have a 'right' or 'wrong' answer. Alternatively, enquiry can be seen as a general approach to learning, permeating all aspects of pupils' work. In this sense, a small enquiry can be carried out within a lesson; it might be based on secondary data, including textbooks and websites. What is important is that pupils are asking questions, researching, with the teacher's help, sources of information, analysing what they find, and coming up with answers. In this way both teacher and pupils are curriculum-makers!

The teacher's role in EBL is to support, facilitate and 'scaffold' the learning. Working in groups, pupils seek answers to their own and others' questions, developing critical thinking and problem-solving skills and gaining new perspectives. As with any 'dispersed' or 'distributed' model of classroom work, it is vital to build in time for plenaries and the opportunity for pupils to report back to the class. Pupils can comment on and learn from each other's progress, developing their creativity and communication skills.

4 Cross-curricularity

Debates in educational circles about whether the primary curriculum is more effectively structured by clearly defined subjects or a cross-curricular integrated approach have been taking place for many decades (Greenwood, 2013). Major reports (the 1967 Plowden Report, the 2009 Rose Report and Cambridge Review) have suggested linking subjects and combining areas of learning, but government policy in England has usually favoured a more traditional subject-based approach. Since 2007 Northern Ireland's primary curriculum has had seven 'Areas of Learning' and a push towards cross-curricular 'Connected Learning' approaches: 'Children learn best when learning is connected' (CCEA, 2007, p. 10).

As an academic subject, geography has always been very eclectic and interdisciplinary, drawing upon and contributing to other subjects. When pupils are 'doing geography', they are not doing it in isolation, but using their knowledge of other areas of the curriculum. Conversely, the best language and literacy learning frequently takes place within a specific content context, which geography is ideally placed to provide. The trick for teachers who are 'curriculum making' is to find the right balance between effectively connecting pupils' learning and maintaining the integrity of the various subjects. Planning topics whose connections are limited to two or three main subjects, with meaningful and appropriate links to other subjects, is a useful way forward.

The topics should have conceptual coherence, with natural, rather than contrived, links; in this way the integrity of the individual subjects can be maintained. It is essential to emphasise the primacy of the main contributing subject, an aspect that becomes increasingly important as pupils progress through the primary phase (see Section 6).

5 Pupil voice

The term 'pupil voice' embraces strategies that offer pupils a role in decision-making in their school. It has become increasingly important in education in recent decades, especially since the ratification of the United Nations Convention on the Rights of the Child, specifically Article 12 (UN, 1989). In this section, the aspect of pupil voice being discussed is pupil input into planning the topics they will be learning.

KWL grids (or KWHL grids – see p. 77) illustrate the pupil voice in action (Greenwood, 2018; 2019a, b). Perhaps best used at the start of a new topic, the pupils are asked to list what they already know (K) and what they want to know (W) about a topic; at the end of the topic, they are asked to discuss what they have learnt (L). KWL grids can be written by pupils, individually or in groups, but are often created by the teacher and whole class as a structural or graphic organiser in the form of a three-columned wall chart (Figure 6).

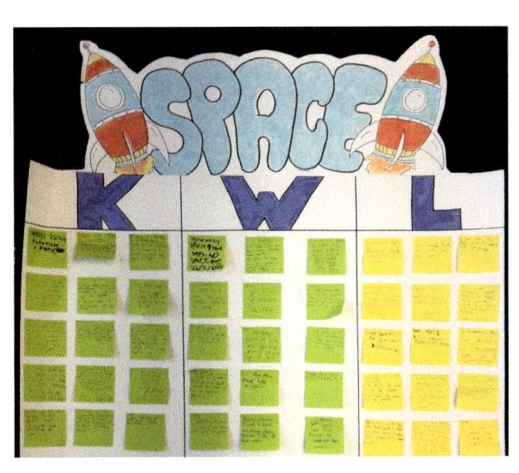

Figure 6: Example KWL grid. Photo © Richard Greenwood.

The KWL grid lets pupils see and be involved in some of the planning process. Listing what they already know (K) allows gaps in pupil knowledge and misconceptions about the topic to emerge, providing the basis for future learning. Recording what they want to know (W) about a topic, as well as involving them in its planning, introduces an enquiry mind-set. The 'enquiry classroom' needs to be a 'safe' place as well as a stimulating one, in which questions are welcomed and valued (see also p. 77). The pupils' questions may also reveal gaps and misconceptions, but again these can prove valuable for future learning. Not all avenues need to be explored; the teacher is still in charge of the topic! The final section (L) gives pupils an opportunity at the end of a topic or series of lessons to reflect on what they have learned. Looking back at the K and W sections, pupils can discuss whether prior knowledge has been confirmed or disproved and record which questions have been answered.

A summary of the research into the effectiveness of KWL approaches (Greenwood, 2018) noted the following benefits:

- an improvement in pupils' ability to generate questions
- pupils experienced greater enjoyment and a sense of being valued
- their greater sense of involvement and engagement led to increased motivation and 'ownership' of the work
- enhanced teacher-pupil relationships.

Catling's (2013) review of teachers' experiences as 'curriculum makers' found that initially many teachers saw the involvement of pupils in planning as 'risky', and were unsure where it might lead. However, as their pupils became 'active curriculum agents' they began to see the benefits. They realised that they needed to develop confidence in their pupils' capabilities and appreciate that they could bring valuable everyday experiences to geography-based topics. However, not all teachers share this optimistic viewpoint. Alexander (2010) reported that some teachers see such practices as just another erosion of their authority, but he challenged this attitude: 'Suggesting that children should have a voice does not negate the importance of the teacher voice' (p. 154).

Figure 7: Key ingredients for making your curriculum shine.

These ideas for personalising the geography in your curriculum are strongly interlinked and can be blended seamlessly together to make it shine (Figure 7). Using them to interpret the prescribed curriculum, and combining them with a knowledge of teaching approaches, your pupils and the subject itself, should enable all primary teachers to be geography 'curriculum makers'.

> To access further support and resources from the *Leading Primary Geography* web page, see page 164

References

Alexander, R. (2010) *Children, Their World, Their Education. Final Report and Recommendations of the Cambridge Primary Review*. Abingdon: Routledge.

Catling, S. (2013) 'Teachers' perspectives on curriculum making in primary geography in England', *Curriculum Journal*, 24, 3, pp. 427–53.

Catling, S. (2015) 'Introduction: thinking about primary geography', in Catling, S. (ed) *Research and Debate in Primary Geography*. Abingdon: Routledge.

Catling, S. and Martin, F. (2011) 'Contesting powerful knowledge: the primary geography curriculum as an articulation between academic and children's (ethno-)geographies', *Curriculum Journal*, 22, 3, pp. 317–36.

Catling, S. and Morley, E. (2013) 'Enquiring into primary teachers' geographical knowledge', *Education 3-13*, 41, 4, pp. 425–42.

Catling, S. and Willy, T. (2018) *Understanding and Teaching Primary Geography*. London: Sage.

CCEA (Council for the Curriculum, Examinations and Assessment) (2007) *The Northern Ireland Curriculum: Primary*. Belfast: CCEA.

Dolan, A. (2019) *Powerful Primary Geography: A toolkit for 21st Century Learning*. Abingdon: Routledge.

Greenwood, R. (2013) 'Curriculum Lessons?', *Primary Geography*, 82, pp. 18–19.

Greenwood, R. (2019a) 'Pupil involvement in planning topics using KWL grids: opinions of teachers, student teachers and pupils', *Educational Studies*, 45, 4, pp. 497–519.

Greenwood, R. (2019b) 'KWL grids: pupil voice in action', *Primary Geography*, 98, pp. 7–8.

Kelly, A. (2010) *The Curriculum: Theory and Practice* (6th edn.). London: Paul Chapman.

Martin, F. (2006a) 'Everyday geography', *Primary Geographer*, 61, pp. 4–7.

Martin, F. (2006b) *Teaching Geography in Primary Schools*. Cambridge: Chris Kington Publishing.

Owens, P. (2010) 'Re-making the curriculum', *Primary Geographer*, 72, pp. 8–9.

Owens, P. (2011) 'Primary Curriculum Overview: How can the GA help?', *GA Magazine*, 17, p. 23.

Pickering, S. (ed) (2017) *Teaching Outdoors Creatively*. Abingdon: Routledge.

Scoffham, S. (ed) (2013) *Teaching Geography Creatively*. Abingdon: Routledge.

Scott, D. (2008) *Critical Essays on Major Curriculum Theorists*. New York, NY: Routledge.

Trevor, C. (2011) 'Primary Curriculum Overview: The view from an advisor', *GA Magazine*, 17, p. 22.

United Nations (1989) *Convention on the Rights of the Child. General Assembly Resolution 44/25*, UN Doc. A/RES/44/25.

Wood, E. (2011) 'Cross-curricular teaching to support child-initiated learning in EYFS and Key Stage 1' in Kerry, T. (ed) *Cross-curricular Teaching in the Primary School: Planning and teaching imaginative lessons*. Abingdon: Routledge. pp. 39–51.

Young, M. (2008) *Bringing Knowledge Back in: From social constructivism to social realism in the sociology of education*. Abingdon: Routledge.

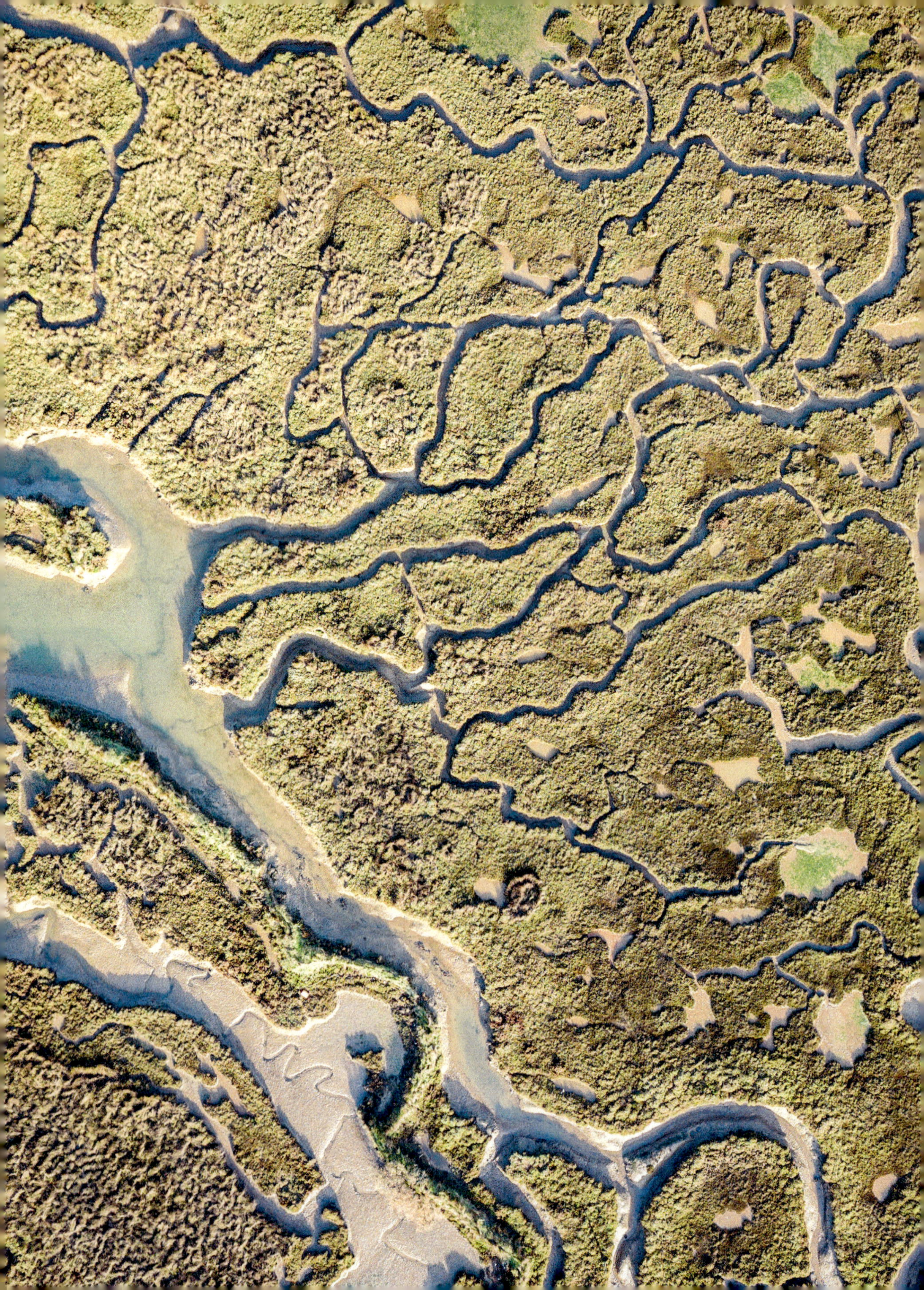

SECTION 6

Integrating geography

Leszek Iwaskow
Julia Tanner
Ben Ballin
Susan Pike

Geography is the ideal 'umbrella' subject as it is able to link with other foundation subjects as well as the core subjects, providing a real and meaningful context and a coherent and comprehensive learning experience. This section offers an overview of integrated teaching and provides examples of varied approaches for integrating geography with core and foundation subjects. It then considers the potential and magic of teaching through topic, especially a geography-based topic, which can animate and inspire learning as pupils focus on real-life examples. Throughout, it stresses the importance of being explicit about the specific geographical learning you want pupils to develop and of having clear and tangible geographical learning objectives.

Introduction to teaching geography in a cross-curricular way

Leszek Iwaskow

Geography is the ideal subject to integrate across a range of disciplines. A geographer is often referred to as 'a jack of all trades'. This could be taken as a compliment, as it suggests a geographer has a good broad knowledge across a number of disciplines and knows enough about each one to be able to bring these together in a practical way. This is an invaluable skill, especially in a primary context, and is particularly well exemplified in the Early Years: young children learn best in an integrated way, not in neat tidy compartments. Play, child-initiated and adult-initiated activities, together with the practitioner's knowledge of the areas of learning, all come together in good Early Years practice, but latent within this is the danger that the teacher becomes a generalist, rather than a specialist – in other words, 'a jack of all trades and master of none'. Do it well, and pupils' learning across a range of subjects and in key skills such as literacy and mathematics can be given a tremendous boost; but do it badly and the geography will be dissipated, the learning will lose its focus, and the work will become shallow and meaningless.

In developing a cross-curricular approach, school leaders should be able to explain the rationale behind the design of their curriculum. In particular, subject leaders need to be able to justify the content and planning of their units of work. It is not good enough to complete the section labelled 'geography' with any activity that somehow satisfies the brief hinted at by the topic title. Teachers will have to think hard about precisely what pupils are expected to learn and remember.

To be effective, a cross-curricular approach must both maintain the integrity of the subject and achieve a high level of geographical learning. Lose the academic rigour and direction and you soon find that what is being taught in 'topic' on a Wednesday afternoon is part of a 'Julie Andrews curriculum' where teachers focus on a few of their 'favourite things'. This was identified in the last Ofsted subject report on geography: '...teachers were selective in what they taught, apparently concentrating on the aspects of the curriculum where they felt most secure. As a result, pupils did not get a comprehensive and cohesive experience in geography' (Ofsted, 2011, p.14).

However, where a cross-curricular approach is used effectively, it can positively enhance the dynamics of learning. Firstly, pupils integrate their learning experiences, broadening their understanding of themselves and their world. Secondly, they are engaged actively in seeking, acquiring and using their knowledge in a variety of interlinked contexts, utilising and improving a range of basic skills including those prime skills of literacy and numeracy.

Subject knowledge

The paramount pre-requisite for successful cross-curricular planning is sound subject knowledge. When reviewing their curriculum, primary schools should be wary of placing too great an emphasis on subject integration. Simplicity, rather than complexity, is the key to effective planning. Care must be taken to ensure that geography does not become peripheral within a topic. Also, there should be a clear balance between the mutually supportive elements of good geographical learning: skills, knowledge and understanding. Themed headings may provide an overarching focus for a module of work, but the geography objectives need to be clearly identified and sufficient time allowed to ensure that the full content is covered. If this does not happen there is a real danger of the geography content becoming thin and pupils' experiences becoming fragmented. A secure subject knowledge base ensures that the subject is being taught in sufficient depth, enabling teachers to recognise and challenge pupils' misconceptions (see web page).

The value of a well-planned and managed cross-curricular approach is that it can develop pupils' knowledge, skills and understanding in a creative way. Where topics and subjects are interconnected with clarity of purpose, pupils' learning can be motivating. A study that crosses subject boundaries can foster a sense of curiosity and stimulate pupils' imagination. It needs to be well organised but not necessarily formal. It can encourage active enquiry, promote discussion and debate and encourage both factual and imaginative writing. The development of the key basic skills in literacy and numeracy can be enhanced by exploring the curriculum for relevant, engaging contexts. The Cambridge Primary Review found that 'far from being a threat to achieved standards in "the basics", a broad, rich, balanced and well-managed curriculum is actually the pre-requisite for those standards' (Alexander, 2010). Geography plays an important part in ensuring pupils become increasingly competent and confident in language, literacy and numeracy. The subject's breadth, spanning as it does a range of disciplines, makes it the ideal vehicle for meaningful cross-curricular links. Pupils can also acquire an array of personal skills during the course of their learning: geography provides a context for communication and teamwork, logical reasoning and data analysis, problem solving, computer literacy and research. It can also encourage pupils to develop the ability to form their own opinions and express and justify their views. It helps foster opinions, perspectives and arguments across a range of subjects.

An effective cross-curricular approach requires a conceptual thread built securely on a clear knowledge base. Teachers must be clear about what needs to be covered and how that fits in with other areas of the curriculum, and know which subjects provide the best links. This is where subject knowledge is essential as it highlights which links are valid. Pupils' progression in geography, or indeed in any subject, depends on being able to link new with existing knowledge and demonstrate understanding. If pupils' knowledge base is partial or sketchy it will limit their understanding; outcomes, particularly written outcomes, can be generalist and superficial. As a result, the potential to make connections and show understanding is very limited. In contrast, if they have a more extensive body of knowledge pupils can make more links and this will be reflected in better developed writing.

Powerful ideas

Central to a successful integrated unit there must be a key idea or concept, based on one of geography's 'big ideas', or 'powerful ideas' (see p. 22). Having a powerful idea provides the glue that binds multi-disciplinary learning into a process that leads to clear and relevant outcomes: a very effective example is shown in Figure 1.

A sense of place

Another powerful idea, which is central to geographical learning, is a sense of place. A locality, including the immediate locality, can be the powerful idea central to a range of linked themes, as shown in the Liverpool case study (Figure 2), which describes how the pupils' local area can open up possibilities for learning across a range of subjects and ages.

Keeping in touch with the curriculum

Ofsted has found that many of the schools that made good use of links across subjects achieved these outcomes:

- they strengthened the relevance and coherence of the curriculum for pupils
- they ensured that pupils applied the knowledge and skills learned in one subject to others, reinforcing their learning and increasing their understanding and confidence
- they made good use of longer blocks of time, enabling pupils to undertake sustained work on themes covering two or three subjects (Ofsted, 2002, p. 7).

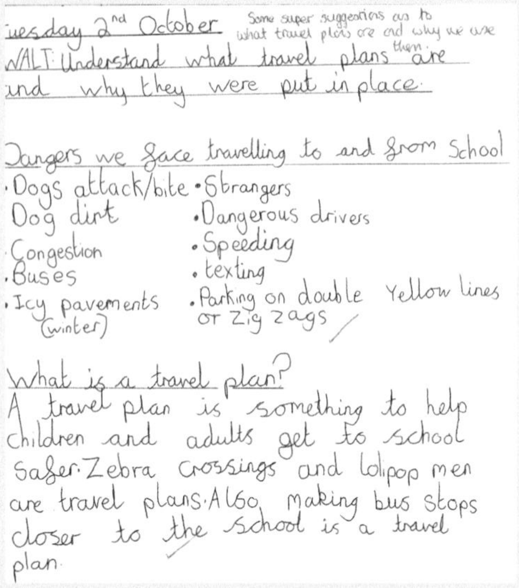

> Tuesday 2nd October *Some super suggestions as to what travel plans are and why we use them.*
> WALT Understand what travel plans are and why they were put in place.
>
> Dangers we face travelling to and from school
> • Dogs attack/bite • Strangers
>   Dog dirt   • Dangerous drivers
> • Congestion   • Speeding
> • Buses   • texting
> • Icy pavements   • Parking on double yellow lines
>   (winter)   or zig zags
>
> What is a travel plan?
> A travel plan is something to help children and adults get to school safer. Zebra crossings and lolipop men are travel plans. Also, making bus stops closer to the school is a travel plan.

The school wanted to devise a unit of work for their classes of 10–11-year-olds that would cover a range of subjects and utilise and develop a range of basic skills. This would also provide a useful baseline for transfer into secondary school, where it could be continued. The main idea, which would be central to the integrated approach, was for the pupils to produce a school travel plan intended to promote and facilitate active, healthy, safe and sustainable travel to school. It was to include a strong focus on geographical enquiry and other skills as well as understanding. The plan was intended to provide a rich context for learning across a range of other subjects including PSHE.

In this example the powerful idea enables the process to evolve naturally: each idea builds on the previous one. Because geography is multi-disciplinary, the links with the other subjects, as identified in the exemplar, occur naturally and are not intrusive. In other words, the unit hangs together and provides clear, complementary learning experiences. There is an explicit connection between subjects and shared skills.

The factual knowledge to be accessed is subject-specific and, in this case, there is a clear core of geographical knowledge. However, the pedagogical skills needed to impart it are shared with other subjects.

The fieldwork investigation provides important opportunities to work collaboratively and, equally, develop individual responsibility, which links well with PSHE and citizenship. As they engaged with the project, pupils developed self-confidence and social responsibility. Since every pupil was involved in different aspects of the learning, they all benefitted and made the best of their abilities. There were numerous opportunities for language development, for example through factual writing and discussion, while the geographical investigations allowed pupils to measure, record and manipulate data. Fieldwork also gave them an excellent reason to use databases, develop graphicacy skills and begin to manipulate geographical information systems (GIS).

Pupils could also become directly involved in road safety improvements in their locality by writing about their findings to their local council, member of parliament or police inspector. They could have an input into the siting of a new pedestrian crossing, or the establishment of a new speed limit, etc., giving them an insight into democracy in action. Presenting their plan to school governors would develop their speaking and presentational skills, as well as their ability to think critically, giving them a sense of achievement. Seeing how their actions can change attitudes would empower them and give them a sense of autonomy. A number of parents from Stanley School reported that their children had castigated them for driving at 40 miles an hour through a 30mph zone.

Figure 1: The school travel plan produced by Stanley Primary School in Blackpool. Download a full case study with travel plan exemplar from the web page.

This Liverpool case study, involving 5–11-year-old pupils across a number of schools, was supported by Liverpool Football Club and fronted by the footballer Mo Salah. The schools' close links with a school in Cairo ensured the exchange of ideas and resources, and was part of the 'travel buddy' initiative (see p. 73). The focus on the locality ensured pupils' engagement and enabled them to make connections and access learning in other subjects.

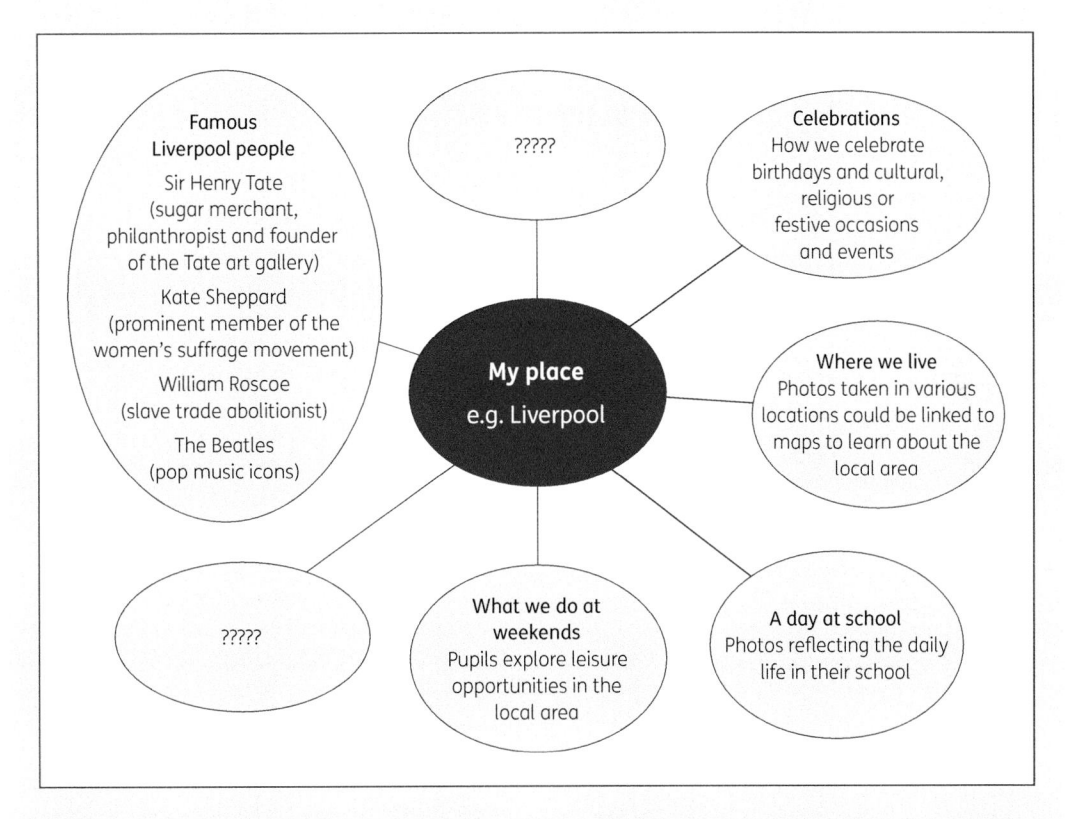

My place e.g. Liverpool

- **Famous Liverpool people**
  Sir Henry Tate (sugar merchant, philanthropist and founder of the Tate art gallery)
  Kate Sheppard (prominent member of the women's suffrage movement)
  William Roscoe (slave trade abolitionist)
  The Beatles (pop music icons)
- ?????
- **Celebrations** How we celebrate birthdays and cultural, religious or festive occasions and events
- **Where we live** Photos taken in various locations could be linked to maps to learn about the local area
- **A day at school** Photos reflecting the daily life in their school
- **What we do at weekends** Pupils explore leisure opportunities in the local area
- ?????

Researching local people can lead pupils to delve into other subject areas: art (the Tate gallery); music (the Beatles); or history (the suffrage movement and Liverpool's role in the slave trade). Celebrations can lead to links with religious education or personal and social education. Where we live is an obvious link to geography: this can include fieldwork in the immediate locality or a study of broader geographical features such as rivers (the economic importance of the Mersey). A focus on Colchester would inevitably link the place to a study of Roman Britain; Bristol, and its association with Brunel, would link well with science and design and technology; Barcelona prompts obvious links with the architect and artist Gaudi (art and design).

However, when planning a unit of work around a sense of place it is important not to let your imagination run riot; bear in mind the time available for the topic. Once the 'My place' mind map has been completed, focus on the content and links with the greatest potential for learning and how these fit into overall curriculum coverage. The focus should always be on core knowledge in the specific subjects.

Figure 2: A cross-curricular study based on a sense of 'my place'.

Topics that worked well were those that took a multi-disciplinary approach without losing touch with the content, skills and objectives of the curriculum. Too often, however, cross-curricular links are unclear or emphasise one subject at the expense of others; consequently, some of the geographical study becomes superficial. Ofsted has reported that a themed week, ostensibly with a geographical context, actually included very little geographical learning:

> 'As part of a themed week, pupils had attended an inter-school Olympics where they competed as and represented an allocated country, Pakistan. During the rest of the week they were involved in activities and lessons linked to Pakistan. The pupils thoroughly enjoyed the opportunities offered: they designed Asian-style clothes, made carpets using traditional designs and learnt about Muslim weddings, mosaics and mehndi patterns. However, pupils rarely explicitly studied the geography of Pakistan. Only in the year 3 class was the opportunity taken to integrate the work into their geography topic of "weather around the world". Overall, despite studying a country in depth over the week, most pupils learnt very little about its geography' (Ofsted, 2008, pp. 17-18).

The outcome is that pupils transfer to secondary school with superficial geographical learning and a weak basis for progression in their geographical knowledge, skills and understanding.

When planning the topic, therefore, the following elements must be considered:

- what the nature of the finished work will be
- what the outcome will look like
- what the topic will cover
- how it will fit into other areas of the curriculum
- which subjects offer the best links.

Implicit is the need to ensure that the necessary generic and subject-specific skills can be developed and nurtured. These are clearly evident in the school travel plan unit, but lacking in the Pakistan example. A poor understanding of the subject links may mean pupils are set general tasks, resulting in an accumulation of information, some relevant, some not. As a result, the geography provides a context for shallow learning in other subjects In a well-planned topic, geographical content is clearly defined and there is a core focus on distinctive geographical knowledge (see pp. 20-2). Geographical skills, pitched at an appropriate level, must be covered: using a range of maps, photographs, sketches and graphs as well as fieldwork skills (see pp. 30-41) and key subject-specific vocabulary on which to scaffold the learning.

The sense of place idea is well suited to a study of a contrasting locality, especially where there are links with other schools, either in the United Kingdom or abroad. However, school links do not always lead to effective learning: reciprocal visits by teachers to their partner schools stimulate initial interest and assemblies can celebrate the link, but embryonic pen pal exchanges can soon fizzle out and the link becomes symbolic or a pleasant memory. However, when the link is curriculum-focussed the learning can become relevant and meaningful, as the case study in Figure 3 shows.

Geographical themes for a cross-curricular approach

When linking subjects, consideration needs to be given to the aims and content identified in the programmes of study. Usually, apart from the core subjects, these tend to be quite broad and flexible. This allows for creativity but at the same time risks a general rather than a specific approach to the planning. This is where multi-disciplinary geography stands out from the other subjects. Many of geography's concepts and themes can provide a 'powerful idea' around which to build a unit of work linking two or three subjects in a tight way while enabling cross-fertilisation of knowledge, understanding and skills.

The 'travel buddy' approach is an effective catalyst for cross-curricular learning. It is often almost impossible for pupils themselves to visit their partner school, but a travel buddy can. The travel buddy can be used throughout the primary years but is especially engaging with the youngest pupils, from 3 to 7 years old.

There are many variations on this theme, and it can start with pupils discussing the question: 'If our class was an animal what sort of animal would it be?' This opens up possibilities to develop discussion, speaking and listening and personal and social development. Pupils may discuss the characteristic traits of various animals (developing their scientific knowledge and understanding). The class then votes on which animal is to represent their class (linking to citizenship and values education). A soft toy representing the animal chosen is brought into class, and pupils discuss and decide on a name for it (promoting personal and social development).

This activity is replicated in the partner school, and the travel buddies are exchanged. Teachers at both schools will have negotiated a number of common themes, some of which may be similar to those in Figure 2, such as:

- a day at school
- my place
- how we spend the weekend
- celebrations
- my family.

For the 'my place' theme, photos of the travel buddy in a number of locations can be linked to a map of the local area. In this way, pupils learn about their own locality. The photographs are exchanged with the partner school and pupils can use stimulus materials to begin to learn about the contrasting locality. Similarly, photos of the travel buddy in school provide a timeline of a typical day at school, and again, these can be exchanged so pupils can compare their day at school with that of the contrasting locality school. As the pupils receive materials from the partner school, they begin to develop an understanding of the geography, culture, religion and lifestyle of the contrasting locality in which their partner school is located. After the completion of the agreed topics the travel buddy returns to its home school to a big celebration linked to what the pupils have learned from their travel buddy's adventures. This provides an excellent cross-curricular stimulus that really captures pupils' imaginations as well as provides a core of geographical learning.

Figure 3: Using a travel buddy to introduce a sense of place theme. Photo © Dorcas Brown.

Themes that may feature in a cross-curricular approach with a geographical context include physical, human and environmental aspects, such as:

- climate
- resources
- landforms
- biomes
- settlement
- development
- sustainability
- diversity
- processes
- interaction
- population
- trade
- energy
- change
- patterns
- culture.

In an integrated approach these themes can all provide clear links to other subjects. For example, links between a primary school in Somerset and a primary school in Kenya provided rich opportunities for learning about sustainability in relation to three separate topics: water, waste and transport. Within these topics there are numerous links to enable learning in science and design and technology, as well as to build on mathematical and language skills. The focus and planning of tasks led to real depth in learning:

> 'Pupils in both schools studied each topic at the same time and exchanged their findings. The pupils from the English school considered themselves to be at the forefront of leading sustainable lives and were astonished to find that, compared to their partners in Kenya, they were very wasteful. Contrasting approaches towards the use of transport underlined differences in lifestyles and attitudes. A Kenyan pupil asked: 'Can you explain why you travel seven miles to get a haircut?' This led to a discussion of 'unnecessary journeys'. Thus, the link went beyond exchanging information to a real challenge that set the pupils thinking about their own lifestyles and revising their stereotypical views of Africa' (Ofsted, 2009, p.13).

In summary

Effective cross-curricular links require the following elements:

Breadth and balance

Pupils should receive their full entitlement to the entire primary curriculum throughout the primary phase. Within this requirement, there is a need to identify which content is best taught discretely and which will benefit from a cross-curricular approach.

Subject core knowledge and coherence

Links should be relevant, and not forced or contrived. There should be a clear link between the different subjects and the topic should not be overcomplicated by trying to link more subjects than appropriate. Basic language and mathematical skills will permeate the tasks set. Learning outcomes should be clearly related (Figures 4 and 5) to the two or three linked subjects chosen, for example:

- extreme weather in geography could be linked with states of matter in science
- rainforests as a region in the Americas could be linked with living things and their habitats in science and a study of the Mayan civilization in history (see p. 92).

Figure 4: Extreme weather in geography could be linked with states of matter in science. Photo © sdecoret/Shutterstock.com.

Figure 5: Geographical work on rainforests links naturally with living things and their habitats in science. Work by Dan Grandfield, Carterknowle Junior School.

If there are no clear links it would be best to teach that subject discretely. Good cross-curricular planning should not include unfocused topic work. It can include several subjects but there should usually be one, or at most two, lead subjects. In the unit on the school travel plan, geography is clearly the lead subject, providing a framework and focus for the topic. The inter-disciplinary nature of geography frequently makes it the most suitable subject around which to build the integrated topic.

The integrity and identity of each subject should be protected

Planning should identify which aspects of the individual subjects are being covered. This is essential in order to check coverage and ensure progression. One of the frustrations for subject leaders in foundation subjects is the almost impossible task of trying to disentangle what has been covered and in what depth. For example, a unit of work on Egypt may focus on life and beliefs in Ancient Egypt. The unit may include a study of the pyramids, linked to work on mechanisms, including levers, pulleys and gears, in science. A map of the Mediterranean Sea and North Africa showing the location of Egypt may be included, but this does not ensure progression in geography: the geography is incidental. If, however, within the topic there is an in-depth study of Cairo or a rural village on the banks of the Nile there will be clearer evidence that pupils have had relevant and meaningful opportunities to apply geographical knowledge, understanding and skills in a purposeful context.

Support for a cross-curricular approach

When planning an integrated unit of work linking geography with other subjects, it is often useful to visit the subject association websites to see if there is any supporting guidance or teaching ideas. You may be surprised, and it may reduce your workload if you can access and adapt teaching ideas and resources. It is also essential if primary teachers are to develop their subject expertise beyond the core curriculum.

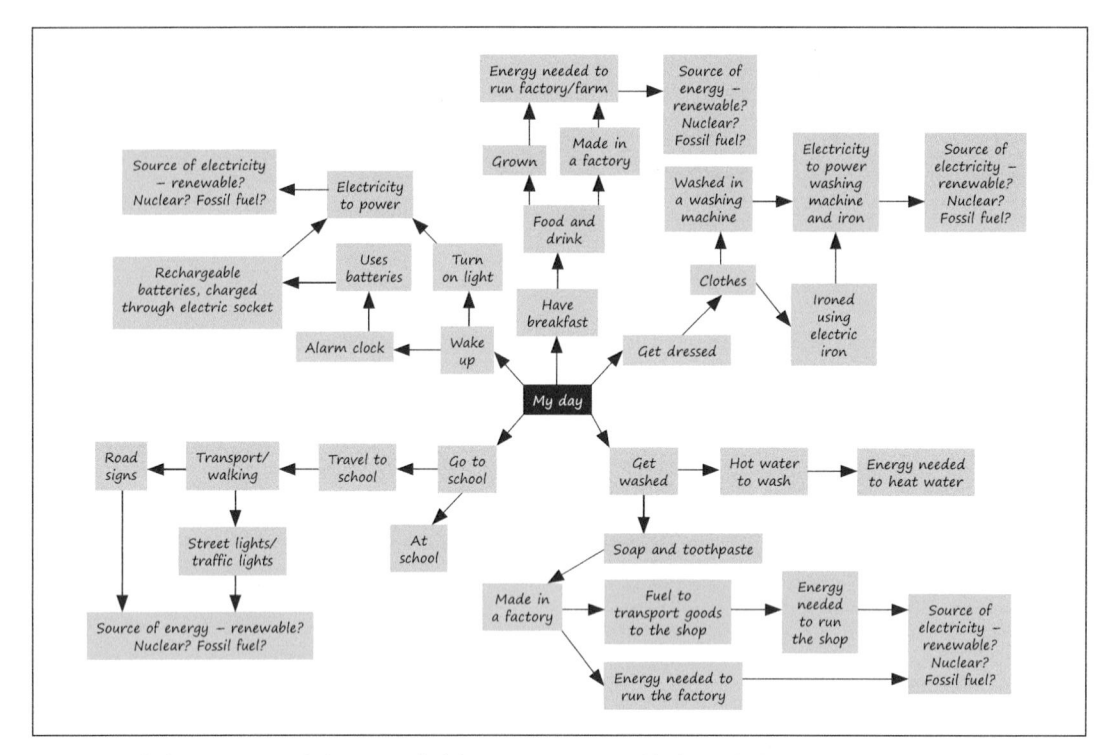

Figure 6: Exploring energy use during 'my typical day'. Source: Geographical Association, 2018.

The Geographical Association website has many links that can help support planning in a cross-curricular way. For example, investigating energy lends itself very well to linking with the science curriculum, especially the study of electricity. Resources, such as the example of 'My day' (Figure 6) supporting the planning of a unit of work linking the study of energy in geography and electricity in science, can be found on the GA website (see web page).

The next section provides ideas to support the integration of geography specifically with the 'core' primary subjects; English, mathematics and science.

To access further support and resources from the *Leading Primary Geography* web page, see page 164

References

Alexander, R. (ed) (2009) *Children, Their World, Their Education*. Abingdon: Routledge.

Geographical Association (2018) *Investigating Energy*. Available at: www.geography.org.uk/teaching-resources/investigating-energy (last accessed 12/6/2019).

Ofsted (2002) *The curriculum in successful primary schools*. London: Office for Standards in Education.

Ofsted (2008) *Geography in schools: changing practice*. London: Office for Standards in Education, Children's Services and Skills.

Ofsted (2009) *Education for sustainable development: Improving schools – improving lives*. London: Office for Standards in Education, Children's Services and Skills.

Ofsted (2011) *Geography: Learning to make a world of difference*. London: Office for Standards in Education, Children's Services and Skills.

Integrating geography with the core subjects

Julia Tanner

This section explores the natural and tangible links between high-quality geographical learning and teaching and the 'core subjects', and suggests meaningful opportunities for cross-curricular work involving pupils in developing, practising and applying concepts and skills from English, mathematics and science. The enquiry approach (Sections 4 and 5) is particularly effective when making links between geography and the core subjects, optimising pupils' communication and numeracy skills and re-inforcing their understanding of scientific concepts.

KWL grids (p. 63) are used by many schools to structure and record enquiries, and a KWHL grid, involving an additional question, 'How can we find out?', helps pupils to think about the process of enquiry by focusing on how they will structure and organise their investigation. Pupils can use a KWHL grid (Figure 1) to pool their prior knowledge (or misconceptions!) in all the subject areas, list their questions, identify possible sources of information, including conducting fieldwork, and ultimately record what they have learnt.

The process of systematically planning and completing an enquiry offers numerous opportunities for pupils to collect, evaluate and analyse information, providing a meaningful context for the development of literacy, numeracy and scientific skills as well as critical geographical thinking skills.

| What do we already **Know** |
| What do we **Want** to know? |
| **How** can we find out? |
| What have we **Learnt**? |

Figure 1: The KWHL grid.

The best geographical enquiries involve authentic learning; they are relevant to pupils' lives and have real purposes, real audiences and, as often as possible, real outcomes. Authenticity in learning tasks engages pupils and enhances motivation and commitment. For example, many schools study energy production and consumption as part of their scientific and geographical study (p. 76). This is much more meaningful to pupils if they investigate energy use at school and know from the outset that their challenge is to present serious proposals for reducing energy consumption to the Head teacher and governors.

Ideally, their proposals should be actioned by the school, reducing energy bills and the school's contribution to climate change. Equally, a study of the physical and human features of a local park becomes far more purposeful if undertaken as part of the exchange of information with another school in a contrasting locality or overseas (p. 73) and develops their writing and other communication skills. An authentic geographical enquiry provides not only an excellent context through which pupils can develop geographical knowledge, understanding and skills, but also a meaningful opportunity for cross-curricular work. Both these examples necessarily involve pupils developing, practising and applying concepts and skills from English, mathematics and science.

Integrating with English

Speaking, listening, reading, writing and drama

Geography offers infinite possibilities for pupils to develop and practise skills in speaking, listening, reading and writing across the full primary age range. Speaking and listening are fundamental to learning. The relationship between language, thinking and learning is complex and multi-faceted (Mercer, 2008). When we use subject-specific vocabulary to name geographical features, concepts and processes, we provide pupils with the language they need to make sense of the world. More importantly, talk is the process through which we formulate thoughts and clarify ideas and opinions, and oral work is a powerful motor for propelling learning in primary classrooms. Alexander (2017) argues that oral activities allow pupils to practise using language for many purposes, including to:

- narrate
- explain
- instruct
- ask different kinds of questions
- receive, act and build upon answers
- analyse and solve problems
- speculate and imagine
- explore and evaluate ideas
- discuss
- argue, reason and justify
- negotiate
- listen
- be receptive to other viewpoints
- think about what they hear
- give others time to think.

Oral work in geography not only promotes deeper thinking, but also provides opportunities to develop the metacognitive skills that underpin effective learning and the interpersonal skills critical for co-operation with others.

Reading and writing skills are also, of course, fundamental to learning. Reading provides access to the vast store of human knowledge and opinion encoded in written form, and in a world saturated by information (and increasingly by misinformation), the ability to find, access, retrieve, understand, analyse and critically evaluate written material is an essential skill. Reading can also be a source of huge pleasure and wonder, stimulating pupils' curiosity and imagination. Geography provides numerous opportunities for purposeful reading and writing. Some geographical questions can be answered through fieldwork in the local area or further away, while others require information that can be found in a plethora of resources, hard copy and digital, as well as in traditional non-fiction information books. Fiction also has an important role in geographical learning, expanding pupils' knowledge and understanding of places, people, environments and situations beyond their personal experience.

Start with a story

Carefully chosen picture and story books are a fabulous cross-curricular resource in the primary classroom (Cremin, 2015). For example, a beautifully illustrated series of books by Kim Lewis (e.g. Lewis, 1991) introduces very young pupils to life on a Northumberland sheep farm, while *Kensuke's Kingdom* (Morpurgo, 1999) raises important issues such as survival in hostile environments, communicating without common language or culture, and respecting others' lifestyles. They are a powerful stimulus for engaging and stimulating pupils, provoking interest, curiosity and questions.

From a geographical perspective, many books have a strong sense of place, conveyed through illustrations or words. They can transport pupils to new, unfamiliar and perhaps unimagined places, expanding their horizons and their world view. The themes in children's literature frequently explore aspects of human or physical geography, including challenging issues of sustainability and socio-economic justice. The ways that characters respond to the challenges provide excellent opportunities for exploring different viewpoints and perspectives, and for thinking about real-life environmental dilemmas at different scales.

Well written and illustrated books also expose young readers to a variety of high-quality models for their own writing. Pupils need plenty of opportunities to explore how authors and illustrators create a sense of place, and to consider the relationship between the setting and the plot. To deepen their understanding of this relationship, they can experiment with relocating familiar stories, drawing or modelling a setting before writing their own story, or devising a story in which a map has a critical role. Numerous ideas for using picture and fiction books as a stimulus for geographical work can be found in *The Everyday Guide to Primary Geography: Story* (Tanner and Whittle, 2013), which also provides a list of over 200 high-quality books for use across the primary age range.

Non-fiction genres

Geography offers infinite opportunities for pupils to work with non-fiction forms of writing, including the six main genres: recount, instruct, explain, inform, persuade and discuss. Figure 2 lists non-fiction forms that pupils may both create and consult in answering their geographical questions.

Fieldwork-based investigations, in the school grounds, local area, or further afield, provide the context for purposeful talk, reading and writing (Tanner and Whittle, 2015). In preparation for fieldwork, pupils should decide what information they need to collect to answer their enquiry questions, agree how to record this data, and consider how they will analyse it back in the classroom. These preparations ensure that pupils engage in geographical thinking, have opportunities to learn relevant vocabulary, and consider how they will present their findings before they collect their data.

In classroom-based enquiries, pupils should be encouraged to identify and use as wide a range of sources as possible, to ensure they are exposed to multiple perspectives. This will also help them to appreciate the huge range of types of non-fiction texts, and to make informed choices about when to use which in their own work. To become skilled non-fiction writers, pupils need meaningful opportunities to experiment with, develop and practise skills in writing for different purposes and audiences. They need adequate time to think, plan, discuss, write and test out ideas. Geography offers endless opportunities for this, as suggested by the examples in Figure 3 and the case study in Figure 4.

Drama and role play

All forms of drama, including small-world play, role play, puppetry, movement, improvisation, debates, simulations and script writing, can enrich the geography curriculum. They offer pupils a safe space to imaginatively engage with unfamiliar places, fictional situations, and complex dilemmas before returning to the real world with enhanced understanding and insight. They also provide an enjoyable and meaningful context for pupils to practise using language for the wide range of purposes identified by Alexander (2017).

Lists	Bus and train timetables	Local/other magazines
Captions and labels	Websites/blogs	Instruction manuals
Notices and posters	Digital presentations	Holiday brochures
Letters and cards	Social media (Twitter, etc.)	Advertisements
Records	Annotated diagrams/images	Newspapers
Invitations	Charts and graphs	Information books
Leaflets	Published statistics	Keys on maps
Word banks	Diaries/journals	Indexes in atlases

Figure 2: Non-fiction forms.

Common non-fiction genres	Geographical examples
Recount (to retell what happened)	- Use a 'journey stick' (Whittle, 2006) to recall the highlights of a walk to the local park and write an illustrated account of it for display in the school reception area. - Following a residential trip, plan, write and perform a special assembly for parents to describe each day's activities and share the most memorable moments.
Instruction (to tell someone how to do something)	- Design a maths trail in the school grounds for younger pupils and write some instructions for them to complete it. - Design a new version of the well-known game 'Battleships' (http://en.battleship-game.org), set in an alternative environment, using four-figure grid references, and write instructions for peers, explaining how to play it.
Explanation (to help someone understand something)	- Create an animated digital presentation about seasonal changes in their country, and why they happen, for pupils in a twinned school with a very different climate or seasonal pattern. - In small groups, create posters that explain the inter-relationships between the weather and climate, plants and animals, and landscape in different biomes, and associated 'quiz sheets' for other pupils to use with them.
Information (to present information accurately and clearly)	- Design and create an information leaflet about the school's sustainability policy for adult volunteers who come into school. - Research, design, publish and sell a guide to family-friendly walks using footpaths and quiet roads in the local area.
Persuasion (to persuade/influence someone)	- Write to the Head teacher to persuade her to support and give her permission for a school grounds improvement project such as a new garden, wall mural or wildlife area. - Following a survey of pupils' view about local play facilities, write to local politicians and officials to campaign for improvements.
Discussion (to present contrasting viewpoints)	- Following a class debate about a proposed housing development in the local area, write a report summarising the arguments on both sides for the school website. - Compare newspaper editorials or opinion pieces on a contested issue, to identify and evaluate their differing standpoints.

Figure 3: Non-fiction in geography.

Integrating with mathematics

Geography and mathematics are natural partners in the curriculum (Whittle, 2017). Much geographical learning requires the application of mathematical techniques, and mathematics teaching is much enhanced by the use of real-world data. Pupils need to use and apply mathematics in real-world, relevant contexts, which geography can supply, but the links between the subjects are deeper than this. Both subjects adopt an enquiry approach, promote creativity in problem-solving, encourage logical thinking, and involve data analysis and pattern seeking. At their best, both foster a sense of awe and wonder at the beauty of the natural and built environment. Although each subject offers a particular and unique 'lens' or perspective through which to understand the world, these are highly complementary.

At Elmwood Junior School we endeavour to create an imaginative, engaging geography curriculum with embedded cross-curricular links. One of the strongest links is with English, as we believe it is absolutely essential that pupils are given the opportunity to express their geographical self in writing. In years 3 and 4 pupils write about Barnaby Bear's adventures, and in years 5 and 6 they maintain personal geography journals, choosing their own format (e.g. letter or diary). Key learning questions are recorded in an A3 'discovery book', where pupils can comment on the world around them, developing key critical thinking skills. Following work on map skills, year 6 pupils imagine and draw their dream island and then describe it using geographical vocabulary.

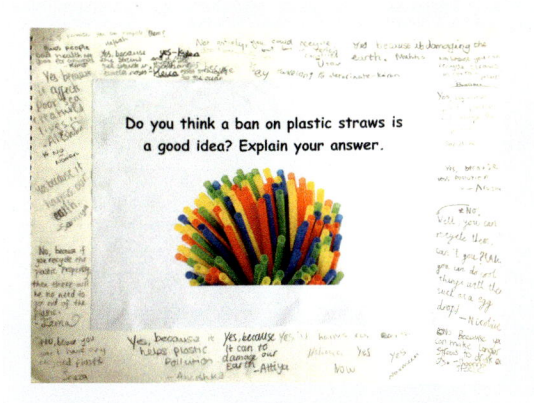

Elmwood Junior School is a large suburban school in Croydon, south London. It has been a Silver Primary Geography Quality Mark (PGQM) school since 2008, confirming this status in 2018. Its policy states that 'Geography can make an important contribution to, and offer a stimulating context for, the development of children's knowledge, understanding and skills across the curriculum'. Teachers carefully plan opportunities for pupils to take part in speaking and listening activities, such as group discussions, debates, and role play, and in writing poetry, letters, reports, and news articles. The subject leader for geography, Gabriella Power, explains the school's approach to integrating geography with English:

Through geography, pupils can explore and develop their writing. A geography theme and context for writing allows them to think geographically and generate ideas, e.g. jotting ideas on a post-it note to generate discussion. Teachers make opportunities for pupils to write about their thoughts and ideas in geography, investing time in creating high-quality writing.

Figure 4: Integrating English with geography at Elmwood Junior School.

Geography offers potential learning activities across all areas of mathematics, as illustrated in Figure 5. Number work, including calculations, for example, is involved in analysing fieldwork data, in calculating distances, and in understanding the economics of Fairtrade. Geographers use measurement to explore and understand aspects of physical and human geography such as wind speed, river velocity, and volume of trade or rate of demographic change. Fundamental geometric concepts such as shape, position, direction, and scale are also key spatial concepts, especially important in using and understanding maps. Many geographical enquiries involve using statistics and graphic representations, providing tangible examples of how making sense and meaning from data is applied in real-life problem solving, enabling us to better understand the world. Numerous ideas for using and applying mathematical tools in geographical work can be found in *The Everyday Guide to Primary Geography: Mathematics* (Tanner and Whittle, forthcoming).

Mathematical tool	Geographical applications and examples
Enquiry and problem solving	■ Any investigation that involves asking and answering geographical questions. ■ Adopting a problem-solving approach, either as part of the enquiry process, e.g. How could we find out…?, or in considering potential solutions to geographical problems, e.g. How can we stop dogs fouling in our local park? How can we reduce our energy use in school and at home?
Logical thinking, pattern seeking, classification	■ Using graphic organisers such Venn diagrams, decision-making trees, flow diagrams, fishbone maps, comparison charts, matrices etc. in problem solving and in presenting and analysing geographical information. ■ Identifying spatial patterns in the environment, e.g. symmetry in semi-detached houses, the location of convenience stores. ■ Sorting, ordering and classifying by criteria, e.g. rock samples.
Number: counting, place value, money, calculations	■ Counting and tallying to collect data, e.g. pedestrian/traffic flows. ■ Using money in geographical role play, e.g. in a role-play area set up as a garden centre, café or travel agents, to understand the role of money in the service sector. ■ Calculating the velocity of a river at different points along its course. ■ Investigating the cost of Fairtrade chocolate and how this is split between producers, processors, distributors and sellers. ■ Calculating distances using scale lines on plans, maps and globes. ■ Using numeric data to calculate, e.g. food miles, water use, energy consumption, value of trade, etc.
Measurement: length, mass, time, area, volume, capacity	■ Estimating and measuring distances in the school grounds to plan and identify a good route for 'the daily mile'. ■ Estimating and calculating area from a large-scale OS map or aerial photograph to determine the proportion of the local area devoted to green space or transport use. ■ Using bus, train and aeroplane timetables to explore time/distance ratios. ■ Investigating time zones, day and night and the seasons, and their impact on people and the environment. ■ Playing Poohsticks to observe the speed of a stream, or using metre rules to measure tidal range on a beach. ■ Making accurate measurements using specialised instruments such as rain gauges, thermometers and clinometers to collect precise data.
Ratio (scale), proportion and percentages	■ Exploring the concept of scale through small-world play. ■ Making scale models to demonstrate the structure of tropical rainforest. ■ Understanding that the scale on a map is a ratio; it shows the relationship between distance on the map and in real life, e.g. 1:1250 on a large-scale OS map. ■ Using scale lines on plans, maps and the globe to compare distances and areas. ■ Assessing the proportion of the sky covered by cloud when making weather observations. ■ Calculating and using percentages when analysing field or survey data collected as part of a geographical investigation.

continued

Geometry: shape, position and direction	■ Finding and identifying shapes in the environment, e.g. in buildings. ■ Using locational and directional language to describe position, bearing and orientation. ■ Making simple maps and plans of real or imaginary places using symbols, and talking about where features are located. ■ Using grid references (alphanumeric, four- and six-figure) to locate places on maps. ■ Using longitude and latitude to locate places on the globe and atlas maps. ■ Understanding the constancy of north (i.e. that it is always in the same place) and using compass directions. ■ Comparing differing world map projections to explore how they distort the shape or size of land masses.
Statistics: data handling and graphic representations	■ Collecting and using numeric data in geographical investigations. ■ Calculating and using fractions and percentages in analysing data. ■ Constructing charts and graphs to present and analyse numeric data, e.g. pie chart, matrix, bar chart, line graph. ■ Using statistics, charts and graphs to generate and answer geographical questions, e.g. comparing climate graphs or population pyramids.

Figure 5: Potential learning activities combining geography and mathematics.

Mathematics and geographical enquiries

Geographical enquiry naturally engages pupils in mathematical problem solving by posing questions that can only adequately be tackled by applying mathematical strategies and tools. In discussing how they can answer their questions, pupils will inevitably sometimes find themselves deciding that they need to ask questions that start with:

- 'How many...?'
- 'How much...?' or
- 'How far...?'

For example, a study of local travel to see how it can be made more sustainable would involve asking questions such as 'How many pupils come to school by car, bus, bicycle or walking?' and 'How far do they travel?' (see Figure 6). These are quantification questions, and to answer them, pupils need to count or measure something to create numeric data. Many fieldwork strategies generate numeric data, e.g. amount of litter left in different stretches of a street, pedestrian or traffic flows throughout the day, or the number of plant species in a square-metre quadrat. Equally, many geographical enquiries involve measuring something, e.g. air temperature, daily rainfall, distance, river velocity, or a survey of people's shopping behaviour. When pupils have collected numeric data, they need to analyse and interpret it to answer their questions. The process of analysis involves organising the data, often presenting it visually, in a table, a bar or line graph, a pie chart, or by locating the data on a map.

Through their geographical studies, pupils will also be introduced to the idea that a range of phenomena can be attributed a numeric value, e.g. the Beaufort scale for wind speed, the Mohs scale of hardness, a Likert scale for assessing environmental quality, etc.

Integrating with science

There is a natural synergy between geography and science. The subjects offer complementary approaches to understanding and investigating the world, drawing on mutually important *practise key skills in real-world contexts, e.g. using percentages when investigating international trade in year 5. Mathematics is integrated with geography in all year groups in the area of map work, linking work on position and direction, including grid references, lines of longitude and latitude, and directions.*

In geography, we provide pupils with opportunities to suggest what they would like to investigate, so that their interests and curiosity are catered for. Pupils really enjoy collecting quantitative data, analysing it and reaching conclusions from it; they seem more engaged when they have actively collected fieldwork data themselves and can see this in numerical formats. For example, year 4 pupils consider the effects of traffic in our local area by counting the traffic at different points during the day. Analysing this data, they reach conclusions, which they then use to propose solutions to traffic problems. We find that pupils enjoy seeing a purpose for mathematics and understand why these skills are important in life. We highlight the links to pupils to show them the importance of mathematics in the world around us.

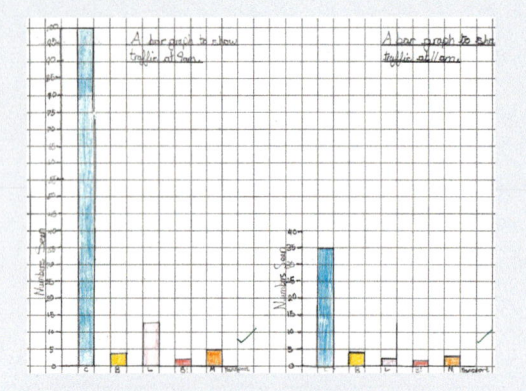

Hey with Zion Primary School is located in the village of Lees, near Oldham in Lancashire. It applied for the PGQM for the first time in 2018, and was awarded Bronze status. The subject leader for geography, Heather Ogden, explains the school's approach to integrating geography and mathematics:

Hey with Zion Primary School has a key focus on the core subjects and we believe that cross-curricular links can be very beneficial in developing related subject-specific skills. Linking geography with mathematics builds on pupils' enthusiasm and allows them to

Figure 6: Case study – Integrating mathematics with geography at Hey with Zion Primary School.

concepts such as cycles, patterns and processes. As Rawlinson and Willy argue, fieldwork offers opportunities for pupils to appreciate how scientific approaches are an integral aspect of geography, enhancing their skills in both subject areas:

> It is important to recognise that the principles of scientific enquiry or investigation mirror those of geographical enquiry, thus engaging in geographical fieldwork addresses many of the demands of the science curriculum (Rawlinson and Willy, 2014).

Scientific investigations involve asking questions, forming hypotheses, making predictions, planning the enquiry, taking measurements, recording and presenting data, and drawing conclusions from the data to answer the original questions (Association for Science Education, 2018). Within this overarching framework, six specific forms of enquiry are commonly identified:

- observing changes over time
- noticing patterns
- grouping and classifying (noticing similarities and differences)
- fair and comparative testing
- modelling
- researching (finding things out using secondary sources of information).

All of these approaches are also used in primary geography, but it can be argued that geography, with its focus on problem-solving, takes the model one step further; geographers use the information acquired through enquiry to generate answers to issues of concern, such as water pollution, deforestation, desertification or global warming.

Figure 7 illustrates how different types of scientific enquiry have a significant role to play in geographical work in primary schools. All of them provide a meaningful context for pupils to develop, practise and apply skills in using a variety of techniques and equipment to collect data in myriad forms.

The natural synergy between the geographical and scientific enquiry processes is complemented by their overlapping subject matter. Science is concerned with the natural, physical world; physicists study the nature and properties of matter and energy, chemists study the composition and structure of substances, and biologists study living things and their habitats. Physical geographers,

Type of enquiry	Geographical examples
Observing changes over time	■ Noticing changes in local woodlands as the seasons change. ■ Observing and recording evidence of weathering processes on the school building over a school year.
Noticing patterns	■ Observing, describing and explaining spatial patterns, e.g. changes in land use from valley bottom to mountain top. ■ Observing, describing and explaining the distribution of volcanoes and earthquake sites on a world map.
Grouping and classifying things (noticing similarities and differences)	■ Collecting and sorting litter from the local park into recyclable and non-recyclable items as part of a project on the 5Rs of waste (refuse, reduce, reuse, repurpose, recycle). ■ Sorting rock samples by their features, e.g. colour, containing/not containing fossils, with/without crystals, in order to investigate the different properties of igneous, sedimentary and metamorphic rocks, and explore how these characteristics influence how different types of rocks are used.
Fair and comparative testing	■ Observing and recording weather measurements (temperature, wind speed, rainfall, etc.) at different places in the school grounds to decide where would be the best place to locate an energy-generating wind turbine or solar panels. ■ Measuring the speed at which 250ml of water filters through different types of soil, to investigate how soil type might affect flooding risks.
Modelling	■ Using a torch as the sun, and a globe as planet Earth, to explore how the relationship between the sun and planet Earth creates day and night and the need for time zones. ■ Creating a model of a river channel and seeing what happens when gradient, volume of water, etc. is changed, in terms of impact on the river and surrounding landscape.
Researching (finding things out using secondary sources of information)	■ Using websites or books to find out about the water cycle, investigate climate graphs for different places in the Americas, or to understand the structure of the tropical rainforest biome. ■ Using published statistics to investigate progress towards Global Goal 6 (clean water and sanitation) for Sustainable Development (www.globalgoals.org/).

Figure 7: Types of scientific enquiry.

such as meteorologists, geologists, and oceanographers, investigate the same phenomena, but through a spatial lens. Physical geography is concerned with planet Earth's natural features, the processes that shape them, and their distribution in space. The most common physical geography topics in primary geography are weather and climate, habitats and biomes, volcanoes and earthquakes, and how mountain, river and coastal landscapes

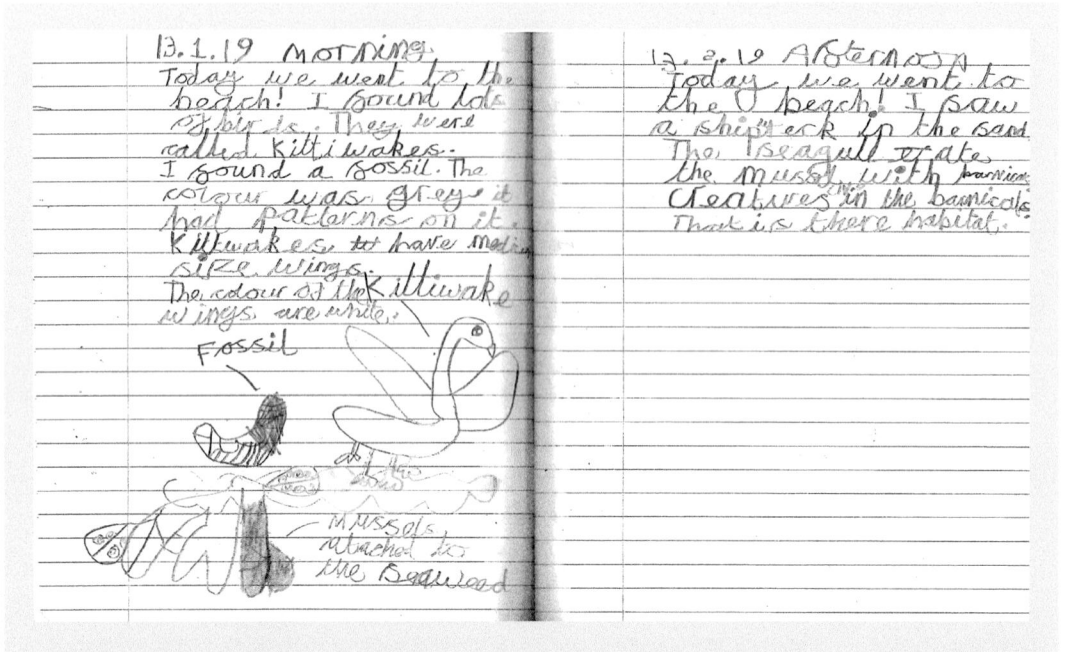

Coatham CE Primary School is sited within a breezy five-minute walk of Redcar Beach, on the northeast coast. As Headteacher Phil Maudsley explains, in embracing the Beach Schools philosophy the school has created extensive and adaptable cross-curricular links with geography and all other subject areas, particularly science.

Our beach offers exceptional opportunities for the pupils to explore scientific concepts and to establish scientific skills through enquiry and hands-on investigation. For example, we have used the beach to construct mini-river catchment models, enabling our year 5 classes to explore erosion and deposition, and the formation of fluvial features. Key stage 2 pupils have also completed beach litter surveys, dovetailing with the current marine plastics agenda. Pupils were outraged at the number of plastic cotton buds they found on the beach. The data from these surveys has been compiled and analysed through graphing lessons.

The amount of space available on the beach allows also pupils to explore bigger concepts. Key stage 1 have modelled the solar system as a scale model, and have explored the movement of particles in solids, liquids and gases by experimenting with movement about the beach. Our EYFS classes love embracing the 'messy curriculum' in the sands, recently exploring floating and sinking by digging holes on the beach, filling them with water and floating and sinking various items of flotsam found in the strandline. EYFS have also observed and recorded the weather on the beach in different seasons. Our classes use 'beach journals', alongside our subject books, to record their findings and experiences.

Figure 8: Case study – Integrating science with geography at Coatham CE Primary School.

develop and evolve. These topics all illuminate how people and their environment are inextricably linked through human choices and decisions that are often predicated on environmental resources and affordances.

Underpinning all of these topics is knowledge and understanding of Earth as a planet, and the structure and processes of the geosphere, atmosphere, hydrosphere and biosphere. There is increasing evidence that these natural physical systems are being overwhelmed by human action that is depleting mineral resources, causing climate change in the atmosphere, exhausting fresh water supplies and fish stocks, and damaging ecosystems on land and water. Pupils are exposed to a daily stream of media stories about these issues. Understanding how these interconnected and interdependent systems work through the integration of geography and other subject disciplines is an essential first step towards empowering pupils to identify potential solutions and take action now and in their future adult lives.

Conclusion

Never has the study of geography been more relevant or urgent. It provides an essential perspective and the knowledge necessary for understanding and confronting the unprecedented global challenges that face humankind. Equally, to become informed, responsible and active citizens, pupils need to develop strong scientific, mathematical and literacy skills. These lay the foundations for success in education and adult life, and for active engagement in community and political life at local, national and global levels. Real-life geographical enquiries offer a fabulous context for developing and applying these essential skills, as well as introducing pupils to an infinitely rich and rewarding perspective on the world.

> To access further support and resources from the *Leading Primary Geography* web page, see page 164

References

Alexander, R. (2017) Towards Dialogic Teaching: Rethinking classroom talk (5th ed). York: Dialogos.

Association for Science Education (2018) Scientific Enquiry. Available at: www.ase.org.uk/system/files/Scientific%20Enquiry%20in%20the%20UK%20V2.pdf (last accessed 12/6/2019).

Cremin, T. (2015) Teaching English Creatively (2nd ed). Abingdon: Routledge.

Lewis, K. (1991) The Shepherd Boy. London: Walker Books.

Mercer, N. and Hodgkinson, S. (2008) Exploring Talk in School. London: Sage.

Morpurgo, M. (1999) Kensuke's Kingdom. London: Heinemann Young Books.

Rawlinson, S. and Willy, T. (2014) 'Get to the core with geography', *Primary Geography*, 84, pp. 5–6.

Tanner, J. and Whittle, J. (2013) *The Everyday Guide to Primary Geography: Story*. Sheffield: Geographical Association.

Tanner, J. and Whittle, J. (2015) *The Everyday Guide to Primary Geography: Local Fieldwork*. Sheffield: Geographical Association.

Tanner, J. and Whittle, J. (forthcoming) *The Everyday Guide to Primary Geography: Mathematics*. Sheffield: Geographical Association.

Whittle, J. (2006) 'Journey sticks and affective mapping', *Primary Geographer*, 59, pp. 11–12.

Whittle, J. (2017) 'Geography and Mathematics: A creative approach' in Scoffham, S. (ed) *Teaching Geography Creatively* (2nd ed.). Abingdon: Routledge, p. 10.

Acknowledgements

Many thanks to the teachers and pupils who contributed to the case studies: Gabriella Power, Elmwood Junior School, Croydon; Heather Ogden, Hey with Zion Primary School, Oldham; Philip Maudsley, C of E Primary School, Redcar.

Integrating with the foundation subjects

Ben Ballin

Finding meaningful overlaps

In his inaugural address as President, John F. Kennedy challenged his fellow Americans to 'Ask not what your country can do for you – ask what you can do for your country'. Something similar applies when it comes to combining geography with other subjects. We need to ask not just what geography can do for other subjects, but what they can also do for geography. In other words, where the 'meaningful overlaps' are; the places where learning in one subject strengthens learning in the other (Wilkinson and Ballin, 2016).

When two subjects come together well, it is possible to identify subject-based learning objectives (e.g. knowledge, concepts, and skills) in both, and thus plan for progression and assessment in each. For example, with a lower primary class, the creation of an autumn leaf display collected during local fieldwork can be assessed for its artistic skills, as well as its ability to convey information about natural features, weather and climate. In discussing it or creating labels, pupils are also demonstrating their grasp of geographical vocabulary. An upper primary local area study, comparing past and present Ordnance Survey maps, simultaneously develops mapwork skills and the interpretation of evidence from historical sources. The key thing is to identify opportunities where such meaningful combinations are coherent, even essential, rather than forced or contrived.

'One of geography's great advantages is its ability to cross the boundaries of arts and science, to enable us to see the big picture' (Rawling, 2008). Such boundary-crossing occurs not only between subjects but also within geography itself. Geography encourages learners to look at the big picture, rather than at facts or technical elements in isolation from each other: for example, pupils' investigation of 'the *interaction* between physical and human processes, ... the formation *and use* of landscapes and environments' (DfE, 2014. My italics. See also p. 22).

What follows are some suggestions about where meaningful connections can be found between geography, the humanities (RE, PSHE, citizenship and history) and the arts (art and design, music and drama), a description of what one subject offers another, and an outline of the principles involved in organising integrated, meaningful and enjoyable teaching and learning across subjects.

Integrating with the humanities

What geography specifically offers to the humanities is an opportunity to explore such connections and interactions in the context of real places. The main overlaps that RE, PSHE and citizenship offer to geography relate to our values as residents of a fragile and often unequal world. Geography offers a real-world context for those concerns and a way of understanding some of the places and processes involved. There is a clear link here to the values and the 'hidden curriculum' of the whole school and the wider community.

Religious education (RE)

RE and geography come together when pupils 'experience the awe and wonder of the natural world' (Pett *et al.*, 2016), either first-hand during school trips, fieldwork and sensory activities, or via secondary sources such as films, music, photographs and stories. Thackrah (2017) describes geography fieldwork with 8–9-year-old pupils as 'an invitation to wonder'; encouraging imaginative exploration that looks afresh at the school site and maps it as an 'everyday wonderland'.

Religion is part of the diversity of culture and beliefs within a place. It is hard for pupils to 'get a handle' on many localities, regions or countries without at least some understanding of their main religions or belief systems.

Meanwhile, specific locations offer a context for how faith and belief are lived out as part of people's 'everyday geographies' (e.g. how a community in a West African village uses its mosque; how a UK school hall is used for assemblies and acts of worship).

At a global scale, many atlases provide maps of world religions. Close scrutiny of these can offer potential surprises: majority Buddhist communities in Kalmykia on the Black Sea, for example, or significant Jewish ones in Argentina. How can such discoveries change how pupils 'see' and understand places? Can mapwork of this kind help break down stereotypes about which religions 'belong' to certain places?

Personal, social, health and economic (PSHE) education

PSHE offers opportunities for pupils to explore and articulate their feelings about places, including familiar ones. Even very young pupils can go beyond 'likes and dislikes' during an investigation of the school site, to 'emotional mapping' (Potter and Scoffham, 2006), where they identify, locate and represent the places where they feel most happy, safe or anxious (Figure 1).

Citizenship

Citizenship builds on PSHE to offer challenges for 'applied geography': the use of geographical understanding in the real world. For example, pupils identifying a lack of play facilities during a local area study will often raise questions about how this can be remedied. Such opportunities to engage with local issues can lend a powerful edge and purpose to (and potential audience for) pupils' fieldwork, data collection and presentation. They can be a way of 'empowering pupils through geography' (see p. 12).

Going beyond the local area, pupils will inevitably touch on ethical and moral questions when investigating international processes and issues around trade, the distribution of

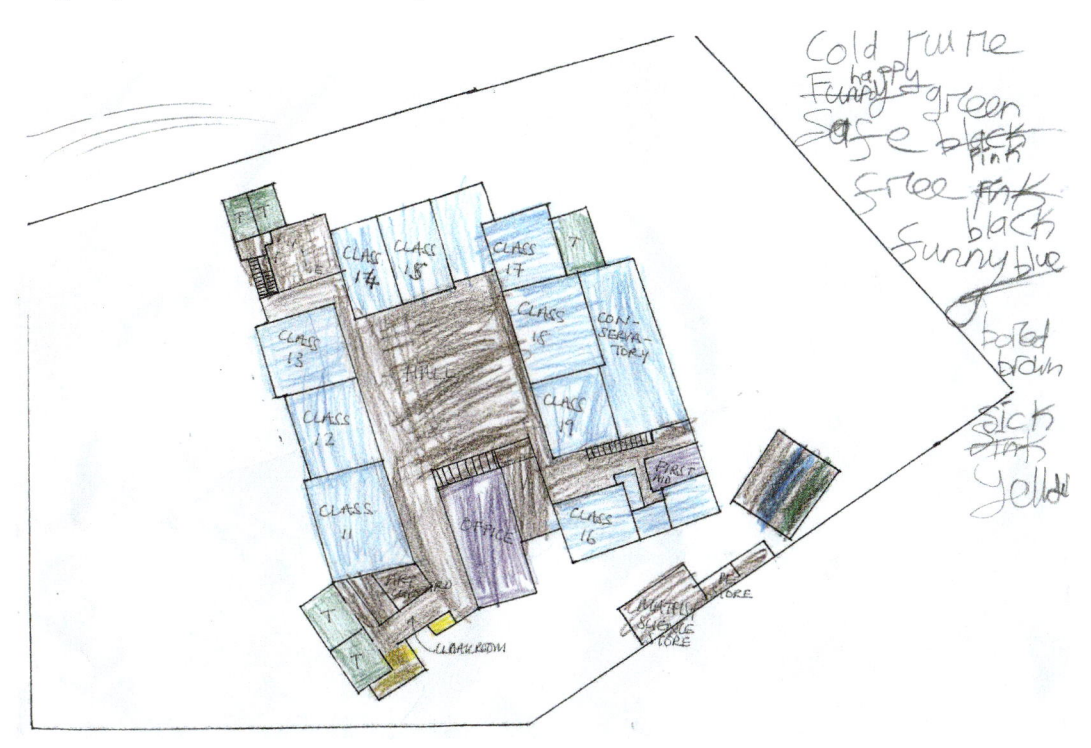

Figure 1: Integrating with PSHE offers opportunities for pupils to articulate their emotions about places and spaces.

This case study describes work with pupils aged 5–7. Online extension activities provide additional challenge, while the example on settlement would also be suitable for older primary pupils.

The two photographs were taken from Heckington Windmill, the UK's only working eight-sail windmill. Most local areas will have significant landmarks that can serve as starting points for an investigation of this kind.

Groups of pupils are given one of the two photographs, placed in the centre of a large sheet of paper (see web page). Alternatively, pupils could visit a local landmark and create their own images for this task. Writing on sticky notes, they discuss and note the main things (human and physical features) that they can see in the picture. Each group compares its image and list with another group. The pupils discuss points such as:

- The photographs were taken from the same place, but in different directions. What things are the same and what are different?
- Why might that be? (This question introduces the key idea of perspective or viewpoint.)

Pupils look at aerial views and/or maps of the site, and locate some of the features from the photographs, in order to develop their map skills, including map reading. Can they work out where the photographer was standing?

The groups go on to explore changes in living memory. They look again at their image, removing anything from their list that they think was not there: a year ago; at the time they were born; when their parents or carers were children; when their grandparents or elders were children. What remains? They suggest features that they think would have been there but have now gone. An older resident could be invited to talk with the pupils about what has changed locally and what remains the same.

Pupils take their sticky notes and place them on a future timeline. What will still be there when they go to secondary school, when they grow up, when they also become elders or grandparents?

Views from Heckington Windmill, Lincolnshire. Photos © Ben Ballin.

Figure 2: A local area enquiry.

resources, human rights and the environment. They will often want to explore potential responses. There are links related to this section to organisations that specialise in global citizenship and sustainable development education and further information (see web page and also pp. 51–2).

History

Isn't history about time and geography about place? If we were to draw a really long timeline, going back millions of years, we would be looking at the geological past, asking questions about how our landscapes formed and the opportunities and constraints that these emerging environments posed for the first plants, animals and human beings. Geography or history? As we moved along the timeline, through ancient times to the recent past, we would see how places at all scales continued to provide opportunities and constraints for human beings, and how the human presence on the planet has increasingly altered and shaped the landscape and even the climate. History or geography? Arriving in the present day, and looking at particular places, we would still be asking questions about continuity and change including, based on what we had discovered, questions and options about how that timeline will extend into the future.

History and geography are inextricably linked to each other: events happen in places; places at all scales change through time. It is not surprising, therefore, that so many primary schools choose to combine the roles of geography and history co-ordinator. It makes sense to do so, especially if this strengthens each subject's distinctive contribution to the pupil's experience of learning.

'Meaningful overlaps' between history and geography can be about content; for example, looking at patterns of change in particular places. Figure 2 provides a brief case study about local content: documenting settlement in the local area (recording what got built when and where, asking why); using modern and historical maps to look at changing land use.

More detailed versions of all the case studies in this section are available from the web page.

Connecting content also involves mapping past and present links between places (e.g. through conquest and trade), asking questions such as:

- Why did the Vikings decide to travel far afield, raiding and invading other places?
- What could they produce locally, and what did they need to obtain from elsewhere?
- What can historical maps tell us about Tudor or Victorian explorers, where they went and why?

Exploring the *relationship between people and their local environment* can also highlight common threads between the past and the present, for example:

- The apparent abandonment of lowland Maya cities around AD 900 and the lessons we might learn from that today (Figure 3).
- The key role of the Nile in ancient and modern Egypt (Figure 4). Both of these case studies are available online.

Integrating geography and history through enquiry and critical thinking

As well as subject content, effective integration between geography and history (or other subjects) can be developed through the pedagogy and teaching approaches adopted. Enquiry learning is key to teaching in both subjects (see Sections 4 and 5). While the specific questions will often differ, the underlying enquiry frameworks and approaches to seeking out answers will often be similar. This can help learners make meaningful connections between the subjects. Figure 5 shows the Development Compass Rose framework used to highlight common threads in a historical and geographical investigation into ancient and modern Greece. A case study of this enquiry can be downloaded (see web page).

The following key questions about the Maya support a geographical and historical enquiry for 9–11-year-olds, into the historical and modern Maya. Each question is in itself a mini-enquiry that takes about one two-hour lesson to complete. At the end of each subject-specific set of seven questions, there is a summative question that draws on the knowledge and understanding gained during the previous six mini-enquiries, and that lends itself to extended writing and other assessment opportunities (e.g. a class presentation). The final, geographical, question looks to the past and the present in order to consider the future. In order to answer the questions, pupils will need to develop their independent and group enquiry skills, testing evidence from a variety of sources. These skills enable them to access, understand and contextualise detailed information about the historical and modern Maya.

Through investigating the interaction between human and physical processes in this particular region, they are developing their locational and place knowledge of the Americas. In comparing the present-day Maya with the past, they are using historical knowledge to help understand the geographical present, and geography to illuminate an understanding of the past: not least because the culture and lives of the modern-day Maya offer some of the main clues to their history. These enquiry questions could serve as a model for enquiries into other times and places: for example, considering how far the environmental limitations of the Vikings' northern European homeland may have driven them to raid, trade and settle in places that offered crops and resources that couldn't be easily obtained in their homeland.

History

- If the Maya lived in the Stone Age, does this mean they were a primitive people?
- What did the Ancient Maya believe?
- What were Mayan cities like?
- Mayan pyramids and hieroglyphs – how were these similar to, and different from, those in Ancient Egypt?
- How do we know about the Maya?
- What happened in AD 900 (catastrophe, or relocation)?
- Why should we remember the Maya?

Geography

- Where do the modern-day Maya live?
- Is this different from where the Ancient Maya people lived?
- What are the main features of the Yucatán Peninsula?
- What can we find out about the environment of the Yucatán Peninsula (e.g. forests and hurricanes)?
- What can we find out about the people of the Yucatán Peninsula (e.g. trade, tourism and the world of work)?
- What is everyday life like in the city of Cancún?
- What might the future look like for the modern-day Maya of the Yucatán Peninsula?

Figure 3: The Maya and Central America.

9–11-year-olds at Emmaus Catholic and Church of England Primary School, Sheffield, enriched their history topic on Egypt and the Nile with a river study (Collis, 2014). They named and located the African countries through which the Nile flows. The pupils then experimented with sand trays and water to explore the flow of water and develop the relevant key vocabulary. This included experiments on how human activity affects rivers (e.g. through dams, pollution, the abstraction of water).

If we look at a satellite image of the Nile taken at night, the lights indicating where people live make a shape like an arm with an outstretched hand. The fertile banks and delta of the Nile are where most Egyptians have always lived, from over 4000 years ago to the present day. Starting with this, we can make meaningful links between Ancient Egypt, modern farming, land use, river/sea transport and patterns of settlement.

Having looked at satellite images of the Nile and related its features to those they had identified in their tray 'rivers', the investigation concluded with a role-play activity, which explored different people's perspectives on a modern-day dam-building project on the Nile. As rivers play such a key role in human development, you can plan similar meaningful connections to studies of places like the Indus Valley civilization; Ancient Sumer or classical Baghdad (the Rivers Tigris and Euphrates); the Shang Dynasty (the Yellow River).

Figure 4: Egypt and the Nile. Image © Egyptian Studio/Shutterstock.com.

Natural
What is this building made from?
Where do the materials come from?
'The question is the same but I think the answer would be different'

Who decides?
Who are they and what are they meeting about?
Is this the government of Greece?
'I wonder if Greece has always been a democracy?'

Economic
Are these people working?
If so, how much do they get paid?
'I'm not sure from their clothes whether these people are poor or rich'

Social
Why are these people there?
How many of them are men and how many are women?
'You can see that in the past, most of them were men'

Figure 5: The Development Compass Rose as a framework for exploring a historic image of a Greek agora as part of an investigation of Athens, Greece and democracy. Text in italics compares past with present. Source: Tide~ global learning, 1995.

Teaching approaches in geography and history are also about:

- Promoting critical thinking (see pp. 47–50) – challenging assumptions, testing evidence, looking for multiple perspectives on an issue or a place.
- Making concepts meaningful and tangible – through fieldwork in modern and historical sites (see pp. 36–40); through relational approaches, such as using stories, images and drama, to bring events and issues from 'long ago and far away' closer to pupils' lives; through enrichment activities that engender a sense of a particular place and time.

Integrating with the arts

'Finding a place in the world... is ultimately an act of imagination' (Bruner, 1996). Geography raises questions about our world and helps provide us with the knowledge, skills and understanding to answer them, while the arts allow us to feel, understand and express what it is like to be a human being in that world. This includes, and goes beyond, curriculum enrichment, because the arts are also 'a mode of knowing the world in which we live' (Big Brum TIE, 2011). For geography, they especially help pupils develop a 'sense of place' (Hume et al., 1995). Claxton highlights the arts' exploratory, investigative nature, more than their decorative or performance-orientated elements. For him, the arts help provide a step in the learning process, where pupils are 'thinking at the edge' of 'what is felt or sensed but not yet articulated' (Alexander, 2010, p. 100).

For example, 4–5-year-olds can take a look around their classroom and school before building models of them using Lego or construction blocks. This act of playful making creates a kind-of-a-map, and this element becomes more explicit if the model is photographed from above and compared with aerial views. However, it has legitimacy in its own right, as part of pupils' emergent understanding of the place and its spatial arrangements.

The same pupils can take Playmobil figures for a 'walk' around their model, making the figures 'talk' about that they are doing and seeing. The pupils are now engaging in a form of imaginative dramatic role play that helps them to understand how people use and relate to spaces. This is a subtle and complex learning experience. As Vygotsky (1976) reminds us, 'In play, action is subordinate to meaning'. It is the meaning-making that really matters here.

The case study in Figure 6 takes the example of a Worcestershire school where pupils aged 7–8 created ceramic tiles with local clay, a process that explored their connections to the local landscape, distant places, work and the natural world. A more detailed version of this case study is available online.

The arts also have a valuable contribution to make to inclusive geography teaching. Evidence from Primary Geography Quality Mark schools suggests that pupils who are less confident in writing or mathematics can sometimes express geographical ideas and responses more effectively through forms such as art and drama.

Art and design

The subject of art and design makes a powerful contribution to the core geographical skill of graphicacy (see pp. 35–6). The very word 'geography' is about writing and drawing the world. How pupils visualise that world is therefore as crucial as how they understand it through words or numbers.

In describing geography's links to history, we said that providing pupils with opportunities to encounter and explore different perspectives is an essential part of good primary geography teaching. It helps promote the enquiry skills of questioning and criticality. Art and design reminds us that there is no one 'right' way to look at the world. It depends to an extent on who we are, how we interpret things, what we wish to show and how we choose to express it.

In this case study, 7–8-year-old pupils worked with local educator and ceramic artist, Rupert Brakspear, using the local clay soil to explore connections with the world around them (Brakspear, 2017).

Scrutinising maps from the UK Soil Observatory, pupils found that their town of Redditch was named after the red clay and mudstone on which it was built. They investigated the properties of soil from the school grounds, and helped prepare it to become workable clay. This clay was used to make and decorate tiles, printed with key words on the theme of shelter. The tiles were fired in a kiln that the pupils helped to prepare.

Some tiles were used for the roofs of hedgehog houses in the school wildlife area, while others were given to visiting teachers from the A M Qattan Foundation, a partner project in Palestine. This led to a comparison with the construction materials used there. Pupils watched a film of a country potter and identified the materials he used, the processes involved, and why he preferred to live and work near to the source of his materials.

Figure 6: Meaning through making. Photo © Rupert Brakspear.

It can be useful to consider map making as a form of art: the art of picturing the world. It is invaluable for pupils to have a wide experience of map formats that include, but go beyond, 'traditional' atlases and Ordnance Survey maps. This variety offers food for thought about what map makers want to show, how they do it, and what this conveys about their 'picture of the world.' The diversity of map formats includes:

- Historical maps (e.g. 'T and O' maps like Anaximander's world map or the Hereford Mappa Mundi, the Bünting 'clover leaf' map (Figure 7), and linear maps such as the 'Britannia Depicta' series);
- Contemporary maps, such as 'satnavs', road maps, online maps, interactive and animated maps, the 'cartograms' on Worldmapper (see web page);
- Satellite and aerial images, such as Yann Arthus-Bertrand's photographs in *Earth from Above* (Arthus-Bertrand, 2017);
- Maps from different cultural traditions or centred away from the Prime Meridian;
- Illustrated maps, including sketch maps, tourist maps, and maps created by artists (e.g. the collection in *The map as art* (Harmon, 2009 and web page);
- 'Teaching atlases' that raise questions about the choices cartographers and writers make when 'picturing the world' (Ballin, 2019; Owens, 2019).

Mackintosh and Kent (2014), taking the example of Harry Beck's influential map of the London Underground, invite pupils to consider it as both an aesthetic and a functional object. It becomes a model for pupils' own maps of journeys around the school, with the aim of using colour, line and key points to create 'topological maps' that are clear, accurate and beautiful.

Mackintosh and Kent (*ibid.*) use other work from a range of artists, sculptors and photographers to help pupils develop their visual literacy: infant pupils explore questions about weather and travel when making clay models based

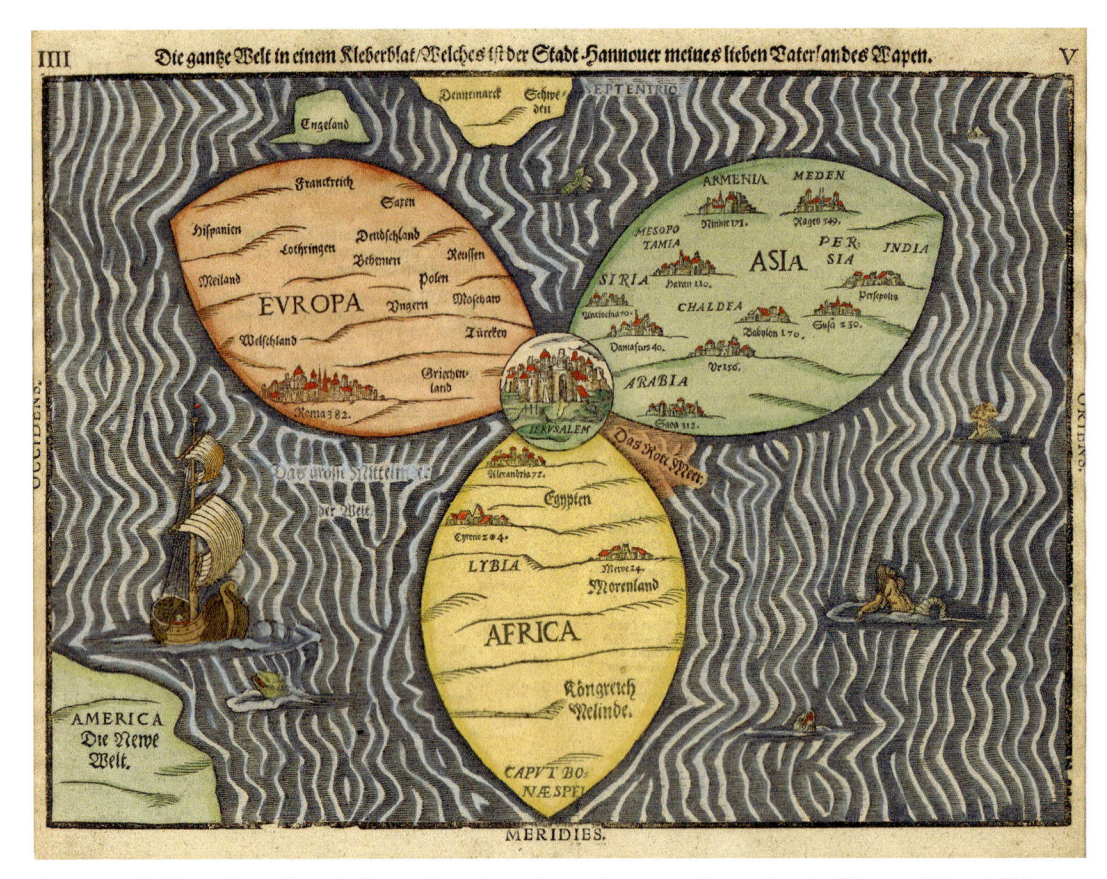

Figure 7: Heinrich Bünting's 'clover leaf' map shows Jerusalem at the centre, the continents of Europe, Asia and Africa as the three leaves, with an indication of Great Britain, Scandinavia and America.

on George Segal's 'Rush Hour'; older pupils gain insights into land use and map reading by looking closely at Hundertwasser's images, and use Henri Rousseau's 'Tiger in a tropical storm' as a starting point for work on environmental themes.

Music

We often privilege the sense of sight in geography, but sound powerfully evokes a sense of place (see p. 31). Try creating a sound map. During fieldwork, ask pupils to close their eyes and listen to the world around them; back in the classroom they try to recreate the soundscape. Stolfa (2005) describes ways of 'talking geography' though musical forms such as folk songs, social dance and classical music. For practical geography/music teaching activities, try a 'Top 10' from Arthur Kelly (2009) or world music approaches from Brake and Jarvis (2016).

Drama

Drama is both a methodology and a subject, and techniques such as freeze-framing, thought-tracking, hot-seating, role play and debating-in-role can help pupils explore different perspectives and develop empathy. Working with professional actor-teachers can help pupils access complex world issues in meaningful and manageable ways, highlighting their human dimensions: 'Drama has the power to embody abstract concepts and data into the lives and actions of people, just like you and me' (Cooper and Easey, 2017).

Conclusion

The key to integrating geography with other subjects resides in finding 'meaningful overlaps' that strengthen learning in both subjects. Sometimes those overlaps are conceptual: every subject offers distinctive ways of understanding the world. Sometimes they are pedagogical (e.g. enquiry learning) and sometimes they arise from the specific topic or opportunity in hand. At best, such integrated planning not only deepens and strengthens learning, but makes planning and timetabling more manageable.

The next part of this section looks at broader topic or thematic planning.

> To access further support and resources from the *Leading Primary Geography* web page, see page 164

References

Alexander, A. (ed) (2010) *Children, their world, their education. Final report and recommendations of the Cambridge Primary Review*. London: Routledge, p. 100.

Arthus-Bertrand, Y. (2017) *Earth from Above* (updated edition). New York, NY: Abrams.

Ballin, B. (2019) *Teaching Atlas* (Upper Primary Edition). Nottingham: TTS.

Big Brum TIE (2011) *Artistic policy. 1. Principles of involvement.* p. 1. Available at: www.bigbrum.org.uk/ourwork/ (last accessed 12/6/2019).

Brake, H. and Jarvis, Z. (2016) 'Musical links', *Primary Geography*, 89, pp. 28–9.

Brakspear, R. (2017) 'What lies beneath?', *Primary Geography*, 93, pp. 8–10.

Bruner, J. (1996) *The culture of education*. Cambridge, MA: Harvard University Press, p. 41.

Collis, S. (2014) 'Refreshing rivers', *Primary Geography*, 83, pp. 12–13. (The article is supported by downloadable resources for the dam-building role-play activity).

Cooper, C. and Easey, N. (2017) 'Intertwined stories: making sense of Europe', *Primary Geography*, 94, pp. 12–13.

DfE (2014) *Geography programmes of study: key stages 1 and 2. National curriculum in England: Purpose of study*. London: Department for Education.

Harmon, K. (2009) *The map as art: contemporary artists explore cartography*. New York, NY: Princeton Architectural Press.

Hume, B., James, F. and Kerr, A. (1995) *A sense of place: activities which develop geographical skills through the study of places and themes for children from five to nine years*. Dunstable: Belair Publications Ltd.

Kelly, A. (2009) 'Sounds geographical', *Primary Geographer*, 68, pp. 34–6.

Mackintosh, M. and Kent, G. (2014) *The Everyday Guide to Primary Geography: Art*. Sheffield: Geographical Association.

Owens, P. (2019) *Teaching Atlas* (Lower Primary Edition). Nottingham: TTS.

Pett, S., Christopher, K., Blaylock, L., Moss, F. and Diamond-Conway, J. (2016) *Trafford agreed syllabus for Religious Education*. Birmingham: RE Today Services, p. 107.

Potter, C. and Scoffham, S. (2006) 'Emotional Maps', *Primary Geographer*, 60, pp. 20–1.

Rawling, E. (2008) 'The Primary Geographer interview,' *Primary Geographer*, 65, pp. 39–40.

Stolfa, S. (2005) 'Let's face the music and dance', *Primary Geographer*, 56, pp. 18–19.

Thackrah, I. (2017) 'Our everyday wonderland', *Primary Geography*, 92, pp. 28–9.

Vygotsky, L. (1976) *Play, its roles in development and evolution*. London: Penguin Educational, p. 551.

Wilkinson, A. and Ballin, B. (2016) 'When 1+1=3!', *Primary Geography*, 90, pp. 22–3.

Integrating geography through topics

Susan Pike

Why teach geography through topics?

Geography works exceptionally well as a starting point for topic-based teaching; such a wide and diverse subject can link to aspects of all other subjects, engaging with people, places and issues. As an umbrella subject for many topics (Rowley and Cooper, 2009), geography encourages a holistic appreciation of how the world works and of the interconnections between geography's 'big ideas' – place, space, scale, environment, cultural diversity, interconnections and sustainability. The enquiry approach lends itself well to topic-based learning and can help avoid bland lessons that include lots of content but not much thinking and metacognition (Pike, 2016). Geography also provides rich opportunities for using a stimulus or 'hook' to engage pupils with a topic; for instance, a challenging question about a controversial local issue, or using an image of a geographical feature to solve a 'mystery' about processes in the natural world (Barnes, 2014).

Greenwood (2013) has devised a useful scale for establishing the level of integration of geography within a topic (Figure 1). He did not view any one of these levels as better than others, just different in structure and content. The examples in this section follow the same pattern, drawing on a variety of levels of integration, but all having geography as a key aspect of learning. They incorporate a range of themes and skills from different subjects (those covered in a national curriculum) and dimensions of learning (those additional areas across and within subjects such as citizenship, well-being, relationships education, personal, social and health education), and put pupils' thinking about the 'big ideas' in geography at the centre of each topic.

Benefits to pupils of topic-based learning

Pupils constantly ask questions about the world, and are innately geographical in their thinking. For example, when introduced to a new topic, 7-year-old pupils in Lusk National School asked all types of questions, with very little prompting, about polar explorers: Why did they go? How did they survive? What did they eat? How did they poo? The simple task of writing down questions for a few minutes reveals pupils' desire to find out more and deepens their thinking as they investigate the topic. Topics can build on pupils' natural curiosity about the world on a range of scales, from the local to the global.

Topics can relate to pupils' everyday experiences in their valued places, like the park; their passions for reading, music or sport; the people and places they are fascinated by, in real and virtual localities. For example, the stimulus for a topic could be

- **Level 1:**
  No integration
  Geography is taught discretely
- **Level 2:**
  Low integration
  The focus is geography, with some elements of other subjects
- **Level 3:**
  Medium integration
  There is still a focus on geography but with more elements of a few different subjects
- **Level 4:**
  High integration
  Lessons are based on the topic rather than geography, with elements from a number of other subjects
- **Level 5:**
  Strong integration
  A broadly-based topic including elements from a wide range of other subjects.

Figure 1: The level of geography's integration in a topic. After: Greenwood, 2013.

pupils' experiences on a walk to the local park, which could conclude with them considering how different people think the park should be used and looked after.

Topics can draw in current issues and events, both local and global. Pupils will be aware of stories in the news, and excited about events such as the football World Cup, but their nascent knowledge is not sufficient to fully understand them. A geography-based topic can help them understand, for instance, the factors involved in staging the World Cup and the issues that arise from it, giving them a more comprehensive and holistic understanding.

Topics can build on pupils' experiences throughout the primary years and across the curriculum. For instance, in a local area study younger pupils can start with observing features in their own school and neighbourhood and, as they get older, conduct investigative enquiries into those known localities. Pupils in Drumcondra National School, while their school was being redeveloped, asked: Where will we go when the school gets rebuilt? Will the yard change? What will the classrooms be like? What will happen to the shed (shelter)? Finding answers to these questions helped them to understand what was happening and prepare for the move from an informed position, allowing them to cope much better with the change.

Topic work can help pupils to empathise with others and begin to see local and distant places differently through, for example, communicating with pupils in other countries or areas, exploring images, watching video and listening to accounts of others' lives.

Advantages to teachers of topic-based teaching

Planning topic-based work encourages colleagues to work together, drawing on the individual skills and experiences of a range of teachers and teaching assistants and developing opportunities for creative original work, both inside and outside the classroom. Topics are also flexible, adaptable and efficient.

Flexibility

Topic-based teaching enables great flexibility and freedom in planning and sequencing lessons: teachers can choose a number of routes through the learning as well as a variety of different levels of integration. Having more time to complete the topic allows tangents to be explored and provides opportunities for pupils to ask questions 'to the topic' and participate in the direction that the topic takes.

Adaptability

Topics can be changed and adapted over time so they remain relevant. Up-to-date material, such as new locations for fieldwork, picture books or news stories, can be introduced. For example, *The Lost Words* (MacFarlane and Morris, 2018) inspired many teachers to think about how they integrate art, language and geography. Pupils can be encouraged to explore topical issues in the news, such as the impact of large events like the World Cup, the Olympics and Paralympics or an earthquake. Topic-based teaching can 'leave space' for other areas of the curriculum, for example the introduction of new subjects or dimensions; it also makes planning more resilient to changes in the curriculum as topics, themes and skills can be tweaked over time.

Efficiency

Teaching through topics is an efficient use of time as it can incorporate a range of learning objectives and skills to enhance pupils' understanding. With careful planning, developing skills can be visited and revisited across a number of topics. For example, younger pupils may be introduced to procedural writing through describing the route that the class mascot travelled during a weekend. In older classes, pupils can draw the route that the class mascot took and then give it to a partner to follow. The pupils of St Mary's National School use maps to plan a route from their school to the General Post Office (GPO), a Dublin landmark. They then write instructions for a partner to follow their route using Google Maps or satellite image.

The class then follows the routes to the GPO, passing a number of other landmarks on the way, and they can refer back to the places they saw online. This straightforward activity incorporates a range of subjects (geography, language, PSHE) as well as skills (using maps, communication); these can be kept as a checklist and used to ensure progression through and across topics.

Drawing on expertise

There can, however, be issues for both teachers and pupils, which generally revolve around the balance of knowledge, understanding and skills within and across subjects. Teachers who come from a school's locality often have extensive knowledge of the area's heritage. They can support a new teacher, unfamiliar with the area, in getting to know more about it, which will help inform their planning. Conversely, teachers who, through travel or previous work experience, are familiar with other localities will also have engaging and innovative ideas for topics. While pupils will have plenty of experience of and opinions on their locality, teachers have the conceptual frameworks to develop pupils' knowledge into understanding and help them come to their sense of place and belonging. For example, the local shops are always significant for pupils, but teachers will see their potential for helping pupils understand settlement patterns and processes by using them as a fieldwork location. Likewise, pupils may be interested in the latest online game but it is their teacher who can plan creative learning opportunities based on it. An important argument and powerful rationale for planning topic-based learning is that it means pupils have to think and work in a variety of different ways, something that will be essential in the future as they '…will need to have the ability and flexibility to draw from many fields and solve problems that have inter-related factors' (Greenwood, 2013, p. 446).

Drawbacks of topic-based teaching

The main issue with topic-based teaching is that it can focus on the *content* to be covered rather than the *understanding* the pupils will develop. To guard against this, teachers need an in-depth understanding of the skills and concepts of the individual subjects involved. Difficulties can also arise with the balance of knowledge, understanding and skills within and between subjects and dimensions of learning.

Skills

Specific skills, for instance map making in geography, can be lost within topics. This can be resolved by making sure the topic covers a good range of skills and suitable progression through the primary phase. One-off skills lessons are still important, but they should be revisited and reinforced over the years. When teaching grid references, for example, pupils should be taught in different contexts and at a more complex level as they progress.

Concepts

The conceptual nature of subjects and dimensions of learning can be lost, especially in place-based topics. For example, in learning about Australia there could be a tendency to focus on what is there, rather than understanding what makes Australia like it is and what it is like to be there. Geography helps pupils *understand* places, rather than just *know* what they could easily Google! Again, it is important that conceptual understanding, especially for subjects such as geography, is mapped out across topics. For example, a topic based on the local area can be revisited every year, looking at different and more complex issues and building on the pupils' developing knowledge.

How can we plan for topics?

Combining subjects and dimensions of learning with a range of objectives needs to be considered carefully through long-, medium- and short-term plans. This planning process can be supported by asking:

- How can the subject links focus not just on content but also on skills and concepts?

- Which subjects are best to integrate in this topic?
- How can we enhance the learning experiences of pupils *in* subjects as well as *across* subjects?
- How do we develop pupils' thinking across topics?
- How can we develop pupils' skills across topics?
- How can we sequence the learning experiences across the topic?

Following on from this, decisions need to be made about what are the key features of good subject teaching and learning, such as geography, as well as in the different dimensions of learning such as citizenship. Having a checklist of three or four features for each subject and dimension, such as that shown in Figure 2, allows each topic to be audited and monitored. For geography, learning experiences are enhanced efficiently through:

- employing conceptual approaches to topics
- sound development of skills across topics
- opportunities for fieldwork, and making and using maps.

The same can be done for other subjects, and these key features often complement each other. For example, in history a key feature is the ability to consider evidence from different sources, which is similar to and can build on the skills developed through the collation of data from different sources in geography.

Figure 2 takes a very familiar and popular topic, Exploring Egypt, and shows how the geography in the topic can be made explicit and how it will not only lead to geographical learning but also greatly enhance the pupils' historical knowledge of events as they gain a more holistic understanding.

Topic: Understanding Egypt	
Subject/learning dimension	Key features
Geography	<ul><li>understanding the impact of the River Nile on past, present and future life in Egypt</li><li>understanding settlement patterns through developing map-work skills</li><li>contrasting localities to develop understanding of similarities and differences between the past and the present</li><li>understanding the impact of climate on people's lives and how it has changed over time</li></ul>
History	<ul><li>understanding why Egyptian pharaonic civilization developed as it did</li><li>exploring the events that led to the demise of Egyptian pharaonic civilisation, and the role of climate and resources</li><li>developing an understanding of what it would have been like to live in Ancient Egypt and contrasting to today; understanding why there are differences</li></ul>
Language	<ul><li>empathetic writing about what it was like to live in Egypt in the past</li><li>reading story books about living in Egypt today and in the past</li></ul>
Mathematics and design and technology	<ul><li>developing mathematical computational skills to design and create a pyramid</li><li>developing spatial awareness when designing and building model pyramids</li></ul>
Citizenship	<ul><li>understanding how Egypt was ruled in the past and how this changed over time</li></ul>

Figure 2: Example checklist to plan for the key features each subject will bring to the topic.

You can download a further example that shows how a geography topic – finding out about what is happening in the world through news stories – can help develop a range of skills, from critical literacy and identifying fake news and alternative truths to locating places on world and national maps. Such a focus provides an opportunity and context to teach about a range of physical, human and geographical phenomena and why they occur in different locations.

St Mary's National School in Dublin plans six-week integrated topics, based on themes linked to the four overarching principles of its School Development Plan:

1. We celebrate our diverse languages, faiths and cultures.
2. We care for our local environment and the world.
3. We encourage everyone to be active and healthy.
4. We keep ourselves and others safe and well.

The topics chosen address challenging questions, and use skills to develop conceptual thinking.

Each topic has common features, such as creative 'entry points', which could be telling a story or going on a field trip. For example, the 'Stories told in tents' topic for 7–8-year-olds is based on *Tales Told in Tents: Stories from Central Asia* (Pomme Clayton and Herxheimer, 2006). This topic relates to all the School Development Plan principles, but especially celebrates diversity. From this story stimulus, the pupils go on to find out answers to questions such as:

- Where is Central Asia?
- How does our community link to this place?
- What do we know about Turkmenistan, Uzbekistan, Kazakhstan, Kyrgyzstan and Tajikistan?
- What do the stories in *Tales told in Tents* tell us about the countries in Central Asia and their cultures?

As a school with pupils from a wide range of different heritages, the decision to find out about countries that are often not heard of is intentional, widening the pupils' knowledge horizons and teaching them about new places and experiences.

Careful and comprehensive planning, specific to the needs of the pupils in your class and to the context of your school, is crucial when developing effective and meaningful topic work. Taking the time to do this will reap rewards in engaging the pupils and optimising their learning potential. There are a number of characteristic foci for geographical topics, outlined below.

Topics based on everyday geography

As teachers we are all aware of the importance of children's places, as we hear pupils' stories about them every day! In some curricula this is recognised, with 'sense of place' and 'sense of space' specifically listed as key aspects of pupils' experiences. Topics can be based on pupils' experiences in both their natural and built environments and their virtual worlds.

Topics in the school grounds

The school grounds offer great opportunities to integrate subjects. They are an immediately accessible environment, requiring little forward planning or investment in additional time. Even very simple topics can incorporate geographical experiences that result in engaging and creative responses from pupils. Opportunities will emerge to incorporate the scaffolding of geographical terms, such as positional language to describe where items are found, as well as spatial awareness, knowing where places are and their representation on a map.

If a school is given or purchases a bench or plant for example, deciding where it will go can be a geographical decision-making topic.

Many other enquiries could be undertaken, for example:

- Where will our hedgehog hibernate?
- Where will we place our buddy bench?
- Where will we plant the plum tree?
- Where would a butterfly like to live in our school grounds?

Figure 3 shows how a similar enquiry, 'Where will we place our beehive?', was undertaken by 7–9-year-old pupils.

Enquiry question	Subject and activity
What is a bee? What do bees do?	- At home or in the locality, pupils observe and/or find out about bees. They return to school with three things that they found out (science and geography) - Pupils describe the actions of bees (language) - Pupils draw and describe the different parts a bee (science and art)
Where do bees go?	- Pupils look at images of bee-friendly environments and learn about what makes them suitable environments for the bees (geography) - Pupils make bees using papier mâché designs (art and design) - Pupils act out a pollinator drama to appreciate how bees pollinate (science and drama) - Pupils carry out an audit of the school grounds discussing what features bees may or may not like. They mark their findings on a base map of the school (geography)
How can we encourage bees to our school?	- Pupils reinvestigate the school grounds with their new knowledge to work out what more they need to do to encourage bees. They explore the importance of direction, aspect and location, and consider where the new features of their school grounds, such as plants to attract the bees, will go (geography and language) - Pupils compile a list of what they need to find or buy to ensure their school is 'bee friendly' (PSHE) - Pupils work out the cost of the changes they would like to make. They consider how the funds can be found or raised (mathematics) - Pupils decide which plants to put in the school grounds as well as where they should go. They talk to significant people (principal, caretaker, etc.) to help them make decisions (geography, science and language) - Pupils draft a plan, on paper, of the ideal environment for bees. They annotate it, verbally or in writing, to explain why they have created it as they have (art, geography and science) - In the following lessons, pupils create a bee garden for their school grounds, drawing on their geographical learning (geography, PSHE, citizenship, art, design and technology)

Figure 3: Enquiring into familiar places (variations on this theme can also be used. For example, where would butterflies like to live?).

Topics incorporating the local area

The immediate locality of the school can be used to understand concepts such as interconnections, on a wider scale than the school grounds, through geography and other subjects and dimensions of learning. The pupils at Kensington Primary School in London focus on the local postal service, as geography co-ordinator Hina describes:

> *'The pupils look at the journey that a letter or parcel takes. Rather than stopping there, we build on the excitement pupils have for the topic, taking our extremely excited four- and five-year-olds to the post box across the road from school. Here they all get to post their beautifully made Easter cards to their home addresses. This brings the learning back to real life and helps them see an outcome from their learning in school as well as strengthening links between school and home'* (Hussain, 2018).

As well as teaching pupils about the process of letter writing, this activity helps pupils understand key ideas about jobs and the world of work:

- What jobs do people do in our area?
- What does a post office worker do?
- Where do the letters go and how does a letter get from one place to another?
- What is it like in the places that the letters go to?

As they explore these questions, the pupils also learn about the places where the processes occur, key aspects of locational and place geography. The school also makes extensive use of ICT, using Digimap along with the fieldwork to plan and map journeys.

Geographical topics also give pupils the opportunity to appreciate places from the perspectives of others (Massey, 2008). Those 'others' could be other children, adults or even an insect or animal. Figure 4 illustrates a further example of using familiar places, with older pupils, aged 10–12. A series of enquiry questions was the starting point for a topic on change in their locality.

The use of pupils' personal geographies as a basis for learning can enhance their well-being within learning experiences. The pupils in the examples above realised that their opinions and experiences of their environments were valued by the teachers; they also experienced time 'to be' in environments such as their school grounds, local park and even valued places, such as outside the local shop! While children's geographies are key to primary geography, we must remember we are using them as a starting point for learning. We must present them with new knowledge and ways of understanding and teach them about the world beyond their own experiences.

The Sacred Heart pupils in the example in Figure 4 built on their prior learning by carrying out a number of further fieldwork investigations in their locality, including:

- Using school records, historical maps and online census data to find out about the locality in the past. They were able to trace the changes in the school's location, as well as the changing nature of the local community (geography, history and literacy).
- Investigating the origins and meanings of place names and street names (English and Irish languages and geography).
- Investigating changing land use over time, using online and paper maps of the area (geography and history).
- Finding out about the local dairy industry, including the processing of milk and other products, which was formerly the local population's main livelihood (science, geography and history).

All these case studies are unique to the local area and the school's particular context. They demonstrate how easily key ideas and concepts can be adapted to different localities, the specific needs of your pupils, and the unique characteristics of your school or setting.

- What was the first location in Finglas?
- Why is Finglas so old?
- Why is Finglas where it is?
- How much did it cost to build Finglas?
- How did some things change and why?
- How far did the stream stretch?
- What did the houses look like in the past?

Pupils at Sacred Heart Boys' National School took part in a project to find signage and other features in the Irish language in their local area of Ballygall, part of Finglas, Dublin. The information this provided about the origins of local place names proved an effective and engaging stimulus to the work that followed, generating questions that were personal, as well as geographical and historical:

The first of these questions alludes to the development of the area from a single village into a number of settlements all with their own parades of shops, schools and churches. To investigate this development, pupils went for a walk around the immediate locality. The question about the stream revealed pupils' curiosity about river processes and features, as the 'stretch' is a meander in the River Tolka. The only teacher-directed activity was to encourage the pupils to enhance their observations of the familiar by finding something 'old', 'new', 'unusual' and 'interesting'. The activity turned the pupils' local area into a learning resource.

Figure 4: Learning about change in the local area through personal geographies. Photo © Susan Pike.

Topics about distant places

Primary pupils are intrigued by the wider world and keen to find out more. They are aware of other places but their knowledge is often fragmentary and disconnected, picked up from a wide range of different media and viewpoints. This can result in pupils developing negative images of distant places (Ruane *et al.*, 2010). Learning about distant places through engaging and meaningful topics can help pupils to a more systematic and comprehensive understanding. It encourages them to question negative or stereotypical views, both their own and those of others, and appreciate places from different people's perspectives. It is also a perfect opportunity for pupils to develop their skills and understanding in geography as well as other areas of the curriculum through:

- corresponding with other children in other parts of the world; imagining life there; writing diary entries (language)
- developing computational skills by working out how far away places are; how long it would take to get there using different modes of transport; analysing climate data and comparing it to where they live (maths)
- understanding why places are like they are; how they have changed over time; what factors have influenced their development (history).

As long as the topics make tangible and meaningful links that enhance pupils' knowledge, skills and understanding, the list could go on to include all curriculum subjects and dimensions.

Finding out about other places not only draws together a number of subjects, it also incorporates other dimensions of learning, such as citizenship, social justice, sustainable development and interdependence, which can be brought together through a place-based topic. Using a number of teaching resources, covering a wide range of curriculum subjects, develops pupils' geographical understanding (see web page) in an effective and meaningful way. Using a variety of sources also helps pupils critically evaluate them. Figure 5 shows how critical thinking about a fiction text can be the stimulus for geographical activities for 7-9-year-olds.

Resourcing distant place topics

Using locality packs and place-based resources requires investment, so to make the most of them it is useful to know how to tackle the following issues:

- Over time, locality packs risk becoming out of date. However, they can still be useful as a reflection of the past, enabling comparisons with the present to be made – an enquiry in itself. Using Mystery Skypes or school partnerships to connect with pupils in the particular locality can elicit up-to-date information; it also allows the historical aspects to be shared with the pupils there.

- They may lack resources, particularly maps. These can be augmented with digital mapping and aerial images; not only do these offer up-to-date information but the zoom facility is particularly effective in introducing locations.

- Locality-based resources may offer only limited coverage of the country as a whole. As with out-of-date material, this can be remedied by locating other places in the country on maps, and asking pupils to research them, exploring any similarities or differences to provide a more comprehensive and representative picture.

- The pack may include activities that are not relevant to your topic. Activities from one resource can be borrowed and adapted for another. Identify where there are gaps in the planning framework and mix, match and upcycle ideas from other resources or topics.

Key questions	Linked geography activities
Settings Can photographs and pictures show what life is really like in a country?	Pupils use Google Earth to find the country and investigate a range of its landscapes. After reading the story pupils devise enquiry questions about the country. Pupils specifically investigate landscapes, finding a range of features, such as homes, schools, parks, sports facilities, etc.
Characters How do people's lives, experiences and perspectives vary within a country and between countries?	Pupils discuss what other images, resources and information they could use to help find out about a country. They use a range of photographs to learn about life in different parts of the country. Pupils exchange enquiry questions with a link school via email.
Plot What are the causes and effects of events in the story?	Pupils discuss the causes and effects of events in the story. They reflect back on how they have explored cause and effect in different geographical topics.
Motive How do writers persuade us to see things their way?	Pupils locate the setting for the story on a map of the country. They find images of the places online.

Figure 5: Critical thinking and geographical activities based on a fiction text. After: Oberman, 2014a; 2014b.

Topics based on physical, human and environmental geography

As described by Catling (pp. 22–5), geographical thinking involves synthesising physical and human geography, understanding how they are interdependent and inter-related and how they are drawn together in the study of environmental geography. Environmental geography is an excellent way of engaging pupils in a study of how human activity and the natural world can have a significant impact on each other, at both local and global scales. For instance, it demonstrates how deforestation depletes soil fertility; or on a global scale, how carbon emissions are changing climate patterns. Similarly, physical processes can have a significant impact on human activities; for instance, avoiding building in areas prone to river or coastal flooding. These are not two-directional relationships but are complex interactions taking place over time and space, as Figure 6 demonstrates.

Topics based on physical geography

Basing a topic on an enquiry question can stimulate pupils' instinct to find an answer and solve the problem. For instance, if you ask 9–11-year-olds 'How did a volcanic eruption hundreds of miles away cause flooding in the Philippines?' to answer it they will need some knowledge and understanding of seismic activity and plate tectonics, so the enquiry question can prompt meaningful teaching of these geographical and scientific phenomena. Once pupils are equipped with this basic knowledge, they can use maps to locate the volcano and area of flooding, developing their cartographic skills. They can use their IT skills to research what happened and present it as a newspaper article. Considering the impact of the flood on local settlements and their inhabitants they will learn concepts of human geography: the vulnerability of buildings in some parts of the world and the challenge of resisting the forces of the natural world.

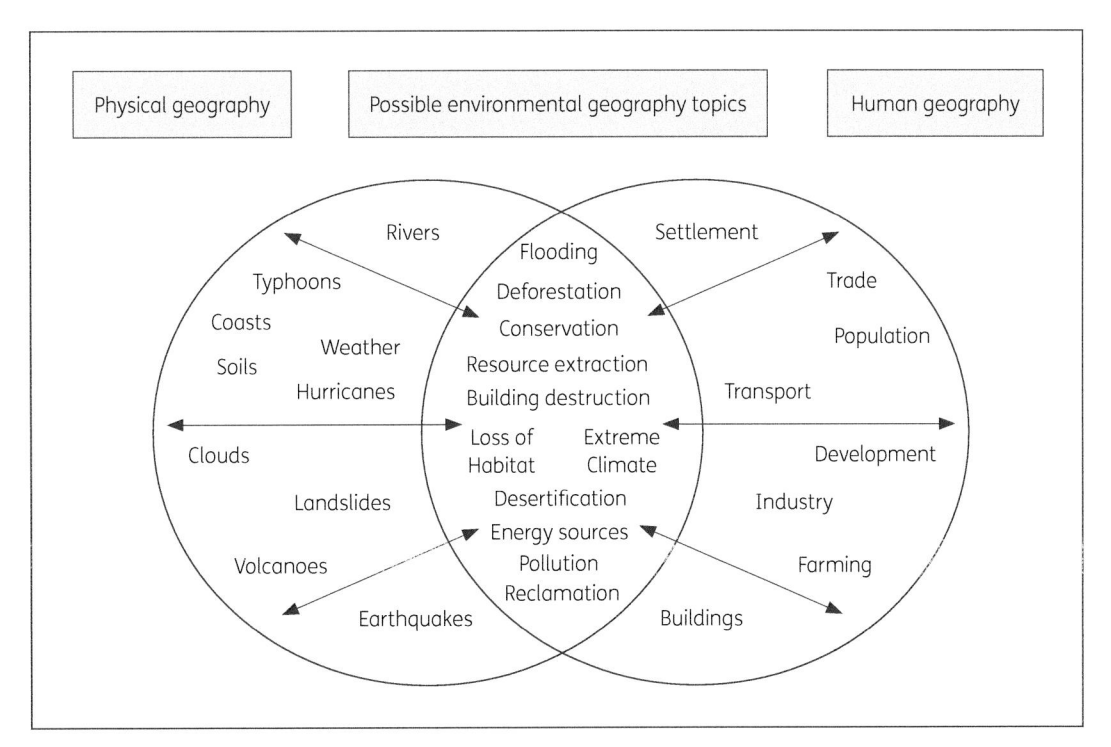

Figure 6: The complex interactions of physical, human and environmental geography. Source: Willy, after Catling and Willy (2018).

Their mathematical skills will help them work out, from the distance between the volcano and the coast and the timing of the eruption, how fast the tremors travelled across the ocean.

The pupils can collate and present their findings to the rest of the school by making a documentary; uploaded to the school website, it could reach a wider audience. By all these means pupils develop an understanding of the interaction of physical and human geography, the complexity of the world, and the repercussions of global events, developing skills and understanding in a range of subjects.

Topics based on human geography

Pupils can also use their personal experiences to understand broader concepts, such as similarities and differences in the processes involved in food production around the world, learning about farming, trade and dependence on the natural world. Figure 7 shows how 5–8-year-olds were able to use their personal experiences and knowledge of food production, from having parents who worked in farming or the meat processing industry, to develop their geographical understanding of food and food sources in a contrasting locality in Kenya.

As well as teaching locational knowledge, specific teaching of topics such as food, using a range of subjects and dimensions, also advances pupils' thinking and language skills.

Older pupils can investigate more complex processes drawing on their local knowledge and using it as a springboard for learning about different places. For example, in learning about global events, such as migration and refugees, pupils could start with their own school and its catchment area to find out more about where people have come from. They can move on to looking at regional, and then national, boundaries, where people migrate from and to and their many reasons for doing so.

Topics based on environmental geography

Many environmental geography concepts relate to controversial issues, requiring pupils to think critically and develop an understanding of different people's views and perceptions. Such issues often have a geographical basis and work very well for integrating a number of subjects and dimensions of learning: for example, a short-term, local community-based issue (a proposal for a youth centre, playground, new road, etc.), or a long-term environmental issue that affects the whole planet (global climate change, soil degradation, deforestation, mining, etc.) that may be felt for generations.

Figure 8 shows how a framework can help pupils explore local or global geographical issues. This type of 'decision making'-based topic provides a wealth of potential learning experiences, and the framework alone cannot convey the full richness of the curiosity and conversations such a topic inspires in pupils.

Resourcing issues-based topics

With the support of their teachers, pupils can generate ideas and enquiry questions for issues-based topics through discussions, research or fieldwork. The data to answer their enquiries can come from many sources, including:

- maps and aerial photographs, especially those taken over a period of time
- stories collected from friends and family, or news items from the media or social media, for instance a local development plan
- statistics collected from surveys or found online, such as GIS data sets of where earthquakes have occurred in recent months
- artefacts or photographs collected on fieldwork, such as potential locations for planting a tree, etc.

For any real-world geography there will be a wealth of people, places and material that can be used as learning resources and audiences, including newspapers, social media, tourist and local council publicity, local developers, councillors, etc., ensuring access to different genres of speaking and writing. Collecting data from and about them through questionnaires can provide a range of mathematical opportunities; this also gives pupils rich opportunities to think

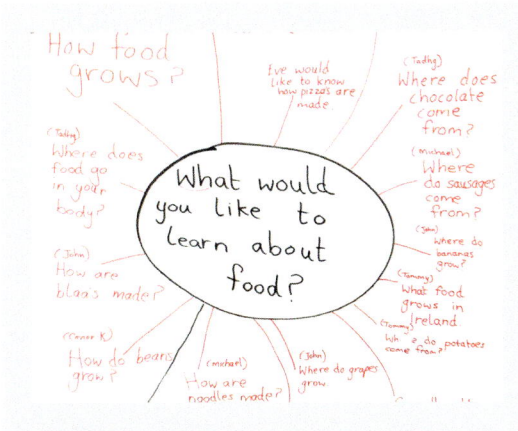

The topic was structured around a number of enquiry questions:

What do we want to know? During a whole-class discussion on the topic, pupils put forward questions they wanted to investigate. They had a particular interest in food sources and how foods were made. There were questions about locally-made food, such as 'blaas' (bread rolls) as well as favourite foods produced elsewhere, such as chocolate (geography, language).

How is food made? Pupils were given images showing the numerous stages of making the blaas and asked to sequence them.

This generated a lot of discussion, developing the pupils' language skills at the same time as their understanding of the processes involved in food production. They also discussed and investigated where in Ireland wheat was grown and how this related to the amount of sun and rain (science, geography, mathematics, language).

Where do other foods come from and how do people in other countries get their food? Using Google maps, pupils investigated, discussed and marked on maps the locations where their favourite foods came from. They speculated about the ingredients of the foods as well as investigating paper, plastic and tin packaging. Drawing on each other's and their teachers' knowledge, they discovered how complex making something as simple as a bar of chocolate was. They then investigated what foods were eaten in other places and how they were grown and processed and used images of food production and processing to help them understand that there is a great deal involved in the production, movement and selling of food before it gets to the table (geography, science, PSHE and language).

Figure 7: 'People, places and food' at Knockmahon National School, Waterford.

critically about the information they receive and how the voices of different groups may or may not be heard in decision making.

Real-world geography

Participating in real-world geography is an essential part of pupils forming their own opinions, thinking about alternative futures and developing as global citizens. When pupils learn about such issues they will want to try to address them, and it is important to support them in this. However, encouragement must be tempered by realism. For example, when investigating where to plant a tree or locate a beehive, if the work is not actually carried out pupils will be disillusioned and dispirited.

It is essential to have achievable goals and be honest and transparent about the pupils' ability to make a difference. In some cases, where pupils can present their ideas and plans to decision makers, through local councils and youth committees, for instance, their desire to act can be really effective. There is always the risk that they may not be listened to; but that can be a good life lesson, and pupils will become increasingly persuasive as a result.

As can be seen from the examples, pupils can contribute to their communities in a multitude of ways, so there is no reason why they cannot be involved in shaping 'their own futures and those of their communities' (Hart, 1992, p. 3). Percy-Smith and Thomas (2010) suggest that

	Younger pupils	**Older pupils**
Enquiry question	Where should we plant our tree?	What will the impact of planning for the Olympics and Paralympics be on our local area?
What do we want to know about this issue?	Where is the best place to plant a tree to enable it to grow and thrive? Find an appropriate place to plant the tree considering its needs, e.g. in terms of shelter, water supply, through careful observation and recording of the school grounds (art, geography, language and science) Consider what it would be like for the tree to be located in different areas through enacting life in trees (drama/play)	How will hosting the Olympics and Paralympics affect us and our area? Analyse news reports to find out more about the Games and the extent of their impact to generate ideas (language). Research more about the issues relating to the Olympics (geography) Scrutinise maps and plans of the proposed sites to determine the changes that will take place and the consequences of them (geography) Consider the ethical dimensions of large-scale events and who will benefit from them as well as those who might suffer (citizenship, geography)
What are we going to do?	How can we show where the best place to locate the tree is? Use annotated sketch maps and plans to show where the best possible locations are for planting (geography) How do we plant a tree? Consider what we need to plant a tree and how a tree is actually planted (D&T, PE and science)	How can we ensure that the impact is as positive as possible for our local area? Set up a scenario or debate, considering the different voices and perspectives (drama, language, geography) Consider the outcomes of the scenario or debate and, bearing in mind the different viewpoints raised, draw up plans of the area to optimise the potential benefits and minimise the drawbacks (citizenship and geography) Investigate the design of facilities to ensure that they are environmentally conscious (geography, science and technology)
What might be the impact?	How do we observe and record change once the tree has been planted and use this in our learning? Take photos and draw sketches during different seasons and in different weather conditions, noting changes and explaining the impact of these (art, geography and science) Write about the changes, e.g. in the form of a diary (language)	What will be the impact of our plans to host the Olympics and Paralympics be? Draw up the blueprint of our plans; use these to speculate on the potential impact of the Games on the residents, local businesses and economy, wildlife habitats etc. (geography, language, maths and science) Investigate past Olympic sites to learn lessons and plan for what to do with the site in the future (history and geography). Use participatory approaches to learning, such as 'Mantle of the Expert', to explore future scenarios (drama)
How will other people respond?	What do other people think about our tree planning? Conduct a survey of other children in the school, parents and governors to determine their thoughts about the location of the tree (citizenship and geography)	What do other members of our community and Olympic experts think about our plans? Invite local councillors in to present findings to and provide assessments of the plans If possible, correspond with other children who have similar experiences in other parts of the world, or a past or future competitor of the Games, to ask their advice Present plans to the school and wider community to gauge opinions and inform further plans

Figure 8: Framing and progression in learning through geographical issues-based topics.

participation should be embedded in pupils' actual daily lives, such as school, rather than in defined formal structures. In fact, in communities susceptible to natural disasters, learning to act through geographical learning is essential. Through such experiences, pupils can also engage in viewing their community through different lenses; for example, they can work as scientists when measuring environmental pollution and as geographers and planners when reviewing plans for urban areas in cities other than their own.

Conclusion

Teaching geography through topics is a relevant and fascinating way for pupils to understand their locality and the wider world through enquiry and critical thinking, using and developing a wide range of geographical skills, knowledge and understanding and enhancing their understanding of other subject areas and dimensions. Geography can be central to topic work, as geographical issues and phenomena act as motivating stimuli and keep pupils engaged in contemporary, varied and meaningful learning across the curriculum.

> To access further support and resources from the *Leading Primary Geography* web page, see page 164

References

Barnes, J. (2014) *Cross-curricular Learning 3-14*. London: Sage.

Catling, S. and Willy, T. (2018) *Understanding and Teaching Primary Geography*. London: Sage.

Greenwood, R. (2013) 'Subject-based and cross-curricular approaches within the revised primary curriculum in Northern Ireland: teachers' concerns and preferred approaches', *Education 3-13*, 41, 4, pp. 443-58.

Hart, R. (1992) *Children's Participation: From Tokenism to Citizenship*. Available at: www.unicef-irc.org/publications/pdf/childrens_participation.pdf (last accessed 12/6/2019).

Hussain, H. (2018) 'Adapting geography through topic-based teaching', *Primary Geography*, 97, pp. 8-9.

Macfarlane, R. and Morris, J. (2017) *The Lost Words*. London: Hamish Hamilton.

Massey, D. (2008) 'A global sense of place' in Oakes, T. and Price, P. (eds) *The Cultural Geography Reader*. Abingdon: Routledge, pp. 257-63.

Oberman, R. (2014a) *Farid's Rickshaw Ride*. Dublin: Trócaire/DCU Centre for Human Rights and Citizenship Education.

Oberman, R. (2014b) *Just Children 2: A tool for integrating critical literacy and global citizenship education across the curriculum at primary level*. Dublin: Trócaire/DCU Centre for Human Rights and Citizenship Education.

Percy-Smith, B. and Thomas, N. (eds) (2010) *Handbook of Children and Young People's Participation: Perspectives from Theory and Practice*. Abingdon: Routledge.

Pike, S. (2016) *Learning Primary Geography: Ideas and Inspirations from Classrooms*. Abingdon: Routledge.

Pomme Clayton, S. and Herxheimer, S. (2006) *Tales Told in Tents: Stories from Central Asia*. London: Frances Lincoln.

Rowley, C. and Cooper, H. (2009) *Cross-curricular Approaches to Teaching and Learning*. London: Sage.

Ruane, B., Kavanagh, A.M., Waldron, F., Dillon, S., Maunsell, C. and Prunty, A. (2010) *Young pupils' engagement with issues of Global Justice*. Dublin: Centre for Human Rights and Citizenship Education, SPD and Trócaire.

Acknowledgements

Thank you to B. Ed2 Geography Specialism students, Dublin City University; Eryn Devine and 1st class pupils in Lusk National School, Dublin; Eaodaoin Kelly and staff, St Mary's National School, Dublin; Jim Ryan and pupils, Sacred Heart Boys' National School, Dublin; Hina Hussain and pupils at Kensington Primary School, London.

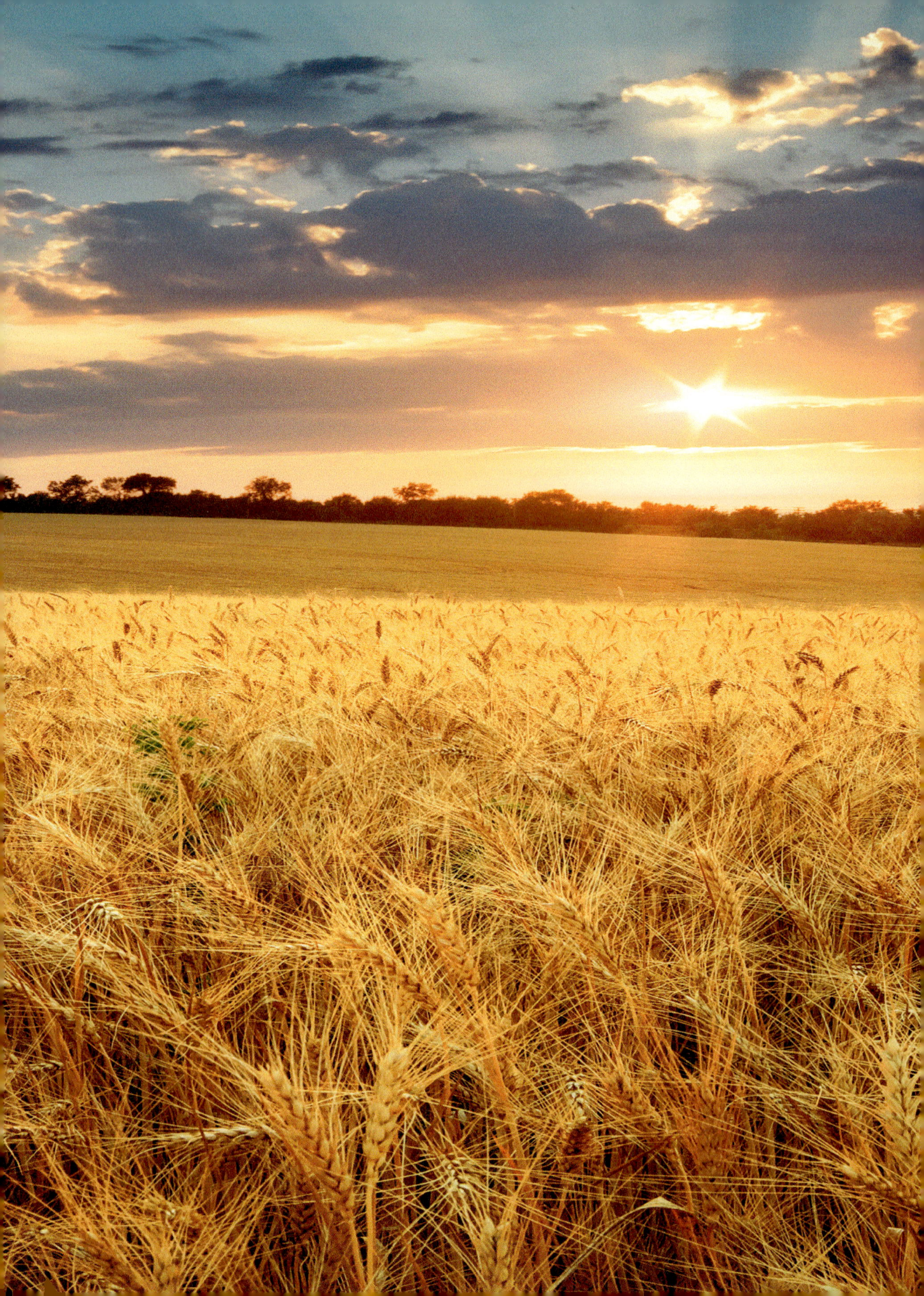

SECTION 7

Effective subject leadership

Paula Owens

This section considers the crucial role of the geography subject leader in school, flying the flag for the subject and giving it identity, profile and direction. It also provides significant support for the class teacher, offering effective and engaging ways of leading geography in the classroom. The section guides you through a range of essential topics including curriculum planning, developing a school policy, progression and transition, assessment and monitoring, individual and school professional development, and research opportunities. Practical advice and ideas will support you in your role and enhance your own professional development and ability to lead others in your school to teach great geography.

Introduction

The breadth of subjects and competition for space in the primary curriculum means that leading any subject well entails a combination of good subject and curriculum knowledge and development, management and leadership skills, and vision. If this sounds daunting, remember that all primary teachers (whether a new subject leader, an aspiring one, an experienced one or even a reluctant one; a class teacher, NQT or trainee) face these challenges and juggle such complex demands to some degree every day. You can't do everything, and you can't do it overnight, but you can learn to identify and prioritise areas for development. Leading geography well is a collaborative act and there are many ways to contribute to effective leadership, so never underestimate the part you can play. This section is designed to help you identify some strategies to lead the subject well in your school setting.

Leading geography in your classroom

All primary teachers are leaders of geography in their classroom. There is a reciprocal relationship between the individual teacher's knowledge, skills and confidence and the subject leader's qualities. Each can support and enhance the role of the other through relevant professional conversations and mutual trust. Relationships in school, at all levels, matter enormously.

If you are a new subject leader, and indeed a relatively new teacher, you might feel anxious about trying to support more experienced teachers who have been at the school longer than you. Conversely, if you are an experienced and knowledgeable subject leader, you might feel concerned about overloading and worrying teachers who may lack confidence in their geography. How can we ensure that all classroom teachers feel confident with geography? A good starting point is to find out informally how the school community feels about the subject.

Informal conversations

Informal conversations can be very powerful and are essential to gauge the temperature in specific areas.

With teachers

Simple leading questions for class teachers could include:

- What is geography like in your classroom?
- Which areas of geography do you enjoy/not enjoy teaching?
- What geography do your pupils enjoy most?
- What aspects of geography do you think pupils struggle with?

And most importantly – do ask:

- How can I support you? What do you need?

Regular informal conversations can tell you a lot about the state of geography in the school and teachers' attitudes towards the subject. It will also help establish relationships with teachers in which they feel comfortable coming to you for advice and support, to ask you questions and have a grumble about what's not going well.

With Head teachers and senior management

Keep the idea of geography alive and thriving, or if need be put it on the agenda, at a senior level. Update senior staff about progress in geography, and raise the subject in the context of whole-school priorities – how might geography support them? For example, pointing out how geography contributes to topical issues and whole-school initiatives such as global learning, sustainability, community engagement and curricular cohesion is a way of foregrounding the importance of the subject, especially if you feel it is, or has been, overlooked.

With governors

Many schools have 'linked governors' who take a particular interest in one area of the curriculum. Having a governor linked to geography can be hugely beneficial, and if you encourage them to 'drop in' to see you or (with their permission) other teachers, an ongoing dialogue about the health of the subject can become part of the school culture. Keep governors informed about upcoming events or successes so that they feel familiar with the subject and what it can offer and can talk well about it at governors' meetings.

With pupils

Pupils' voices are a vital part of any evidence gathering, process and action. Find out what they think about their geography classroom experiences. The sensitive and effective subject leader will ask pupils about their likes and dislikes, not as a test of how well they are doing or a way of checking up on what's been taught, but in a way that is non-threatening to both them and their teacher. Before asking pupils what they think, it is helpful to talk to their class teachers – ask them to identify something that they think has gone particularly well in geography and use this as a reason to visit their classes and praise pupils for their efforts. This can be a natural precursor to asking pupils why they enjoyed doing that aspect of the subject or to explain what they found out.

These kinds of conversations normalise such dialogic processes in everyday school contexts and help to keep dialogue about geography alive. They raise the status of the subject in all classrooms and help teachers and pupils realise that geography is something that *matters*. Raising the profile of geography in your school is probably one of your biggest challenges, yet ordinary, everyday conversations about the subject can be incredibly helpful in establishing a culture in which geography can thrive.

Formal conversations

Once you have established a culture of informal, professional conversations, you will begin to get a sense of the capacity for geography in individual classrooms. These conversations, along with other sources of information that we will discuss later, will help you identify areas where you might take a more structured approach and initiate formal conversations. Here are some examples of what you might do.

With teachers

A **questionnaire**, in electronic or paper format, can give you a general idea of what teachers are doing, need or want in their classrooms. This will provide valuable evidence for your geography file and action plan. You will probably do this no more than once a year, so think carefully about the questions you will ask. They will need to reflect school priorities, the school vision and areas you have identified for further investigation, where they will help you decide what actions need to be taken.

If there is time, you might ask for a brief interview with **individual** teachers or year groups. It is very time-intensive, but asking questions face to face, noting responses, often gathers much more information than a questionnaire. It might be that responses to your initial questions warrant further exploration and necessitate a follow-up interview.

A **staff meeting** might focus on the questionnaire, with time for individuals to write their comments before a short discussion. This format might give people the opportunity to talk openly about their areas of concern; however, if there is an imbalance between highly confident and less-confident teachers of the subject it could have the opposite effect. You need to identify staff you feel might benefit from further conversation.

With Head teachers and senior management

At least once a year you will need to have a formal meeting with your Head, or members of the senior management team, to contribute to the setting of school priorities and the action plan for the subject for that year. You will also need to make a case for a budget, and it is essential to have an annual summary of strengths and weaknesses and an action plan for the coming year. Records of these meetings can go in your subject leader's file (Figure 1) where they will help evidence whole-school thinking and curriculum making for you, the senior management team and any outside agencies who might be assessing the quality of the subject and its role within the whole-school curriculum.

Your subject leader's file will build over time to include many important documents. It needs to be useful for you and your school. It should also be something that a new subject leader can pick up and use easily should you leave the school or change roles. Ideally it will be an electronic file accessible to all staff, and/or a paper file kept in an accessible place. Suggested content includes:

Policy and curriculum
- a copy of the school's current geography policy
- the geography part of the School Development Plan
- a record of the geography budget against expenditure
- the geography part of the latest Ofsted report
- a curriculum management audit, plus a copy of the subject leader's action/development plan, list of jobs to do and when etc.

Planning
- a copy of the school's geography scheme of work, annotated to show amendments, and a curriculum map showing when the units will be delivered in the year
- copies of teachers' planning from each year group
- monitoring schedule and reports, including teacher and pupil feedback
- assessment information relevant to your role as subject leader (it may be useful to have this element as a separate, dedicated, assessment folder, with annotated examples of pupils' work throughout the school)

Fieldwork
- fieldwork and outdoor learning schedule for the coming year
- generic and updated risk assessments and templates for the immediate local area
- a record of geography-related visits in and out of school
- a list of contacts for local fieldwork trips and names of parents who may be suitable as additional support

CPD
- CPD attended and CPD needs for the coming year
- any other useful notes and readings, e.g. co-ordinator's/subject leader's diary, dates for staff meetings and in-house training sessions

Lists
- a categorised list of resources
- useful organisation contacts, publications and journals such as *Primary Geography*
- contact details for possible visitors to give talks to the pupils (parents, local councillors, etc.)
- a bibliography including reference books (see web page)

Figure 1: Your subject leader's file.

With governors

You may find there is a running rota for formal subject reports to governors and that you are needed to present one about geography. This is an ideal opportunity to showcase your strengths and successes and make a case for support in any required areas. You can use much of the same documentation as for senior management. It is helpful in both cases to include some pupil voices.

With parents

You may have spoken to parents about the geography their children are doing in school, especially if the pupils have been on field trips, but there may be occasions when it would be useful if parents had a broader understanding. Some schools do a series of formal talks to parents, on different curriculum areas, throughout the year, and class teachers are required to write reports and talk to parents at Parents' Evenings. As a subject leader, you may also need to advise other teachers about what they might say at Parents' Evenings. Placing a formal statement about the subject on the school website, with examples of planning, policy and pupils' work, can be extremely helpful here.

With pupils

Surveys or set questions about the subject (Figure 2) for pupils to answer are essential for shaping the development of the subject at a whole-school and classroom level. Encourage class teachers to do this themselves and feed the responses back to you and into their planning. It is best if all classes answer the same questions. These might be very open, such as:

- What do you enjoy most about geography, and why?
- What don't you enjoy about geography, and why?

Responses like these are very helpful if you are redesigning the geography planning to improve the learning and teaching experiences, but if you are concerned that pupils may have no basic understanding of what geography is for, you might start by asking questions such as:

- What is geography all about?
- What does it mean to you?

Each school will have a unique context, and this will influence the questions you need to ask.

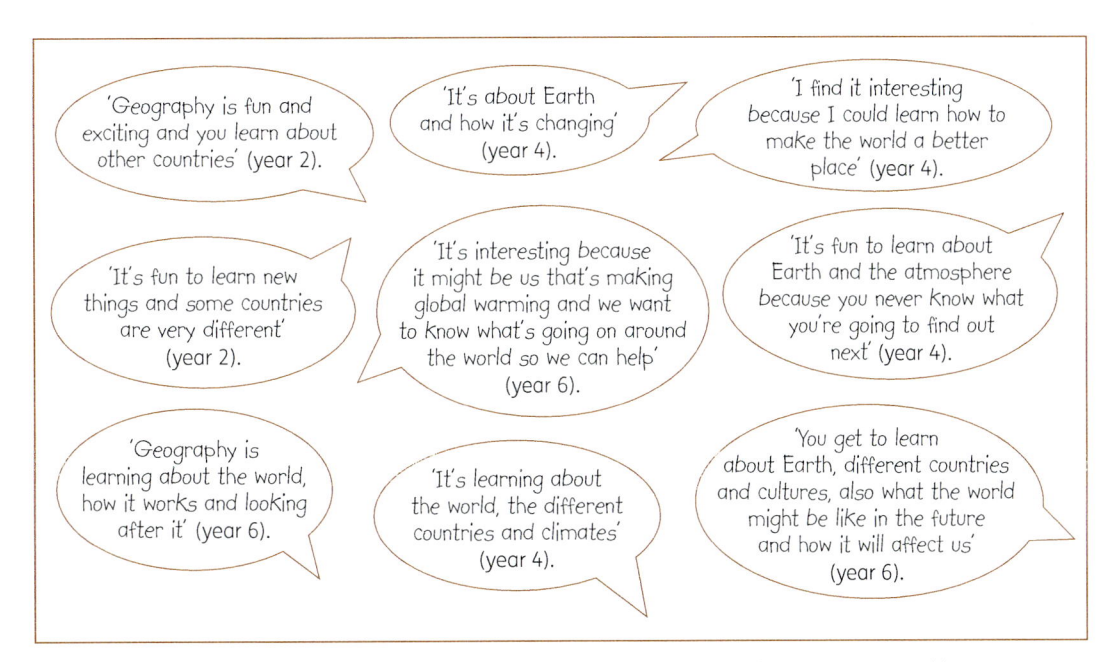

'Geography is fun and exciting and you learn about other countries' (year 2).

'It's about Earth and how it's changing' (year 4).

'I find it interesting because I could learn how to make the world a better place' (year 4).

'It's fun to learn new things and some countries are very different' (year 2).

'It's interesting because it might be us that's making global warming and we want to know what's going on around the world so we can help' (year 6).

'It's fun to learn about Earth and the atmosphere because you never know what you're going to find out next' (year 4).

'Geography is learning about the world, how it works and looking after it' (year 6).

'It's learning about the world, the different countries and climates' (year 4).

'You get to learn about Earth, different countries and cultures, also what the world might be like in the future and how it will affect us' (year 6).

Figure 2: Pupil responses are essential for the development of the subject. Extracts from Halterworth Gold PGQM application, 2011.

When everyone is incredibly busy juggling all the subjects in the primary curriculum, collaborating with class teachers about the questions to ask will ease the process. It will also help if older pupils complete their own questionnaires and help younger pupils to do theirs. This inclusive and participative model is a great way to engage pupils in the process. If time is very tight, the class teacher can ask questions, elicit verbal responses and then summarise them as notes. Both informal and formal conversations need to be conducted in a way that makes class teachers feel the purpose is to support them, rather than cause additional work.

Indirect channels

Geography postbox

An 'All about geography' week might feature a special postbox in the corridor for staff and pupils to post ideas, suggestions and any concerns about the subject. Alternatively, the postbox could be placed in the reception area and parents invited to add their thoughts. It could be part of a display, with some key questions about the subject to invite feedback about geography in the school.

Classroom observation

Classroom observation can be a powerful opportunity to see geography in action and gauge its impact in the classroom. However, you will probably find yourself in the majority of subject leaders who do not have this luxury; or if you do, you will have severely limited time in which to do it. As well as time-consuming for you, being observed for a whole lesson can be daunting for the teacher. Having consulted with the class teacher, decide on a focus and observe that part of the lesson – for example, the lesson starter or plenary.

Lesson starters can sometimes be too heavy on the writing of learning objectives and too light on getting pupils' brains into geography gear. Five minutes observing one teacher's starter session is manageable and can yield useful information. If you could set up a timetable for five minutes each afternoon over the course of one or two weeks, you could cover several classes and build a good body of relevant evidence. To prepare the ground, you could ask for a short slot at a staff meeting and talk about your focus and why you have chosen it. Give teachers a clear idea of what you will be looking at, and why, and give them some examples of relevant activities they could try out.

Ideally, you should record what happened during the lesson on an observation sheet, summarising briefly, in a non-judgemental way, lesson successes and areas for development (Figure 3).

Summary of evidence: Pupils questioning a picture and class brainstorming activity. Really good relationships with the pupils. All pupils were engaged. Pupils generally knew what they were learning. Use of the United Nations Convention on the Rights of the Child. Clearly went through the success criteria. Engaging and interesting activities that were clearly differentiated. Pupils had a good prior knowledge of the topic. Some technical vocabulary used by pupils and staff. Well-chosen resources clearly differentiated for each activity. Example video used to show weather forecast. Good amount of work from all pupils and pupils could comment on what they have learnt from the session.

Areas of strength/progress made: Good range of activities and well-pitched towards ability groups. Good mapping activity with pupils discussing the symbols and the maps. Support staff well delegated and the questioning with the lower ability particularly well pitched. Pupils were able to comment on how they were using their literacy skills in their learning. Success criteria clearly explained and linked to the learning objective. Good progress and output from all pupils across the activities.

Areas for further improvement: Swap the mapping activity and teaching points for the middle ability to allow the pupils a greater flow in their learning. Have a more focussed success criteria to provide more clarity for the pupils. Move around more to provide demonstration and instruction while teaching. Higher achieving pupils need more scaffolding to provide even better outcomes.

Suggested actions: Use a wider range of questioning to promote deeper thinking. Pick your activities carefully and cut out excess activities to provide a more streamlined beginning. When showing a video, stop it at key points to allow pupils to fully digest the ideas/take notes.

Figure 3: Example observation notes.

Essential geography resources

As a subject leader, you need to ensure that teachers are properly equipped to teach the subject. The ideal resource list for the geography classroom will vary between schools, according to their needs and budget, but some must-haves should make any list.

Globes, maps, atlases and compasses

Do invest in at least one **inflatable globe** for each class, preferably more. They come in a variety of sizes and types – political, physical, a mix of both. Some can be written on. You can buy these very cheaply online, but their quality and accuracy are very variable. Check that they show, for example, South Sudan and name changes like Eswatini (Swaziland). If you do have some out-of-date globes it's not the end of the world; just make the out-of-date information a teaching point and ensure everyone knows where the glitches are.

Standing globes are useful as they are a visual representation of the subject and can be referred to quickly, as well as being something pupils can explore by themselves. Aim to have one per class. They are a lot more expensive than inflatable globes, though.

Maps come in a wide range of types and scales – world and UK maps; Ordnance Survey (OS) maps; maps with different projections and styles; tourist, picture and story maps. Ideally, each class will have a wall map of the world and/or the UK and a readily available supply of other maps to explore and use. A class set of new OS maps would probably be prohibitively expensive, but old, worn OS maps can be laminated and cut up for jigsaws and playing class games. Maps and laminated OS map keys are great to add to a book box for pupils to read and explore at will.

Ideally, each class will have at least one **atlas** per two pupils; realistically, however, these may have to be shared between a year group or even a key stage or age phase.

Do aim to have a few atlases in each classroom so they can be referred to on a regular basis. They should of course be up to date, but if you have any with outdated information use them as a teaching tool to make points about change.

It might be a luxury to have a class set of compasses, but ready access to this geography tool is essential. Many mobile phones incorporate **compasses**, and as long as pupils have lots of practice with the basic compass a class phone or tablet can link the basic tool to a contemporary app. Perhaps you could even have a compass rose painted on the playground!

Fiction and non-fiction books

What relevant and up-to-date geography books are there in each classroom? This is the opportunity for some joyful collaboration with the English subject leader, to identify relevant books that might be purchased collaboratively (see Section 6 and web page).

Electronic resources

Internet access

One of the biggest problems in schools can be reliable access to the internet, via laptops or tablets in the classroom and/or a dedicated computer suite. This is of course a problem for all subject leaders; however, geography lessons need access to online materials and digital maps on a regular basis, so if there are issues with internet access, this could automatically become one of your priorities.

Digital mapping software

Along with globes, atlases and paper maps, digital mapping software is an essential piece of kit. Some software, like Google Earth, Google Maps and Bing Maps, is freely available. ArcGIS Online, also free to use, is an invaluable source of global information, although it can be tricky for younger pupils (and some teachers) to use without guidance and training. The National Curriculum requires pupils to be familiar with

OS mapping formats and conventions. ArcGIS Online has an OS layer for Great Britain and may be a useful free option. However, the Ordnance Survey's Digimap for Schools subscription service offers digital mapping of Great Britain at all scales, from topographical level, essential for younger pupils to see house shapes and names as well as the school grounds in great detail, to small-scale maps showing Great Britain as a whole. There are numerous advantages to using Digimap for Schools in the primary classroom, including:

- it offers whole-school access to maps of Great Britain at a range of scales
- it is appropriate for younger and older pupils
- it provides a suite of annotation tools allowing pupils to label, highlight, measure, and add photographs and other graphics
- all maps can be easily saved and printed, with a storage facility for class maps
- map layers include two historical layers showing the same place in the 1890s and 1950s, useful for exploring historical changes
- aerial imagery layers show detail at a very high-quality, using data from OS aerial reconnaissance
- maps are updated each year
- the programme links to the Geograph project, offering access to online photographs searchable by feature terms
- the programme is supported by free-to-access teaching resources and progression maps.

Images and artefacts

High-quality images and artefacts can help geography come alive. The value of photographs and other images, including 3-D virtual reality ones cannot be underestimated, especially when studying places that cannot be explored first-hand. Class teachers may have useful photos, postcards and artefacts from their own travels to bring into the classroom, and pupils can be encouraged to do the same. Published resources include sets of photos on particular places or topics. Whatever the source of your geography images and artefacts, they must meet certain criteria, of which all teachers should be aware. You may decide your own criteria, but there are some key principles to think about:

- Do the images and artefacts challenge stereotypical thinking?
- Are they up to date?
- Do they offer different views and avoid the 'single story' of people and places?

For example, if you have been using the same photopacks for several years, consider how accurate their representation of people and places is now. If you have been learning about, say, a village in Kenya, and have displayed images of life in simple homes, do you balance these with images of high-rise buildings and city life in Nairobi? Do your images portray life in a country in just a single way, and how positive is that way? Finally, don't forget to catalogue all resources so they are easy to access and available to everyone.

Personal experiences and links

Teachers' geographical experiences

We all have experience of different places and can use that as a starting point to help bring geography alive in the classroom. Teachers may have come from overseas to the UK to work and/or have travelled extensively. Do encourage them to bring that knowledge into the classroom and share details of everyday life in different places that it might otherwise be impossible to find out about. Think carefully about the alignment between their relevant geography experience and the places they are expected to teach about. Recognising teachers' personal geographical experiences can be beneficial for both teacher and pupil. You cannot teach geography well by relying on personal experiences alone, but they do offer valid starting points and enhance other sources of information.

Pupils' geographical experiences

All pupils come to school as budding explorers and geographers. They already have a good deal of geographical knowledge, whether of a purely local specific area or of the wider world in more general terms. Facilitating the sharing of pupils' own experiences and knowledge is a powerful and collaborative way to ensure an inclusive geography curriculum and is a most worthwhile, freely available resource. It also helps you to establish what pupils think about the places they already know about and challenge any misconceptions, while providing motivational learning contexts.

Meaningful class links

There is a real world outside your classroom with people you can connect to and learn from. Initially, think local: keep lists of parents, other local people and businesses that might come and talk to the class or even the whole school. Perhaps you have pupils who have lived in other countries whose parents might be persuaded to come in and talk about their experiences. From shopkeepers to farmers, these people have lives and jobs that offer a direct window into living geography and comprise a fantastic resource.

Further afield, from national organisations to your local MP and small-business owner, there are people who might be willing to give up their time and come and talk to your class. Keep a register and contact details of both potential and prior visitors, with feedback on how useful the event was and whether you ought to invite them again. Some local businesses and amenities, including the nearest recycling centre, can be useful for reciprocal field visits. These kinds of links support ongoing information gathering, deepen collaborative learning and can be included in pupil-led meaningful enquiries. They also give a purposeful context and help to develop relationships between the school and the local community.

Looking to the wider world, a class link with a school in another part of the UK and/or another country can be hugely beneficial to learning (see pp. 45 and 72). Connections can be made via post, email, Skype or a range of online social media software that is suitable for the classroom. The benefit of the latter approaches is that they are instant. However, this section is headed 'Meaningful class links' for a reason: any school linking activity needs to be a serious undertaking. To establish and sustain a mutually beneficial relationship takes time and persistence. It is not a 'quick fix', and if there are other aspects of geography teaching and learning that need development it may be best to postpone school linking projects until you can give them the time and attention they require.

News and media

Geography, being very much about the here and now, feeds on current, real-world issues and events (as described in Section 4). The news is a free resource that teachers can access and disseminate in their classrooms. Ideally, each classroom should have a display of news-related items, relevant to other subjects as well as geography. It might be as small as a 'Question of the Week', or as big as a world map annotated with newspaper headlines. News and news-related topics can support meaningful, collaborative geographical learning and teaching (Figure 4), particularly when given a spatial element, and they can be wonderful fuel for engaging active minds right across the curriculum and the school. This is a quick, easy way to bring some critical thinking about geography into the classroom and can form part of a toolkit of ideas you can make available to class teachers.

Valuing geography

Encourage teachers to run geography quizzes, leader boards, map problems and other geographical challenges each term or as a constant thread of activity within the class. Your support can be very basic, from providing jigsaws and timers or a 'Best news story of the week' (see Figure 4), to online mapping quizzes such as GeoGuessr (see web page). Learning to name and locate countries in continents, South America for example, or the counties of England, can be supported by fun, online quizzes, enhanced by the motivation of a leader board, either for the class or the wider school context. 'Geographer' badges and certificates can all enhance the learning and value of the subject: certificates can be easily made, and badges can be bought online from the Geographical Association. Appointing a 'Geographer of the Week' need cost little or nothing but can instil great pride in the lucky recipient.

These are just a few of the ways that subject leaders can help classroom teachers foster high-quality geography; class teachers might reciprocate with suggestions and ideas for subject leaders. It is only one part of the story, but building a mutually beneficial relationship with class teachers is a key foundation for more visible leadership work throughout the school. A good understanding of teachers' areas of expertise, needs and concerns is a sound basis for thinking more strategically across the whole school. Sometimes, however, there may not be this clear sequential outcome: you may be tasked with providing whole-school subject leadership from the start. Then you have to find the time to form relationships with individual teachers at the same time as planning whole-school changes. A good subject leader will know that sometimes the best thing they can do is to listen and talk to other teachers and pupils, so use some of the strategies suggested here to allow others to reach out to you if you cannot immediately reach out to all of them.

Leading geography in your school

Geography as a subject, or as part of the humanities or an area of learning, might be given dedicated time and focus for whole-school development; it may have already had a recent overhaul, or it may be awaiting its turn in the limelight. Whatever the current situation for you and your school, you will need to bring some coherence to geography through whole-school subject leadership. If you have had time to contact teachers and pupils across the school and instigated informal conversations about the subject (pp. 114), you may have already identified some common areas for development and can begin to prioritise areas for change in order to develop curriculum and practice in ways that harmonise with both national expectations and the school's own vision and ethos.

4–5 years	5–7 years	7–9 years	9–11 years
Spot of the day Record the place in the school grounds where someone has 'spotted' something relating to the environment, e.g. 'Ahmed spotted a robin singing' or 'Lisa spotted our first spring daffodil'. Add the week's sightings to a plan of the school.	**Tell the news** Ask pupils to talk about local news they have heard at home or in school and discuss. Use a map to locate the story, or watch a children's news programme such as Newsround and discuss the issues raised. Use globes and atlases to locate international news items.	**Ask a question** Display an image and/or headline from the news and ask pupils to add their own questions throughout the week. Choose a time near the end of the week to select some of the best questions and discuss some answers. This could be preceded by group research time for pupils to investigate a question.	**Issue of the week** Choose an issue, e.g. deforestation, trade, renewable energy, flooding/extreme weather impacts, and ask pupils to collect headlines and news stories for a display board. Link stories to a map.

Figure 4: Ideas for using current news items. All of the examples can be adapted for use with older/younger pupils. See also p. 102.

You may also, as a member of the Geographical Association, decide you are in a position to apply for a Primary Geography Quality Mark award (PGQM). This is a framework designed to help you evaluate and evidence how well your subject is doing, and it offers you a toolkit for thinking through leadership areas such as creating a vision, devising an action plan and planning next steps. The PGQM is a recognition of good leadership and you can use it to evidence progress and success across the school. In exploring some of the leadership areas in this chapter, exemplars and examples of practice are drawn from schools who have achieved the award. You can find out more about the PGQM below and via the web page.

Developing a vision

What can geography do for your school? How can geography contribute to your unique setting and learners? As geography is such a potentially vast subject, having a vision about what the subject can do, and how, is a very powerful starting point. Figure 5 has some prompts to help you as you consider how to develop your vision for geography. The most successful geography visions have three simple things in common:

1. they support and harmonise with the overall school vision
2. they are simple and easy to understand
3. most importantly, they incorporate contributions from pupils, staff and other school stakeholders.

If you have already carried out a formal, or informal, survey about what geography means to pupils and staff in school, you can draw out some common themes and use these to build your vision statement for geography. There is no exact or 'right' way of deciding on the final 'vision', other than it should be as inclusive as possible, and pay heed to the points already mentioned.

Devising a vision doesn't have to send you off in a completely new direction either: start by examining what you already do well in your school and how geography contributes to this. You can also consider what might be done better and the potential role of geography in achieving this. A successful vision will remind everyone of the purpose of geography. Figure 6 shows three different examples of a vision for geography.

Need
What do you need geography to do for your school, pupils and community?

Where next?
What outcomes are you hoping for? How can you accomplish your plans and aspirations for geography – and the school?

Everyone
Consider how pupils, staff and governors can contribute their ideas to a geography vision. A successful vision is inclusive and underpinned by genuine participation.

Share and apply
Unless it is put into practice, the most profound vision is meaningless. Think about how your vision can genuinely inform planning, policy and practice and ensure this happens. Make it visible and accessible to all.

Figure 5: Geography vision compass rose.

Episkopi Primary International School, Cyprus

We offer the pupils a broad and balanced curriculum that builds on their knowledge, skills and understanding of geography through visits and enquiry. Our curriculum provokes and answers questions about the world both physical and human. It is a focus within the curriculum for developing cultural awareness, understanding and resolving issues about the environment, and recognising the importance of sustainable development. It can inspire pupils to think about their own place in the world, their values, and their rights and responsibilities to other people and the environment.

The subject lead explained the vision in the school's PGQM application:

This vision informs the geography curriculum that we deliver. As part of the half-termly meetings of the Humanities Team the current planning is reviewed and updated in line with the pupils' and National Curriculum needs. This is further supported by pupil conferencing where their views are responded to (Episkopi Primary School, 2016).

Hawkshead Esthwaite Community Primary School

The vision influences the geography curriculum, which is underpinned by a recently revised policy and schemes of work for teaching geography. The importance of global learning has over the last two years been incorporated into our school vision, to:

- *help pupils learn to respect and understand their environment now and into the future*
- *encourage pupils to think about, care for, and respect other people*
- *help pupils to develop the skills, knowledge, values and attitudes needed to be pro-active global citizens equipped for the 21st century, in an ever-changing world*
- *enable pupils to grow up with the desire and ability to make a difference in the world at a local, national and global level*
- *help them to think about and develop an understanding of moral, social, religious and ethical issues that will enable them to develop a reasoned set of values, attitudes and beliefs* (Hawkshead Esthwaite Community Primary School, 2015).

Student teacher of primary geography, Winchester University

Year 3 B.Ed. students at Winchester University were asked to give presentations on 'Conducting a staff meeting' as part of their end-of-year assessment in primary geography.

One very simple and straightforward approach to a vision statement draws on ideas from school practice:

Geography is EPIC

Explorers

Passion

Inspire

Creativity

(Courtesy of Sharon Witt, University of Winchester, 2018).

Figure 6: Example vision statements for geography.

Episkopi's vision statement works well because it has a clear purpose and is reflected in the curriculum, as it should be. It is also evident that staff and pupils have contributed to it and that it responds to individual, school-specific and National Curriculum needs. The vision statement clearly directs the reader to the school policy for geography, showing continuity of thinking and cohesion. It also shows the emphasis placed on cultural and environmental issues. A visit to the school and conversations with staff and pupils revealed that it was a vision that genuinely informed and shaped geography in an inclusive way.

Hawkeshead school built their vision statement around their focus on global learning and their experience as a Centre of Excellence in this field. In their PGQM application, the school subject leader explained how their geography vision was part of their school vision. This vision statement works well because it is highly personalised to work with the school's focus and area of specialism: global learning. Rather than being a separate entity, it is actually part of the wider school vision statement.

The Winchester student's very short and snappy vision statement works well because it identifies the key drivers of the subject and is easy to remember. It can support practically any whole-school vision because of its simple and generalist approach so it has a wide appeal and replicability, but remember – to have meaning and potency your vision statement will need to reflect *your* school context.

Perhaps you already place an emphasis on strong links with the local and/or global community, have an active programme of fieldwork, strength of experience in ICT or a focus on sustainability; maybe these are areas that you wish to initiate or strengthen. Geography can help to lead, inform and inspire many whole-school issues such as local traffic problems, pollution or even community tensions over planning proposals. Giving geography its place through a relevant vision statement is yet another way to raise awareness of the value of the subject and unify the school community.

Having agreed a vision for geography, you can use it to drive curriculum aims, inform policy and bind practice together. As well as constituting an important piece of documentation, consider how it can be made visible in the school; for example, in geography classroom and school displays. Geography in the school will then have a clear and confident identity and an accessible common frame of reference for conversations at every level.

Creating a school geography policy

There is only one thing worse than having no geography policy document and that is having a document that no-one knows about. It should be a simple affair, designed to be of practical use; a template is provided on the web page. Other templates are widely available online, but you need to make sure that your policy document reflects what you are doing rather than being overly generic as this may render it worthless.

A school policy document for geography needs to:

- reflect actual practice – what it says is what is happening
- be current and familiar to all members of staff
- be led by the vision statement for geography and reflect the values of the school
- be useful and informative
- be brief and concise
- be accessible, easy to find and understand.

The document should run to no more than two pages and should be prefaced by the geography vision statement. It should answer the following questions:

- What geography does the school teach, i.e. do you follow a national curriculum?
- How is geography taught? For example, do you teach it as a standalone subject, or is it topic-based? Or is it a combination?
- What teaching and pedagogical approaches, e.g. enquiry-based learning (see Sections 4 and 5) does it follow?

- How does it ensure access to the subject for all? How are pupils with an additional educational need, or who are gifted and talented, catered for?
- What do you do for fieldwork? Does every class have a regular outing, and when?
- How is the subject monitored and assessed? Who is responsible for this?
- How are resources managed to ensure accessibility and relevance?
- How are health and safety aspects managed?

School A
- Introduction and vision
- Subject aims
- Planning and organisation
- Teaching approach
- Access and entitlement
- Differentiation
- Special needs/higher achieving/gifted and talented
- Assessment
- Resources
- Monitoring and evaluation

School B
- Philosophy and aims
- Subject organisation – long-term planning
- Teaching and learning – geographical enquiry
- Assessment, recording and reporting
- Resources to support primary geography
- Health and safety issues
- Monitoring, evaluating and review

Figure 7: Example geography policy headings.

An example of headings used for geography policy documents can be seen in Figure 7, and some extracts from different policies are given in Figure 8. There is a whole exemplar policy document available online (see web page).

Some schools may have a separate policy for, for example, sustainability; other schools may incorporate this into each policy document. Schools should show how they are addressing issues of sustainability, and geography is the ideal context in which to do this.

If you inherit a policy document, test it against the extracts above. If it does not reflect what is happening in your school, you have to decide whether the policy needs rewriting or the practice needs re-aligning.

Ideally, a policy will be revised with all staff at a staff meeting, so everyone can go through it together, but this can be very time-consuming. Since it is a document that states what is happening in school, you could use your observations to complete it, highlighting and giving reasons for any changes you have made, and give it to staff to check over.

If it doesn't already include them, it would be useful to add a full inventory of geography resources and contact details for potential visitors and sources of fieldwork support.

Make sure everyone has an electronic copy and upload a copy to the school website so that parents and carers can access it. Keep a paper copy in your file, in the staffroom and with a central store of geography resources and do refer to it in your conversations with staff on a regular basis.

Planning a curriculum

A broad and balanced curriculum, with genuine coherence and purpose, matters. Geography has an important role to play in the curriculum – not only as a rigorous, standalone subject but also because of its synergy with other subject areas. An important aspect of being a classroom teacher and subject leader is evaluating how well the school geography curriculum you offer your pupils is fit for purpose (see Section 5).

(a) Teaching, learning and geographical enquiry will be planned to ensure continuity and progression as required by the National Curriculum. Learning, activities and resources will be directed towards pupil needs to enable all pupils to progress and demonstrate achievement.

(b) Special thought will be given to the provision of appropriate materials/resources and the choice of places to be studied with regard to equal opportunities, especially those of gender and race within the chosen communities.

(c) The experiences will be gained through individual, group and whole-class work.

(d) Teachers will deliver the units to be taught at each key stage as identified in the school's two-year rolling programme.

(e) The range of activities will include:
- observing and asking/formulating enquiry questions
- collecting and recording evidence
- analysing evidence/drawing conclusions
- fieldwork
- using instruments to take measurements
- map, globe, atlas work – drawing, reading and using these
- using secondary sources of evidence (photos, pictures, TV, radio, books, newspapers, visitors, ICT) to inform their studies
- the use of ICT; including Google Earth and mapping programmes
- educational visits
- homework where appropriate.

(f) Lessons will include access to good-quality, well-maintained and effectively organised resources.

(g) Differentiation: Each pupil is encouraged to work at age-related expectations. However, those working below them may need to embed learning from the previous year. Those working above age-related expectations will use and apply their learning in broader contexts. Some investigations can be sufficiently 'open-ended' to allow for differentiation by outcome, but most activities will be targeted to individual or group requirements.

(h) Special needs/higher achieving/gifted and talented: Individual needs will be met through task differentiation and in certain circumstances a Learning Support Assistant may be available to provide in-class support. Enrichment days focusing on mapping skills have been and will continue to be developed and used for each year group.

Figure 8: Example geography policy extracts from two schools.

A school geography curriculum is not necessarily the same thing as a national curriculum for geography. For those schools obliged to follow its programmes of study, a national curriculum is both a minimum entitlement and a statutory requirement. How schools teach, adapt and augment their national curriculum determines their curriculum, and much depends on contextual design and implementation. As a subject leader, you need to ensure that your geography curriculum conforms to any minimum entitlement, while supporting and advising as to how it might be developed to work well in your school context as part of the wider curriculum.

Ensuring national curriculum coverage

As subject leader, you will know what the statutory requirements for geography are; however, you also need to think about the opportunities for geography to support other learning areas and act as a cohesive curriculum 'glue'.

Different curricula operate in the different countries of the UK, and geography is placed within slightly different contexts, although the subject retains its familiar blueprint through its key concepts (see p. 22). It is taught as a discrete subject in England, while Wales is moving to a model that offers 'Areas of Learning', in which geography will sit with history, citizenship and RE in 'the Humanities'. Scotland takes a similar approach, placing geography within the 'Social Studies' area of learning, while in Northern Ireland geography can be found in the theme 'The World Around Us'.

A curriculum audit is the ideal way to check for coverage of statutory requirements and if you can get the time from your Head teacher it is best carried out in a formal staff meeting or staff training day. If you are new to the role, or if the school has undergone curriculum change or had a turnover of new staff, doing an audit can establish a baseline and get you thinking about your priorities.

Ask staff to come to a meeting with a copy of their planning. Ask them to work in year groups to begin with; if you have mixed year groups, you can adapt this as necessary. They could also work in key stages or age phases. Give each group a printed copy of the statutory requirements for the subject. Ask them to check against their planning and use a highlighter pen to highlight everything that they cover. Colour-coded pens for different year groups can be effective here. You will probably find that some people are doing more than they need to, some are not doing enough, and some are covering areas in geography they thought was something else altogether.

Using this information with earlier informal conversations and classroom surveys can help to identify where the 'gaps' are in terms of content and progression. Figure 9 has some prompts to help you think about the geography content and coverage, starting with statutory requirements and then expanding to ask questions about other important curricular aspects such as enquiry and inclusion.

Managing change

Ofsted (2018) is clear that curriculum coherence and intent are important lynchpins of a whole-school curriculum, so any geography curriculum needs to work well within the wider school curriculum. To achieve this, the geography subject leader needs a feel for what already happens and what needs to change, so that you can at least show that you are working towards this coherent curriculum. If you are in a school where not much time has been available to audit and evaluate the geography curriculum, the mention of change may conjure up the daunting prospect of endless revision. How do you deal with this scenario? The first answer is not to panic! The results of your audit show that you have a plan, and that you know where the strengths and weaknesses are. Secondly, bear in mind that you cannot change everything overnight.

Change needs time to become embedded and effective. Use the audit findings to prioritise, and write these priorities into your action plan. The 'areas for scrutiny' in Figure 9 may help you decide your priorities. The 'Adopt, Adapt and Innovate' mantra (Figure 10) can be very useful for both curriculum planning and managing change. Find out what is already being done well – you are rarely in a situation where everything needs to be thrown out and rewritten – and there is often much good practice that works and can be kept from the existing curriculum (**adopt**). Then think about what might work with a bit of adjustment (**adapt**). Lastly, think about what new material can be brought into the curriculum (**innovate**).

If you are following a statutory curriculum, what you *must* cover is already set out. *How* you choose to cover it, and how you link it with other subjects, experiences, areas of learning and dimensions is up to you – and *your* context.

Area for scrutiny and discussion	Questions to ask	Priorities for action plan
Coverage of statutory geography requirements	How well is each class and year group covering a minimum entitlement? Where are the gaps? Where are the successes?	Year groups and areas of the curriculum for targeting. Staff requiring additional support. Remember to keep what works well!
Differentiation and access	How well is planning differentiated? Is it inclusive and does it take account of gifted and talented as well as those with additional educational needs?	What support do I need to put in place? Where are 'shiny' examples to share?
Progression across the school	Does the current curriculum allow pupils to both enjoy and achieve and is there room to consolidate, build, develop and embed?	How does this support assessment and challenge learners?
Fieldwork engagement	Is everyone doing fieldwork regularly? Is there progression and cohesion across and within key stages and their planning? Where do classes go and why? What additional support is needed?	Do staff need additional training in risk assessment? Do you need to build their confidence in taking pupils out-of-doors? Do the guidelines need updating? Do 'new' areas for exploration and enquiry need to be found?
Enquiry and participation	How well does enquiry drive learning? Are there opportunities for pupils to build on their personal geographies and ask critical questions? Is knowledge balanced with skills so that pupils develop core knowledge alongside essential geography skills?	Do staff need CPD on critical thinking or guidance about consolidating knowledge as well as ensuring enquiry and exploration?
Resources	Do the resources support the planning? Where are the gaps? How dated are the resources? How much budget is there?	What are the most urgent resources to drive curriculum coverage? Do you need to acquire mapping software, for example, or better hardware?

Figure 9: Evaluating the whole-school geography curriculum.

Curriculum planning and managing change

Adopt → Adapt → Innovate

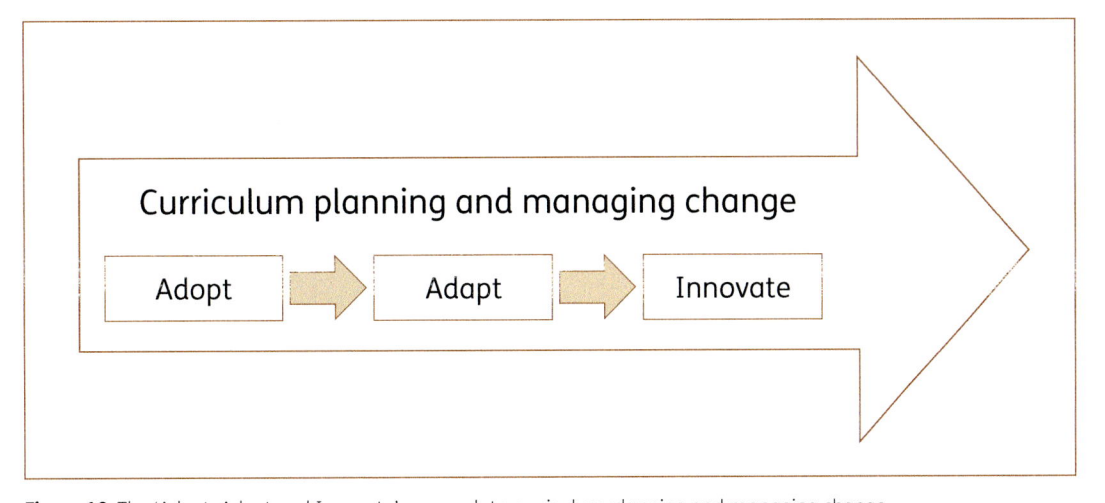

Figure 10: The 'Adopt, Adapt and Innovate' approach to curriculum planning and managing change.

Visualising a whole-school scheme of work

You might use a coverage framework (you can download one from the web page) to ensure you cover the requirements and to add some ideas and aspirations. This framework is just one example and draws on text from the current National Curriculum for England, but you could copy and paste your own national requirements into a similar grid. By devising your own framework, you can agree with staff what will be taught and to which year group. Some elements will be ongoing and you can help people plan these in. A one-page document like this can be a useful way both to ensure that any curriculum requirements are tailored to your school and to visualise what needs to be covered and when.

Once you have your personalised 'bare entitlement' sketched out across the school, you can begin to enhance it with the geographical activities and contexts that will bring it to life. Your vision for the subject will help guide these 'lenses for geography' and give purpose to the kind of learning you want to realise in the classroom.

Using ready-made schemes of work

Many schools use publishers' schemes of work as a basis for their geography curriculum. If your school desperately needs some instant support for geography you might choose this route; or you may find a published resource that supports and augments what you are already doing. The school may have bought in a whole-school curriculum, and you may be presented with a geography scheme of work that you feel it isn't suitable for high-quality geography. Whatever your situation:

- check you are covering the prescribed, minimum entitlement
- adopt, adapt and innovate to personalise the curriculum and add value
- match the curriculum aims to your shared vision of geography.

Checking the minimum entitlement can be quite difficult with bought-in schemes of work as the intended coverage may be lost when the schemes are adapted to a particular school's needs. Using a framework can help to check whether the requirements are covered.

Rigorous, high-quality geography

If your school uses topic-themed approaches, incorporating geography into history and/or science learning, it can be easy to lose the bits that are the essential 'geography'. Non-specialist teachers particularly may not be familiar with what high-quality geography looks like. How can you help teachers to quickly check whether their planning contains opportunities for high-quality geographical learning to take place?

Core geographical concepts

Using a framework can be helpful; so too can a simple, memorable 'touchstone' that highlights some of geography's core concepts. Catling (p. 22) explains in detail the concepts underpinning geography, but if you need a quick check that some geography is actually taking place '**Place**', '**Space**' and '**Scale**' (Figures 11 and 12) are three core geography ideas that can be relied on as an instant and easily remembered litmus test, no matter what curriculum you are following. If you can find these ideas evidenced in planning and practice, then geography is happening.

Figure 11: Remember the core ideas of place, space and scale. Photo © Maradon 333/Shutterstock.com.

Concept	Key questions
Place Place is at the heart of geography. According to the philosopher Yi Fu Tuan (1977), places are spaces given meaning; a product of **human and environment interactions**, redolent of **culture** and **diversity**. We can enquire about and measure a vast array of data about 'place', some of which is factual and some emotive. Enquiry about place ranges from the rudimentary, but essential, recognition and naming to the descriptive, comparative, explanatory and analytic.	What is this place like? What physical and human features does it have? What happens here? How does it compare to…? Who lives here and why? What do the people who live here do? How is the place changing and why? How are people changing this environment? What might it look like in the future?
Space The 'whereness' of geography matters. Without a spatial element, the learning might be beautiful and relevant and engaging, but it won't be geography. For example, a rich description of the Amazon rainforest without any spatial context is a good piece of prose, not geography – a failing noted by Ofsted inspectors. The spatial element also helps pupils to better understand **environmental impact** and **sustainability**.	Where is this place? How can it be mapped? Why is it here and not there? (In the case of rainforests, for example, their spatial location explains how the global climate system functions.) What is special about this location? How does this place connect to other places (**interconnections**)?
Scale The study of geography also requires an understanding of scale. We 'zoom' in and out of places to examine how they are nested inside each other and to discover how we can both generalise and be place-specific. For example, while studying a country in Africa we zoom into the continent, locate the country in question and consider how its location within the continent shapes its characteristics. We can explore country generalities and core knowledge such as the location, and name key geographical features, but by zooming in further to town, village and family level, we can add detail, variety and complexity. Zooming in to contrasting aspects of places avoids the 'single story' and guards against stereotypical representation. Recognising scale enables us to see Africa as a continent, not a country; it allows us to explore differences between local, regional, national, international and global meanings and how they work together. Younger pupils need places near and far explored at a very accessible local scale as well as at a global scale. As their cognitive development allows them to think in more abstract terms, they can start to fill in the complex array of scales in between and discern the arbitrary political distinctions between different places.	How does this place change as we 'zoom' in and out? How do places 'fit' together? What more can we find out by zooming in on a place? How can we identify and explain different patterns by considering different scales? How does scale provide different 'stories' about a place and offer alternative perspectives? How do places on a different scale work together – the local and the regional, or the national and the international, for instance? How can scale enable pupils to relate the local to the global?

Figure 12: A checklist for the core concepts or 'big ideas'.

Links across the curriculum

Helping non-specialists to understand place, space and scale can avoid the sort of 'Africa Week' topics that fail to explore both rural and urban stories of diversity, and where learning is superficial.

Figure 13 explains how place, space and scale work together to ensure that learning is indeed geographical while highlighting links to other subject areas (see also Section 6).

Literacy Geography gives context to literacy, from its vast vocabulary of place names and features to its rich descriptions and issues that require persuasive text. Geography stimulates passion and prose through poetry and storytelling, made all the better through close observation of real landscapes.	**Mathematics** Geography gathers data about the world and presents it in a range of media, using an array of mathematical skills. Maps develop knowledge of scale, position and pattern; geographical processes and features can be described and analysed using number and comparative data.	**Science** Geography provides science with a real-world setting and spatial contexts for conceptual understanding. Both use enquiry although geography can offer broader ways of investigating the world through fieldwork.
Art Geography can help art look more closely at the world around us and see the processes that signal change. Annotated field sketching, maps as art and photograph analysis are just some of its techniques.	*What is this place like?* *Where is this?* **PLACE** — **SPACE** **GEOGRAPHY** **SCALE** *How does this place change when we zoom in and out?*	**History** Geography helps explain change that has taken place over time and offers reasons why. It adds vital aspects of explanation concerned with human and physical processes.
ICT Geography gives a motivational context for using ICT through enquiry, from GIS and GPS, to digital mapping and a host of research and communication techniques.		**DT** Geography is a futures-orientated subject that investigates practical design solutions – from owl boxes to solar lights – and seeks to understand how they might help us live more sustainably and/or how they are impacting on landscapes and lives.
RE Geography identifies, enquires and celebrates diversity of peoples and cultures around the world. It investigates what makes places special, and why, by a closer examination of where, why and how.	**Music** Geography enquires about the characteristic sounds of a place and can inform and inspire musical composition through its breadth of landscapes, from rural to urban and the wondrous to the everyday.	

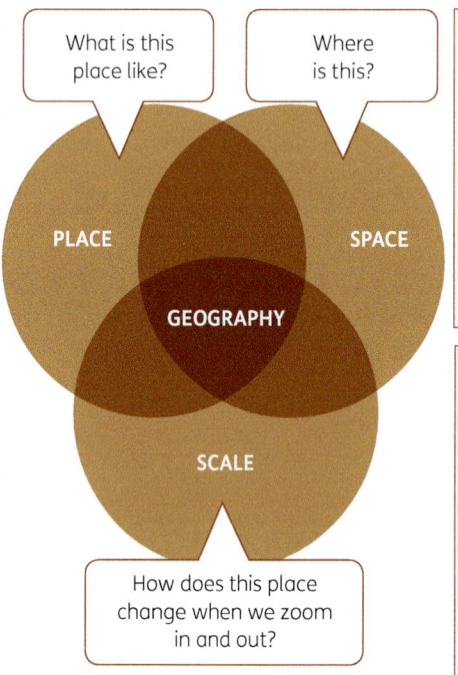

Figure 13: Place, space and scale, and possible links across the curriculum.

Balancing core knowledge and values

To understand geography, you need a good deal of knowledge and vocabulary about the world. Grid references, postcodes or latitude and longitude, and for the most part names of countries, places, capital cities and geographical features, all comprise factual knowledge, mostly undisputed. However, places are more than just lists of facts: they are where people live, work, play and interact with the environment, causing change for better or worse. Our perception of places influences our emotional response to them, but we don't all perceive places in the same way; we may have very different ideas about what we can do there and how we want them to change. Understanding that others may have different views, values and opinions to you is another vital aspect of geography, and of critical thinking (see p. 47). Ofsted (2011) reported that schools needed to develop both their core knowledge and their sense of place; Figure 14 is a reminder that we need to balance factual knowledge with emotions, perceptions and values: a *sense of place*.

Place study

Within the various curricular requirements for primary geography there is always scope for choice. When deciding on a 'region of South America' or a 'non-European country' to study you need to consider, for instance:

- Is it relevant?
- Is it current?
- How does this curriculum ensure progress in geography?

For example, if a majority of your pupils are from Poland it may make sense to study a region of Poland rather than (or as well as!), say, a Spanish region. If you have a teacher from Australia, it makes sense to build their knowledge and experience into the geography curriculum. A subject leader can find opportunities to make sensible links to other curricular areas and create a cohesive curriculum that offers progression.

Each pupil's prior knowledge about places will depend on who they know, where they have been and all the various media that they have

---

Core knowledge
Facts: location, vocabulary and process

Example: *St Pancras Station is an international railway station in London. It is north of the Thames and home to the high-speed trains that bring in many commuters each day from south-east England. You can travel from here directly to France via the Channel Tunnel.*

Sense of place
Emotions, perceptions and values

Example: *Rescued by Sir John Betjeman, the beautiful architecture of St Pancras Station contains iconic symbols of meetings past and present. It's a great place to catch up with friends, people-watch or browse the shops. It feels special to me as I associate it with travelling home.*

Figure 14: Core knowledge and sense of place.

engaged with. Only when pupils are helped to make sense of their prior knowledge in relation to geographical ideas, such as place or environment, will their experiences be useful in terms of developing capability in geography. Starting with personal geographical imaginations can be useful (Figure 15), but we also need to think about the 'gaps'. It is helpful to regard any national curriculum list of requirements as a kind of framework; the beginning of a global jigsaw that helps to create, over time, a functioning mental map of the world. Teachers should therefore be looking for links and connections between the places specified in the curriculum, rather than thinking about this as an exclusive list or requirement.

Being flexible and responsive

Geography is a subject that deals with the here and now. This is part of what gives it excitement, dynamism and relevance. There are always going to be events in the news – global and local – that offer opportunities for some focused geography work, even if it's just for a one-off lesson. Unexpected opportunities might arise from a sudden snowfall at school, giving the opportunity to learn more about the weather from the wider issue of rapid climate change and its associated impacts, such as hurricanes and drought or from a natural disaster such as an avalanche on Everest or a flood in Wales. The geographical opportunity might even be seemingly mundane, such as the closure of a local shop or the building of a housing development on green space.

As subject leader, you can give staff permission to embrace unexpected news-related opportunities and equip them to do some rigorous geography using the framework and questions in Figure 9. Pupils' learning can be cross-checked against statutory requirements and planning documents annotated, as the dynamic documents that they should be; you will always find plenty of corresponding opportunities. More importantly, the learning

Figure 15: Starting with personal geographical imaginations to develop map skills. Photo © Paula Owens.

will be fresh and lively and will change from year to year. In response to major events, the Geographical Association often puts useful links and support ideas on its website.

Creating an action plan

From your information gathering and investigations you should be in a position where you can create an action plan. This will necessitate some prioritisation. As stated earlier, you cannot hope to change everything overnight. Identify with staff where the most urgent areas are, decide what your budget can support and create your plan. This will guide your actions throughout the academic year and help you keep track of what has been done and how successful it was. Your school may have a set format for an action plan, or you can use the Geographical Association Primary Geography Quality Mark framework. Either way, remember that you are thinking how best to improve your pupils' learning and enjoyment of the subject while ensuring that everyone is kept up to date with what needs to be done, for example liaising with senior management to ensure coherence with school priorities. You will be asking yourself: Why am I doing this? What is the impact? How do I know? Figure 16 shows an extract from an action plan for geography that makes clear what the successes were from the previous academic year, giving something positive to build on.

Your action plan will be a part of your subject leader's file (see Figure 1). It should be a working document – annotated, evaluated and adapted as the subject progresses – so don't be afraid to write on it or change priorities if circumstances change. A purposeful, flexible action plan will help everyone to move the subject forward.

Celebrating geography

We have discussed how class teachers might be encouraged to celebrate the subject and help make it more valued and visible within the school (see pp. 10 and 121–2). Discuss with staff at whole-school staff meetings how you might celebrate the subject more widely.

Badges and certificates can be used in class and assembly, but you might also want to create some geography 'Ambassadors' or 'Champions' to buddy up with other pupils and classes. You might have an exhibition of local area work and invite parents in, collaborate with other staff and pupils to write an article for *Primary Geography* or get pupils to write a geography blog for the school website. Enlist the support of pupils to keep the subject visible, to help them feel positive and confident about the subject.

Assessment and progression

Before discussing assessment, we must revisit some thoughts about planning (see pp. 126–8). The two processes are complementary and interdependent, and are most successful when they support each other in the curriculum. Any statutory curriculum requirement is a bare minimum and schools should tailor it to their pupils. A worthwhile and effective geography curriculum will:

- meet the needs of *all* learners
- teach knowledge and skills
- challenge, excite, support and motivate pupils
- give pupils opportunities to know, understand and apply what they have learnt
- draw on content that is relevant, topical and inclusive
- make coherent links to other areas of the curriculum
- augment core knowledge with empathic knowledge, recognising that values can shape and present the world through different lenses
- incorporate progression, revisiting, consolidating and extending knowledge while practising and honing skills
- be flexible and responsive to current events
- be designed so that its effectiveness and impact on pupils can be easily evaluated.

Leading Primary Geography

Successes (What happened and what impact did it have?)
Humanities cluster meetings continued (although decision was to focus on opportunities in history)
New curriculum and scheme of work taught successfully with a few areas identified for improvement
Gifted and talented year 6 pupils took part in geography quiz at Robert Smyth Academy and will do so again
Large world and UK maps displayed in corridors
Assessment procedure investigated by co-ordinator

Targets (What will we do?)	Success criteria (What is the impact on pupils/staff?)	Activities/ responsibilities (Who does each job?)	Resources (What/how much, cost, staff development needs)	Timescales (When does each job get done?)	Monitoring (Who/how do we check that success has been achieved?)
To assess pupils' knowledge, appropriate to their age	Pupils will achieve the NC objectives Pupils demonstrate a good understanding of places in the world	Developing a whole school assessment tool to monitor progress and achievement of NC geography Key stage 1 and 2 quiz Focus pupil studies Pupil interviews	No additional costs involved Staff meeting time needed Subject co-ordinator release time	Autumn term (disseminate materials to staff) Initial quiz to be carried out by all key stage 1 and 2 pupils by Autumn term	Subject leaders to monitor
To demonstrate that geography is valued within the school	Active involvement of: All teaching staff Global Ambassadors Green Ambassadors Pupils show increased enthusiasm for geography	Pupil-led groups are actively involved in developing aspects of geography (Global Ambassadors, Green Ambassadors) Displays around school Visitors to year groups and whole school assemblies Website Focus days (Explorer Academy/African keyhole garden/ culture days) Revise policy	Ambassadors to meet during selected assembly times External designer/printer to cost welcome and 'values' signage Class displays Explorer Academy – £600 (£300 from GLP funding and request sent to FSA) African Garden Day – funded through 'Send a cow' charity Request for funding for resources made to local garden centre. Approved	Ambassador groups established by 1 October Welcome signs/ values to be completed in Autumn 1. Tuesday 15 September Monday 21 September Meeting with garden centre (re funding) on Wednesday 9 September	S Panter/A Galpin to monitor

continued

| To promote 'learning through enquiry' and critical thinking skills | Planned activities to allow pupils to engage in 'enquiry' in curriculum time Pupils gain an increased global understanding through engaging with different viewpoints (layered thinking) | P4C training for level 1 accreditation to be carried out by at least two members of staff and then disseminated to teaching staff during staff meeting time Planned P4C activities and approaches evidenced in planning and pupils' work | TBC October 2015 £295 per person for level 1 training (funded through GLP fund) | Provisional dates for P4C training – 1 and 2 December | S Panter/A Galpin to monitor |

Figure 16: Extract from action plan. Source: Fleckney Primary School PGQM application, 2016.

Assessment

Why assess?

When planning a route, you need to know the starting point and the destination – a neat analogy for the link between planning and assessment. If you have clear expectations you can plan teaching activities that will enable pupils to make appropriate progress. Not everyone will have the same starting point, and pupils' progress is rarely steady, linear and generic: assessment allows us to respond sensitively to the varying pace of travel. A PowerPoint highlighting examples of progression can be downloaded from the web page.

Assessment is a crucial part of the planning, teaching, evaluating and assessing cycle (see Sections 4 and 5) but it can seem daunting and unwieldy if there is no clear understanding about why it is being done, or how. Assessment has many purposes and guises, but all are arguably driven by these three key questions:

- What is the impact (of teaching and learning) on pupils?
- How do I know?
- What do I need to do next?

Assessment helps establish what pupils already know; then it is a way of monitoring their progress towards the planned destination (or destinations, because they may be different for different pupils). The assessment process involves a wide range of actors: pupil, teacher, subject leader, senior management team, parent and policy-maker. It starts in the classroom with the planning process, knowledge of starting points, desired outcomes and appropriate routes and modes of travel. Figure 17 shows the flow and links between planning and assessment.

It is important that pupils enjoy their learning, and some of the strategies discussed at the start of this section will help you to find out what they like and dislike about their geography lessons. A record of sound bites from different age groups can be a useful evaluative tool when tweaking or re-designing the curriculum (for examples, see Figure 2).

Benchmarks and pitch

For all pupils to achieve their full potential the planned learning needs to be pitched at the right level. It should provide opportunities both for individuals to make good progress and for whole classes to assimilate and consolidate a progression of ideas. If we get the planning right, assessment becomes more manageable: we can identify those who are struggling, as well as those who exceed expectations, and put appropriate intervention in place. In this regard, effective planning is also context driven, sensitive to change and flexible.

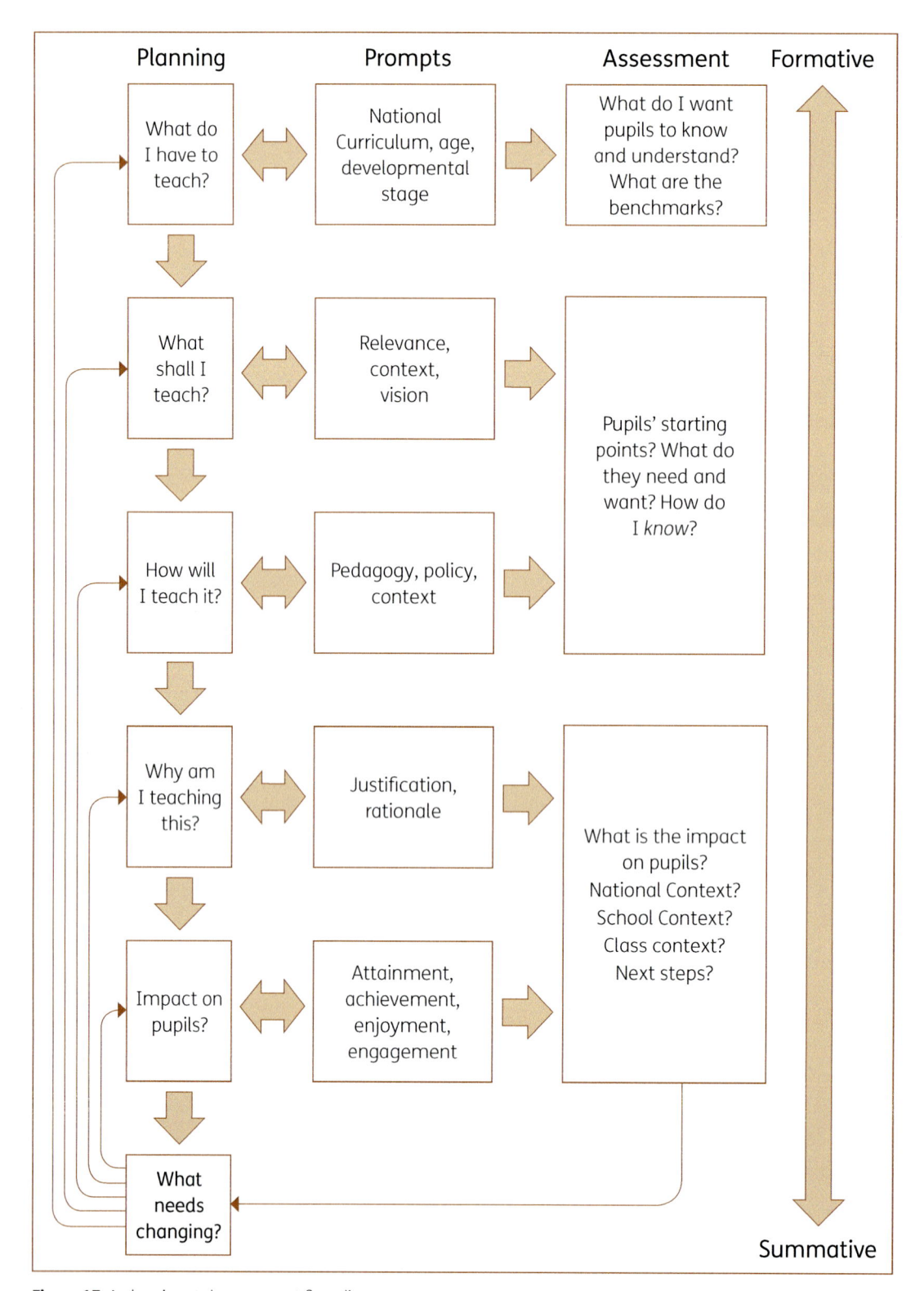

Planning	Prompts	Assessment	Formative
What do I have to teach?	National Curriculum, age, developmental stage	What do I want pupils to know and understand? What are the benchmarks?	
What shall I teach?	Relevance, context, vision	Pupils' starting points? What do they need and want? How do I *know*?	
How will I teach it?	Pedagogy, policy, context		
Why am I teaching this?	Justification, rationale	What is the impact on pupils? National Context? School Context? Class context? Next steps?	
Impact on pupils?	Attainment, achievement, enjoyment, engagement		
What needs changing?			Summative

Figure 17: A planning and assessment flow diagram.

A set of age- or phase-related national benchmarks for expectations of achievement in a subject, or in an area of learning, can guide our expectations, so we know what outcomes to aim for and pitch our planning appropriately. The GA offers detailed assessment guidance and a clear progression framework with benchmarks for pupils aged seven, nine, eleven and thirteen (see web page). No matter what curriculum you follow, the rigorous GA benchmarks constitute a common currency for assessment. Three key conditions for achievement in geography, linked to geography's 'big ideas' (see also p. 22), underpin these benchmarks:

- contextual world knowledge of locations, places and geographical features
- understanding of the conditions, processes and interactions that explain features and distributions, patterns and changes over time and space
- competence in geographical enquiry – the application of skills in observing, collecting, analysing, mapping and communicating geographical information (Geographical Association, 2014).

If we look at the key stage 1 and 2 curriculum for geography in England (DfE, 2013), we can identify the content that should be learnt during the primary years. Combining this with, for instance, the GA benchmarks for progression in geography can produce a workable framework for planning and assessment (see web page for download) and even identify some 'I can' statements that might guide learning.

Adapting this basic framework to take account of individual and school contexts, as well as other curricular opportunities for meaningful links, can contribute to a coherent and purposeful curriculum. Such 'curriculum making' is something all teachers do when they select content to teach and decide how they will teach and assess it, aiming for a recipe that will nourish learners on their journey. Figure 18 poses some questions that we might ask about planning and assessment in order to make a high-quality and nourishing curriculum.

Curriculum Making

Finest ingredients?
Local or globally sourced?
Fresh/seasonal?
Home grown?
Expensive or thrifty?

Who is dining at the curriculum table?
Diners?
Special dietary needs?
Cultural needs?
What time of day is the meal?
How hungry are the diners?

How tasty is it?
Spices and seasoning?
Will diners come back for more?

How is it made?
Do you make the recipe fit the ingredients you have to hand?
Do you select the ingredients needed for the recipe?
How long will you cook it for?

Whose recipe is it?
Traditional and well-used?
An old one but with a new twist?
A new one, untried and built around what is available and what they will eat?
Recipe? It's take-away!

How digestible is it?
Are the nutritionists happy?
Does the diet nourish?
Is it a quick bite, a treat or a three-course meal?
Is it healthy eating?
Is it part of a balanced diet?

Figure 18: Curriculum making to nourish pupils' learning journey. Image © NotionPic/Shutterstock.com.

Progression

The 'big picture' of expectations and outcomes is informed by our understanding of how pupils progress in geography: moving from concrete to abstract thought that develops in ever more complex ways. As pupils' knowledge and understanding of geography grow, their vocabulary and reasoning become more complex: they become more able to link ideas together, make reasoned arguments and investigate and analyse at different scales of enquiry. This progression is not linear: pupils need to revisit knowledge and conceptual understanding, often progressing at different rates.

Geography is a subject with a lot of 'stuff' to know and a vast vocabulary, including place names, is needed to support this knowledge. Ideally, pupils begin by learning about their locality in more depth while also gaining a sense of the wider world. Gradually they begin to fill in the gaps of their mental world map like pieces of a jigsaw. As pupils develop the ability to think more critically and at a range of scales, the planned learning should offer them opportunities to apply their knowledge.

Figure 19 describes progression as being more like a spiral pathway in which pupils extend their breadth, depth and range of enquiry and learning over time. While progression of both the class and the individual pupil can be planned for, progress can be unpredictable and uneven. This is where monitoring and day-to-day assessment strategies come into their own.

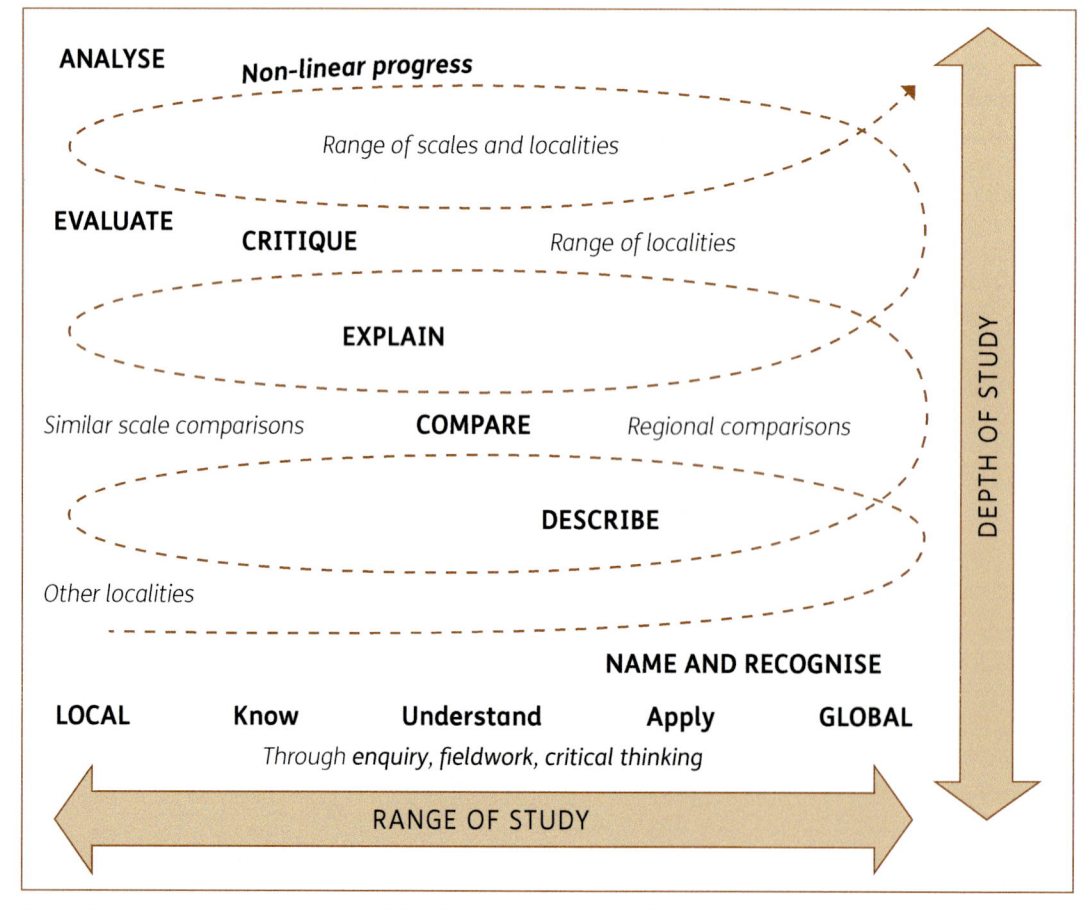

Figure 19: Spiral progression towards breadth and depth in geography. After Bruner, 1960.

Supporting pupils with additional educational needs and disabilities (AEND)

Pupils with AEND will need additional support and more finely tuned progression statements, so that what might otherwise be unnoticeable progress can be planned for, observed and recorded. Some schools, particularly special schools, devise their own statements of progress, but in England there are statutory guidelines for the use of P-scales in these circumstances (DfE, 2017b). Outcomes for geography are given on a detailed eight-point scale; for example, P6 states:

> 'Pupils understand the differences between the physical/natural and human-made features of places. They use pictures or symbols to show familiar places and what they are for, such as making simple plans and maps of familiar areas. They show what they think about different people and environments and answer simple questions about places and people (for example, "What can you buy in this shop? What can you do in the park?")' (DfE, 2017b, p.16).

Such detailed expectations can only be met and evidenced if they are planned for.

Monitoring progress

Having planned with assessment in mind as far as outcomes go, we can also plan in opportunities for monitoring progress and supporting pupils along their learning pathways. Two terms that are used frequently when assessing pupils' work are summative assessment and formative assessment. These two strategies work together to give a rounded picture of a pupil's progress over time and might be thought of as a continuum. With these twin assessment approaches we can investigate and support learning through a mix of observation and dialogic interventions, modelling strategies that pupils can develop for themselves. Keep in mind the purpose of assessment as something that helps pupils make the next step.

Summative and formative assessment work together over different timescales. Summative assessment is a snapshot in time, involving a judgement against a set of criteria and/or a marked test with quantitative outcomes. It is particularly useful for medium- or long-term assessment and subsequent planning. Formative assessment is a process of engagement with pupils; it requires teacher skill and judgement and should permeate each and every lesson (see Figure 17).

Summative assessment

Summative assessment is, as the term suggests, a summary judgement. It can take many different forms; it is useful as a tool to inform progress at the end of a topic, term, year or phase of schooling. It is particularly useful for transition between phases and to help inform reports to parents and future teachers. There is no statutory requirement for formal tests in geography during the primary years, but this does not mean that some testing is not useful – it has its place. Testing can be done in ways that do not intimidate pupils and can help to consolidate learning. Bear in mind, though, that while testing may sometimes tell you what pupils know or remember it may not reveal the extent of their understanding. It is also important to remember that summative judgements are just a small part of the overall picture of pupil progress.

When planning is pitched around progression and expectations, it is easier to identify pupils who are 'achieving as expected', those who are 'working towards', and those who are 'exceeding expectations'. You can identify particular areas of challenge within a topic, as well as individual pupils' needs, and this can feed back into your planning. Summative judgements of this kind can be used to gauge progress between year groups and across the school. When data about progress and achievement is set in a common framework (see web page) there is scope to gauge progress against national expectations too.

Some national curricula have an assessment system in which pupils' progress is judged against best-fit levels of attainment. Where there is no statutory use of levels, schools are free to devise their own assessment strategies; as a result, many now use their own skills progression system to make summative judgements. However, there are advantages to using a national system: it sets how well your pupils are doing into the bigger picture beyond the school gates.

A good summative assessment strategy is to keep samples of pupils' work, annotated to explain their contextual impact. The GA asks teachers applying for the Primary Geography Quality Mark (PGQM) to provide evidence of pupils' work to illustrate different aspects of achievement. The best kind of evidence is an image of either a piece of work or a pupil in the process of learning, clearly and comprehensively annotated to explain the context, the teaching support and the outcome. A portfolio of annotated pieces of work, photographs or recorded conversations with contextual explanation can be valuable assets for both class teacher and subject leader.

Figure 20 is an extract of text from a portfolio of evidence for a GA PGQM award. The teacher also used images of pupils' work from nursery to the end of year 6, with contextual commentary, as a general and summative indication of where each year group was on their learning journey.

You might keep individual pupil portfolios or rely on a class portfolio – selected pieces that convey the different levels of challenge within the class. These can be quick snapshots of achievement or more considered pen portraits. They can be qualitative or quantitative, from tests. You will want to record pupil starting points at the beginning of a topic, either from concept maps in which pupils display their initial thoughts, or through recording general aspects of a class conversation to identify misconceptions.

One simple activity that can be repeated twice a year, or even termly, is to get pupils to draw part of a world map using markers on a gently inflated balloon. Take images of the resulting maps and keep them to chart progress.

Nursery
The pupils used Bee-Bots to move around different maps. They were developing geographical vocabulary linked to direction and location. They could say whether their bug was on the land or in the sea, on the mountain, bridge, river etc. They had also been working on location and direction in PE and, following walks around the building and grounds, had been describing where places were around the school.

Reception
The pupils investigated Burnt Ash Road. They talked about the human features, what the place was like, what people were doing, the traffic etc. They took photographs of the road, the buildings and other things they could see. On returning to class they used photographs they had taken to make a large picture map of the road. They could tell the difference between human-made and natural objects and could express opinions about the environment. Most pupils were increasing their geographical vocabulary.

Year 1
Pupils developed their map skills by drawing a story map of the Stick Man's journey. They began to develop the idea of route or plan, began to use drawn symbols to represent areas and places, used positional and directional vocabulary and could draw and mark a route on a map.

Year 2
Pupils carried out research into the local area. They looked at aerial photographs and used a large map to locate their houses and places that were important to them. They could describe routes between locations and describe the local area using geographical vocabulary.

Figure 20: Summative assessment evidence. Source: Brindishe Lee Primary School, London.

If this is tied in with planning, it becomes a tool for learning. For example, reception pupils might be asked to mark the poles, and even the imaginary line around the middle called the Equator, on their 'world'. In year 1 they might add a recognisable continent shape such as Africa, as well as the poles and Equator. Then they could add where they live; and so on. Recording progress in this way can also help to make learning engaging and challenging as pupils see their progress and think about how much better they are getting at geography. Approaches such as this can help to chunk learning into more accessible and digestible servings that can be linked to form a clear understanding of bigger concepts.

Formative assessment

Formative assessment is the result of engagement with pupils; it requires teacher skill and judgement and should permeate each and every lesson.

> 'An assessment functions formatively to the extent that evidence about student achievement is elicited, interpreted and used by teachers, learners or their peers to make decisions about the next steps in instruction that are likely to be better, or better founded, than the decisions they would have made in the absence of that evidence' (Wiliam, 2011, p. 43).

As teachers, we are continually monitoring pupils through observation, interaction, questioning, discussion and dialogue and all of these can tell us much about what is going on in a pupil's mind and how well they are coping with new challenges. Mackintosh (2008) sums up an approach to formative assessment very well:

> 'My approach to assessing pupils' progress in geography is through continuous dialogue and 'listening in' to pupils' geographical conversations while enjoying practical activities on their geographical journey. For this to be useful the teacher needs to know where the journey is going, in skills as well as content' (Mackintosh, 2008, p. 5).

What is crucial, though, is how we interpret what we learn about a pupil's developing knowledge, skills and understanding and how we help them achieve the next step on that journey. Formative assessment happens at close and immediate scales of interaction and requires constructive feedback if it is to be helpful and effective.

In Figure 21 a teacher explains how learning was supported during a geography lesson with 7–8-year-old pupils who were sorting, grouping and comparing features following local fieldwork in the town centre. Knowing her pupils' starting point and that some had previously struggled with language, she used props in the form of photographs to help vocabulary association and use. Her teaching assistant was given a specific role to work with those pupils who required some verbal support.

Each group of pupils was given a set of photographs and asked to sort the features they show according to the labels provided into different types of land use. This activity was designed to help consolidate knowledge from an enquiry and used both formative (questioning, probing and prompting) and summative (observing, judging, and recording) assessment strategies. After each group had sorted their images they were asked to walk around and look at what other groups had done. There was immediate feedback time for pupils to discuss what they had done with each other and whether they wished to change anything.

Self and peer assessment

A lynchpin of any assessment process is putting pupils at the heart of it. Making pupils partners in their learning by sharing intended outcomes and helping them to become more self-aware is good practice across the curriculum and has a key role in geography. Assessment should be part of the relationship with learning for all of us, not something that is 'done' to pupils. A reflective self-aware approach is a valuable attitude to learning that we can model in the classroom. Two effective participative strategies are self and peer assessment. Figure 22 shows three examples.

Some pupils found this task very challenging. The terms 'residential', 'agricultural' and 'industrial' were very difficult for them to use and remember. They worked with the teaching assistant (TA), each pupil taking responsibility for one type of land use. The TA showed them a picture and they were able to begin to recognise their type of land use.

As the task progressed, most of them recognised examples of land use that other pupils should be collecting. A few pupils still needed support with this and could recognise features such as shops but could not describe features or say why some might be grouped together. Gradually, most of this group began to be more confident with some of the language used as the lesson progressed and began to employ it appropriately. The TA used questioning techniques and interactive dialogue to enable pupils to practise and refine their responses and subsequent understanding.

The strengths of this kind of assessment activity were that it was enjoyable and challenging for the pupils, demanded collaborative and thinking skills and gave pupils the opportunity to make progress with their learning. It was relatively easy for the teacher to assess pupils' knowledge and skills from the outcomes they produced, and the language used.

Figure 21: Example of supported learning. Source: Jennie Till, Minterne Community Junior School, Sittingbourne.

Two of the examples are from 8–9-year-olds at the end of the same unit of work. One (Figure 22a) is for pupils to complete their self assessment quickly, by ticking those statements they think they can do. The teacher has prepared statements covering the range of intended outcomes for the unit of work. These outcomes were built into the planning and while the teacher has arrived at her own judgment about what each pupil has achieved, this is an opportunity to see what the pupil thinks they have achieved.

The second example (Figure 22b) allows each pupil to go into more depth and identify what they have achieved in their own words. In this example, pupils have been asked to identify what they need to get better at as well, so in effect, they are setting their own target. The teacher reports that the pupils' self assessment mirrored her own judgements almost exactly. Younger pupils may not be able to write as much as older pupils, but they can judge their own work in more accessible ways. Instant verbal feedback, a quick show of thumbs up or down and teacher-annotated work using pupils' comments are just some of the ways to record their thoughts. Photographs, video and audio recordings, as long as they are presented in context, are also useful ways to gather evidence. Figure 22c is an example of a self and peer assessment sheet for Early Years pupils that includes teacher feedback.

Peer assessment might take the form of assessment buddies, talk partners or even whole-class feedback. Essentially, we are asking pupils to be critical, in a helpful way, of each other's work. This skill requires a classroom culture in which pupils are not afraid to make mistakes and know how to be honest, kind and to listen to each other. In this learning environment assessment is a shared enterprise and therefore much more effective. One teacher explained that she now celebrates a 'mistake of the week' in which a pupil makes a mistake but learns something new from it. Such critical and reflective thinking techniques help pupils to develop resilience.

a)

RATE YOURSELF!

Mapwork and skills

I could find the places we studied on the aerial photograph. I could find the places we studied on the maps we were given.	I could find the places we studied on the aerial photograph. I could find the places we studied on the maps we were given. AND I could use local maps and aerial photographs to help me find answers to my own questions. I could make my own maps to show the information that I found out.	I could find the places we studied on the aerial photograph. I could find the places we studied on the maps we were given. AND I could use local maps and aerial photographs to help me find answers to my own questions. I could make my own maps to show the information that I found out. AND I could use ICT to organise and present my fieldwork findings and explain how these places compared. I could use maps to explain some of the environmental problems in our locality.
✓	✓	✓ ✗

Environmental quality

I can give my own views about the environment of Warden, Warden Point, and Leysdown and I can see how people do things to affect these localities.	I can give my own views about the environment of Warden, Warden Point, and Leysdown and I can see how people do things to affect these localities. AND I can give reasons for my views and how people affect the environment. I recognise how people can do things to look after their locality.	I can give my own views about the environment of Warden, Warden Point, and Leysdown and I can see how people do things to affect these localities. AND I can give reasons for my views and how people affect the environment. AND I understand how people can improve and damage their locality.
✓	✓	

b)

My Review and Assessment of the Geography Project

I think I have achieved my learning target because I can read maps and put myself on maps. I think that taking sheep away and building more houses on fields is wrong because your desroying there home.

I need to work more at understanding about the damaging on the beach and how much warden has changed.

I am most proud of key maps because I understand all of that and I understand that people have different opinions.

What I would do differently next time I will try and pay more attention to are Environment.

c)

LO: 14.04.18 ➢ To investigate places ➢ To use and interpret globes, atlases and maps To be successful I need to:	What did I think?	What did my friend think?	What did my teacher think?
✓ Find places on a globe or in an atlas or on a map	🟢	🟢	✓ ✓
✓ Write a thought shower about why we go on holidays	🟢	🟢	✓ ✓
✓ Write in full sentences	🔴	🟢	✓ ✓
✓ Use adjectives to write a description about a place I have visited	🟡	🟢	✓ ✓

🙂 😐 ☹

Figure 22: Examples of self and peer assessment in practice.

One simple technique is to ask pupils to look at each other's work and say, using given criteria, what they like best and what could be made better. Initially, you could provide example phrases for pupils to select from. If this process is started in the Early Years, pupils become both more resilient and more perceptive and reflective learners. When using peer or self assessment, it is important to build in some correction time at the end of the lesson, rather than leaving it until the next day.

The pupil-buddy system can be used across, as well as within, classes and year groups. In the commentary below, part of a PGQM application, one school explains how they match older with younger pupils. It is a reflective assessment from the teacher on the healthy and inclusive nature of geography within the school:

> 'Pupils in year 6 'buddy' a reception pupil and work with them on a weekly basis. We have been sharing geographical skills and knowledge to encourage an early love of geography that will stay with the pupils as they progress through the school. Ollie from year 6 and Oscar from reception are looking on a map of Europe for Spain, since Oscar's family are from there' (Sacred Heart Primary School PGQM application, 2015).

Lesson observations

In an ideal world, we would all have time to go and observe at least part of another teacher's geography lesson as this can help us become more reflective practitioners. The geography subject leader should of course be able to devote some time for this across the school, but even where this happens, the time allocation is likely to be very small. If you can manage some observation time, focus on one part of the lesson, such as the introduction or the plenary, and go in for just five or ten minutes. You may also ask the teacher if they have something particular that they feel they need to work on and would like you to focus on. This detailed focus can be more productive for both a subject leader and class teacher and can inform whole-school practice. For example, the subject leader suggests to staff some lively and effective lesson starters for geography and says she will visit class teachers to support them in implementing the ideas. This can also provide an opportunity to talk to pupils about their learning experiences and find out what they think and enjoy about their learning (see p. 117).

If you are doing a more formal, written lesson observation then you must give teachers plenty of warning and discuss with them what your focus is going to be. Offer your feedback as soon as you can and record any changes on your action plan for the subject. Figure 23 gives an example of a formal lesson observation.

Reporting to parents and carers

Keeping parents and carers informed about progress is very important. It is usually formalised at the end of each school year with a written report, though parents' evenings also offer an opportunity to talk about pupils' work. While your school might have specific guidelines about report formats, it can be helpful to think about a short comment for the subject using the context of learning and progression statements to identify successes and areas for development. For example:

> (Year 2) We have been out on fieldwork, investigating where we live and comparing our locality with a town in Kenya. Anya has been an enthusiastic learner and used maps and atlases well to find the places we have been studying. She is starting to get more confident at creating her own drawn and annotated maps and is developing her understanding of symbols. Anya is able to describe some similarities and differences between where she lives and the locality we have been studying overseas.

Reporting to governors

A short, written report each year to the governors about what has been covered in geography can be very helpful in raising the status of the subject – a point made at the beginning of this section. Many schools have

> **Classroom Observation Recording Sheet**
> **Fleckney Church of England Primary School**
>
> | Teacher | Support Staff | Year Group | Observation date and time |
> |---|---|---|---|
> | R.H. | None | 4 | 25.1.16 1.15pm |
> | **Subject** | **Grouping** | **SEN** | **Number of pupils** |
> | Geography | Class | 2 ESPs 0 EHCPs | 23 |
>
> Notes and context of lesson
>
> Children have looked at what Fleckney is like (physical and human features, land use etc). Now looking at Edale in preparation for residential visit and to compare to Fleckney.
>
> Clear LO (to understand OS maps) and re-cap on previous learning
> Teacher's subject knowledge is excellent.
> Children very knowledgeable about land-use in and around Fleckney – confidently using terminology such as residential, industrial, commercial, agricultural etc.
>
> Various styles of learning in use – talk partners, 3-2-1 share, mixed ability pairings and group work.
>
> Children enthusiastic and eager to learn – current learning is clearly linked to up-coming residential to Edale. Techer entions, "When we go…" which really focuses the children and set a buzzing atmosphere.
>
> Children introduced to OS maps – quick discussion about what maps are/show etc.
>
> Children given time to explore an OS map of Edale and key to symbols. Very practical – annotations on map and large paper to make notes. Encouraged to think about what ways Edale is similar and different from Fleckney.
>
> Mini-plenaries throughout to refocus children and allow assessment for learning opportunities. Teacher is then able to support a group that are finding the activity challenging.
>
> Children then present their findings to the class.

Figure 23: A subject leader's formal lesson observation record. Source: Fleckney Primary School PGQM application, 2016.

a named governor for each subject, and this can be very helpful. A supportive governor who is familiar with the aims for the subject might come in once a term, for example, to observe teachers in class. A copy of the report to governors can be put into the subject leader's file as a quick summary of what has been achieved and next steps.

Transition

Transition from one phase of learning to the next can be challenging for the pupil, teacher and parent or carer. There are two key crunch points: starting and leaving school, and in between there are the changes and upheaval that each class move brings. Managing the different protocols and expectations of early to older years settings can also be daunting for the pupil. It can be very helpful, especially for geography, to draw on pupils' own settings and backgrounds and build from there.

Encourage new pupils to bring in artefacts from home that they can share with each other in ways that celebrate families and community. Use a world map to celebrate diversity and connections and simple maps and aerial images of the local area to talk about where they live. Provide opportunities in class to make and use table maps for small role figures; outside, provide cars and sand pits for 3D play and observation stations to encourage attention to place and vocabulary. Have a teddy, such as Barnaby Bear, or other soft toy, that pupils can take turns to host for the weekend and bring back to talk about where they have been and what they have done (see p. 73). Some parents may be able to come in and help in class and may have stories, skills and job experiences to share – this is true across the school but is especially helpful when pupils are first settling into what is a very new world to them.

The idea of a buddy from an older class works well, as does having some regular helpers from other classes who might come in and play with younger pupils for short periods of time – if only for the first few weeks. Older pupils can act as guides at break and lunchtimes too, helping younger pupils find their way around their new world. Activities should include taking the pupils around the school to explore and notice features of their new surroundings, with opportunities to draw and make models and simple maps. Mapping people can also be very useful to settle pupils new to a school (Figure 24). Where is the Head's office and what happens there? Where is the kitchen and who works there? What does the school secretary do? Who makes sure the school is warm every morning and who locks the gates at night? Tackling these questions helps pupils to feel that they belong.

Summative class records and portfolios can form the subject of the conversations between the two class teachers that usually take place when pupils move up at the end of the year. There will be many topics for discussion but a quick résumé of who is meeting expectations, who is exceeding them and who is being challenged will help the next teacher plan their geography accordingly. In addition, if there are parts of the geography curriculum a class has struggled with or particularly enjoyed this can be flagged up

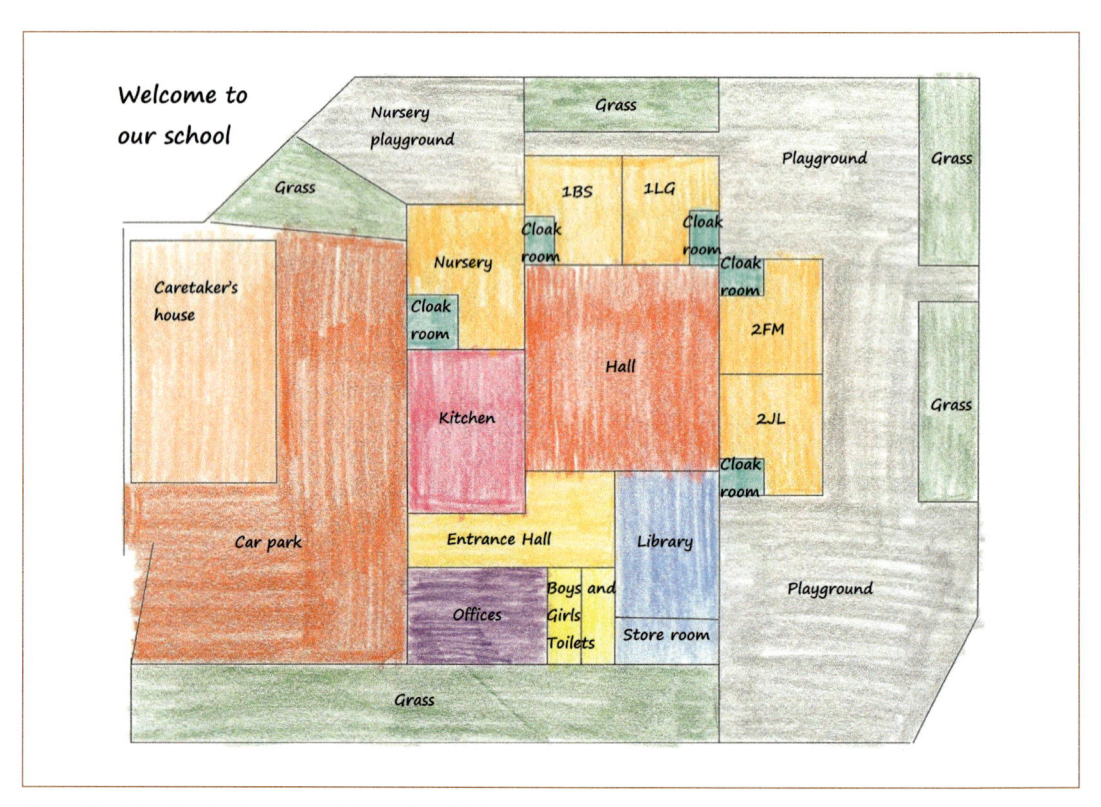

Figure 24: A simple school map can help pupils settle in.

here too. Who has needed additional support and who has shone when doing fieldwork and outdoor learning, and how could they be further challenged or called on to support others? Has there been a pupil who has struggled with spatial awareness or direction finding, for example? Does one pupil have a parent who is particularly helpful and available for field trips? All of this information can be very useful.

There is often talk of getting pupils 'secondary ready' but this idea needs to be taken in context. Primary pupils are, hopefully, living the primary school experience for its own sake and not merely as preparation for secondary school. If you have a rich and engaging geography curriculum and pupils are reaching expected benchmarks, they will be well placed to cope with the demands of a secondary curriculum. What they may be less well placed to cope with is the transition to an unfamiliar location and a much larger setting. They may not be prepared for the stress and uncertainty of this move; here are some strategies to help them to be more emotionally resilient:

- if you can, make links with the local secondaries and talk to the staff
- share examples of pupils' work, as well as summative assessments
- ask if year 7 can collaborate on some work with your year 6 – if only exchanging emails, letters and Skype calls
- collaborate with your local secondary through fieldwork or other activities that can be shared.

Taking stock

As subject leader, the end of the school year is the time to revisit your geography action plan and think about what your priorities might be for the following year. The timing of this is likely to be dictated by budgets so may be around April, though where budgets are small or non-existent, it is more likely to be at the end of the summer term.

Karen Falcon, an advisor with Hampshire County Council, has these prompts for teachers to ask about the nature of geography in the school:

1. Where's the geography in your planning, teaching and assessment, and what geographical learning do you want pupils to achieve?
2. Is it the 'right' geography; is it appropriate and relevant and will they be able to engage with it? Indeed, is it geography? Whole-school International days are great for getting all the pupils involved but are significant geographical concepts being made explicit?
3. Where are the skills? Which specific skills are being targeted, and how do the activities enable the pupils to practise and develop them?
4. Are the pupils being challenged to apply their knowledge to different levels of thinking?
5. Does the learning take them on a journey that they are also aware of?
6. Does the work that they do expose them to and explain different scales?
7. Does it connect to the pupils and is it meaningful to them? (Falcon, 2019).

Professional development

Understanding and meeting the professional development needs of your colleagues matters. Informal conversations, curriculum audits and surveys will enable you to gauge the specific needs of individual teachers. How much practical support you can offer depends on the size of your geography budget and how much time allocation you can get during staff meetings and school INSET days. You will need to keep your own CPD up to date too, but prioritise the areas where your colleagues could benefit most. Here are some approaches that you can take:

- Membership of the Geographical Association for the school means that not only can you access additional online support – courses, think pieces and resources material – you also qualify for reduced prices for resources and at training events. More importantly, you will receive the *Primary Geography* journal and its online back catalogue.

Do make staff aware of the journal: photocopy relevant articles or send them PDF files that they can tailor for their curriculum needs and interests.

- Arrange for teachers to observe each other's, or your, geography lessons, and discuss outcomes from your informal observations of theirs (see p. 146).
- Download the reading list from the web page, and stock the staffroom bookshelf with relevant items that teachers can borrow or dip into.
- Use time at a staff meeting to review a resource or storybook or demonstrate a teaching technique, such as using compasses and map reading.
- Attend a GA CPD event in an area of need and follow up by sharing the key points at a staff meeting.
- Attend the GA Annual Conference and disseminate what has been learned.
- Find out what free CPD opportunities are available in your area. Check the Geographical Association website for twilight CPD. Check with Digimap for Schools or ArcGIS if they have a trainer who can come in for free and demonstrate their software to staff.
- Invite a geography consultant to come in and work with you on a one-to-one basis or to lead a CPD session.
- Join, or start, a local Geographical Association branch.
- Attend, or host, regular cluster meetings with like-minded colleagues from other schools to share ideas and practice.
- Hold transition meetings to ensure continuity between stages or phases of education.

The Primary Geography Quality Mark (PGQM)

The PGQM is an evaluative tool and accreditation as well as recognition for schools and teachers. It is a framework prompting process and reflection that any school in the world can use, from academies to state schools, faith schools, independent and special schools. There are categories linked to impact of achievement, teaching and curriculum, relationships within the school, and leadership. The PGQM categories support and provide evidence for aspects of the Ofsted/Estyn inspection frameworks, which is particularly helpful for schools facing an inspection process but also widely applicable to schools around the world because of the framework's rigorous whole-school approach.

The following extract from a PGQM application describes how one school approaches professional development:

> 'At Tinsley Meadows, we believe that it is essential to give our teaching staff the correct tools and resources so that they feel confident in delivering quality geography sessions. To do this they are offered chances to watch good practice across the school. The subject leader (SL) also works with the senior leadership team (SLT) to ensure that the school has a current Geographical Association membership so that we are able to use current and up-to-date resources.
>
> At the beginning of each year, teaching staff are sent a questionnaire in which they are asked to highlight the things that they think went well the previous year and anything that they feel they need in order to deliver excellent geography. This helps the SL to put together the relevant CPD and informs the geography action plan for that year' (Tinsley Meadows School PGQM application, 2016).

As subject leader, doing a PGQM can be a powerful way to pull together the threads of geography and produce a coherent, evidence-based narrative. Download a case study from the web page that explores one subject lead's path from starting in the role to applying for the PGQM. It will certainly be useful for an Ofsted or Estyn visit and show that you know the strengths and weaknesses of the subject in your school. The PGQM will also show that you have a plan for moving the subject forward.

You can gather evidence for the PGQM over the course of a year and submit it online. A team of moderators from the GA will evaluate your application against the award criteria. One certificate is issued to the school and one to the subject leader. The award lasts three years before requiring renewal. There are three different levels of award:

- Bronze means there is some lively geography happening in the school and the subject leader is developing it, with potential for growth.
- Silver means there is excellent geography teaching and learning happening across most of the school and pupils are achieving well and making good progress.
- Gold is as for Silver but means the geography is embedded throughout the school. There should also be evidence that the school and subject leader have spread the influence of their geography beyond the school. This could be, for example, by writing an article for *Primary Geography*, running a workshop for other teachers, or working with other schools on a transition project.

If your geography is flourishing, why not celebrate it by applying for and submitting a PGQM award? Get the local press involved and shout out about your brilliant geography provision!

Evidence-informed teaching

Teaching is a profession that thrives on the application of sound, evaluated, evidence-informed teaching, and this applies perfectly to primary geography teaching. Much of your geography content may be prescribed by a national and school curriculum, but how it is taught is much less prescriptive. Whether you are a subject leader or class teacher you can benefit by using research-based evidence to improve your geography lessons and to identify CPD events for addressing particular areas of your development. As Biesta *et al.* (2011) argue, theories have consequences: why would we not want to draw on good, reliable evidence of something that will enhance our pupils' learning?

Part of what it means to think professionally as a teacher is to be critical about the evidence we use, its source and how we apply it. However, reading about and/or carrying out research can be difficult to fit into the everyday ongoing demands of teaching, so here are some sources of sound geographical subject and pedagogical knowledge using reliable research evidence:

- Peer-reviewed journals that offer a generally accepted source of reliable evidence, especially when that research has been validated through several studies and different authors.
- The seminal texts on best practice and research, whose authors have done much of the work for you, reading and evaluating peer-reviewed articles to sift out the best and most relevant research.
- Practitioner journals offer an easily digestible source of teaching approaches. In particular *Primary Geography*, which takes examples straight from the classroom, is an invaluable 'go-to' resource. Many articles are written by practising teachers, so the journal can also be an outlet for you to share your classroom practice or action research. This gives other teachers the opportunity to 'adopt, adapt or innovate' your work with their classes, contributing to a vibrant primary geography community.
- Small, informal, classroom-based action research projects can also provide reliable evidence.

An overview and examples of such sources of research evidence can be downloaded from the web page.

Action research

As teachers, we are continually, often subconsciously, carrying out a piece of research as we teach. We ask ourselves 'Why am I doing this?'; 'What impact is this having and why?'; 'How do I know?'. It is a small further step to consciously rationalise and sequence a process of action research. Newman and Legget (2019) argue that this is a powerful way for educators to drive improvements in their own practice. In its simplest form (Figure 25), action research comprises posing a research question, building this into your practice, evaluating outcomes and incorporating the results into new practice and policy.

Some common features of action research include:

- Identifying a problem or need
- A space for communicative reflection
- Reflexivity
- Systematic review of practice
- Professional growth
- Contextualised and relevant enquiry
- Improving practice
- Openness to change
- Agency and empowerment (of practitioner and pupils)
- Questioning assumptions
- Critical stance
- Collaboration
- Trust
- Sustainability.

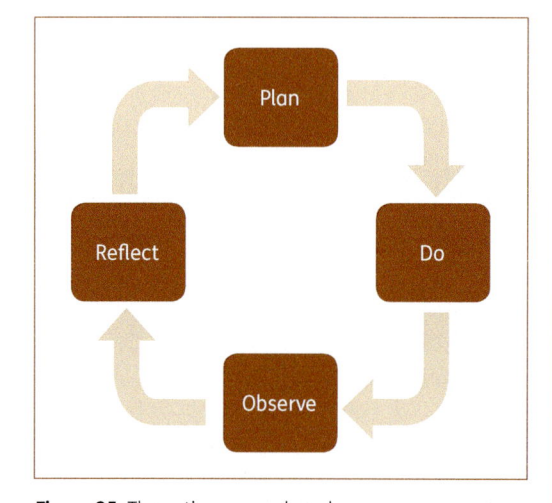

Figure 25: The action research cycle.

Whether evaluating an individual pupil's progress or the impact of geography across the whole school, it is useful to think analytically rather than just descriptively. Why are certain practices and particular content in place, and how effective are they? How do they support the development of reflective and reflexive commentary? This is the approach advocated by the Primary Geography Quality Mark process – it draws on the best available evidence to inform our teaching and learning.

Sometimes, we might want to formalise our classroom research. This doesn't have to be an overly complicated process; it could just involve one lesson. Alternatively, it could be a longer study over a period of time.

Cultivate a community of practice and learning wherever you can: in your school, in your local network and with the wider world. By collaborating with colleagues, you can get access to research that you haven't had time to read; professional conversations with the wider geography education community can yield advice about the impact-feedback cycle of action research. The primary geography community of practice is thriving, with active committees, journals, conferences, get-togethers and a strong social media presence. There are many ways to get involved, contribute and feel supported.

Subject association support

Whether you are an experienced teacher and subject leader, a new teacher or a trainee, a subject association can provide you with support, ideas, opportunities and enrichment as well as collegial companionship at both virtual and face-to-face levels.

Joining, participating in and belonging to a subject community of practice, such as the GA or RGS (with IBG), shows that you value your subject and supports your professional development. The benefits of belonging to the GA include:

- discounted resources and courses

- regular updates on geography and wider education news, policy and practice
- a network of professional support
- a journal of theory and best practice for teachers and subject leaders delivered to you three times a year
- access to online courses and refreshers to develop your and others' professional learning and development
- guidance on teaching sensitive and controversial issues
- opportunities to join study tours
- the chance to get directly involved in a diverse array of activities such as writing journal articles, presenting courses, joining committees and working on resources (see web page)
- the opportunity to apply to be a recognised consultant for the Geographical Association, working on projects in a variety of contexts
- taking part in the PGQM accreditation scheme with guidance and support from a team of mentors and moderators (see p. 150).
- Joining a special interest committee such as fieldwork and outdoor learning, international, physical geography, sustainability and citizenship, just to mention a few.

Wales does not have a separate subject association for geography but there is a version of the PGQM for Wales, and Welsh-speaking moderators assess evidence and visit schools. Just as the version for England aligns with the Ofsted inspection framework, the Welsh version of PGQM aligns with the Estyn framework. The subject association for Scotland is the Scottish Association of Geography Teachers.

The Royal Geographical Society (RGS) also offers a wide range of CPD opportunities and teaching resources. You can find out more on their website (www.rgs.org). If you enrol as a Fellow of the RGS (with IBG) you are eligible to apply for their Chartered Geographer (Teacher) accreditation scheme.

CPD

Because so little time is spent on geography during initial teacher education, primary teachers can go into geography lessons lacking sufficient subject knowledge to teach the subject with confidence. Indeed, some may not have studied any geography since they were 14. If you are a teacher in this position, the first thing to do, with the guidance and support of your subject leader, is to sign up for some subject-specific CPD, including joining a subject association. Since a leadership role in the humanities is often given to newly qualified staff who are not geography specialists, newly appointed subject leaders may find themselves in the same position, and need to take the same action. At the start of this section we identified some ways to prioritise action areas; this will guide your choice of training.

It may be that geography has not been a priority in your school, so time and resources for CPD may not be available. If this is the case, do speak to school leadership teams about the value of the subject and how important it is that teaching is underpinned by rigorous, confident subject knowledge. Subject associations like the GA and the RGS (with IBG) have bespoke sections on their websites with guidance and support for subject leaders. There are also a number of GA online courses and resources with reduced rates for members.

In-house CPD

Many schools have very valuable in-house staff training schemes for geography, led by experienced and knowledgeable subject leaders. In-house schemes can be supported by resources from your subject association. Speak to members of staff about their needs, provide brief weekly or monthly updates, and share journals like *Primary Geography*, encouraging all staff to try out ideas and disseminate the outcomes.

Sharing expertise

Although in-house staff training can be excellent, if it is your only source of CPD it risks becoming inwardly focused; seeking external sources of expertise can add a rich cross-pollination of ideas. For example, for one staff meeting you might swap geography subject leads with another school, asking each leader to explain how geography is implemented at their school and how they are looking to develop. This can be a catalyst for positive change and development for you, the school and most importantly, the pupils.

One of the requirements for the highest level of PGQM award is the school's work in the wider educational community. These schools are expected to show how they have reached out beyond the school, for example writing articles for *Primary Geography* and other related journals, working with the GA on a small local research project and sharing the research online, collaborating with other schools in the area or presenting a workshop at a local or national conference. Some schools have found it helpful for a buddy group of teachers from different schools leading the PGQM to meet regularly to share progress. High-quality CPD and evidence of its impact across the school is something that will help tell a story of high-quality geography learning and teaching.

Further ideas for CPD

Collaborative work on practical teaching ideas can be helpful for staff who would welcome support but may not wish to be singled out; it also generates a great collegial atmosphere and a celebration of successful, effective practice (Figure 26). You could:

- ask all staff to bring one geographical resource and share how they might use it as a stimulus for pupils' learning. For example, a book, a picture or an artefact that supports a particular aspect of the geography they are currently tackling

Figure 26: Share ideas and generate a collegial atmosphere using a geographical stimulus. Photo © Shaun Flannery/Geographical Association.

- lead a whole-school project to investigate and improve one aspect of the subject (see earlier suggestions for research and evidence-informed teaching, p. 151)
- explore and develop pupils' ability to pose higher-level questions and develop critical thinking across the school through the vehicle of geographical enquiry (see p. 47)
- have a whole-school focus on local fieldwork, and feed back the impact of this from each year group.

Social media can extend CPD collaboration to other, distant schools and other relevant contexts. Twitter, for example, can be a useful platform to search for articles, advice or examples of work from other schools. It can help you develop a personal learning network, not just in your local area but globally. Likewise, Facebook and Instagram can be platforms for special interest groups that you can join for updates and support. Technologies such as Google Docs and Dropbox also support collaboration between colleagues who cannot always get together.

Conferences offer concentrated, intense CPD with plenty of practical learning contexts and face-to-face conversations with likeminded teachers from all phases of education. The GA Annual Conference, held each spring, is an invaluable way to develop your expertise. Anyone can bid to run a workshop or present a lecture, and if you are successful you may get help with travel and accommodation.

Charney Manor Primary Geography Conference is a small but influential gathering of primary geography educators. It takes place each year, usually during a weekend in February, and is unique in its focus on primary geography.

The GA local branch network offers the opportunity to meet up regularly with other professionals in your area. Branches throughout the country are listed on the GA website. There is often an invited speaker and the chance to network and share practice. If your area does not have a local branch, you might feel inclined to set one up! If you are interested in this do get in touch with the GA directly.

Having a 'geography buddy', either in your own or another school, can be a source of confidence-building support. It might be a teacher from another phase of education that you can work with to help ease transition – a colleague from a junior school if you are in an infant setting, or a colleague from a secondary school if you are in a junior school. This could be developed into a local network of buddies to ensure comparability and coherence between primary and secondary transition, for example. If you are applying for a PGQM, the GA can put you in touch with other applicants in your area. The buddy system can help you support each other through the process.

Quality assurance

Sharing your geography journey with other schools and the wider education community also feeds into the vital process of quality assurance. How well are you really doing, in the context of the geography beyond your school gates? What is the reputation of geography within, and beyond, your school? What would inspectors say about geography in your school, compared to other schools?

It is vital to compare the nature and quality of geography in other schools with your own. Summative assessment has been described as a means of evaluating your achievements (see p. 141); for example, using a set of national standards such as that provided by the GA. Conversations with teachers, visits to and reading about geography in other schools can all help develop this picture. However, arguably the most effective quality assurance is to complete the PGQM (see pp. 150–1). This provides you with a portfolio of evidence, gathered over three terms, showing that you have carefully considered the intent, implementation and impact of geography teaching and learning across the school. Should Ofsted inspectors wish to find out more about the geography in your school, it shows that you have identified what is happening and evaluated what needs to be done.

Even if you feel that much work remains to be done, you can show that you know what needs doing and why. Having examples of pupils' work will also help you explain the progression of geography within the school and across a sequence of lessons.

Something the PGQM can also do is to both evidence and accredit quality assurance. GA moderators examine all applications, carefully checking that they fit the criteria and are fully representative. This may mean moving some schools down to a lower level than that applied for; equally, it can mean moving some schools to a higher level (Figure 27).

Subject leader impact and inspection

Inspectors coming into a school will of course be guided by their own current inspection frameworks, but as far as geography is concerned, they will want to see learning that is thriving throughout the school, involving all pupils and offering a diverse range of content and teaching approaches, with clear progression and enthusiastic learners. A current PGQM accreditation is a reliable way to show just how well geography is being planned for and implemented and to demonstrate its impact on pupils' learning. An exemplar framework of the Ofsted Criteria for the Education Inspection Framework (EIF) (2019) and its implications for primary geography can be downloaded from the web page. Some of the real opportunities for primary geography the framework offers are outlined in Figure 28.

Regardless of what changes the future may hold, the absolute necessity for pupils to have access to high-quality geography education will remain. Their future is too precious to ignore this pivotal subject, whatever the shape of the curriculum.

GOLD — You lead with strong support from other members of staff and high-quality practice is embedded.

SILVER — Your leadership influences the whole school and impacts positively on teaching and learning.

BRONZE — You are enthusiastic and your influence is beginning to impact on others.

Enthusiastic geography is happening and there is potential for growth.

Excellent geography is happening across the majority of the school.

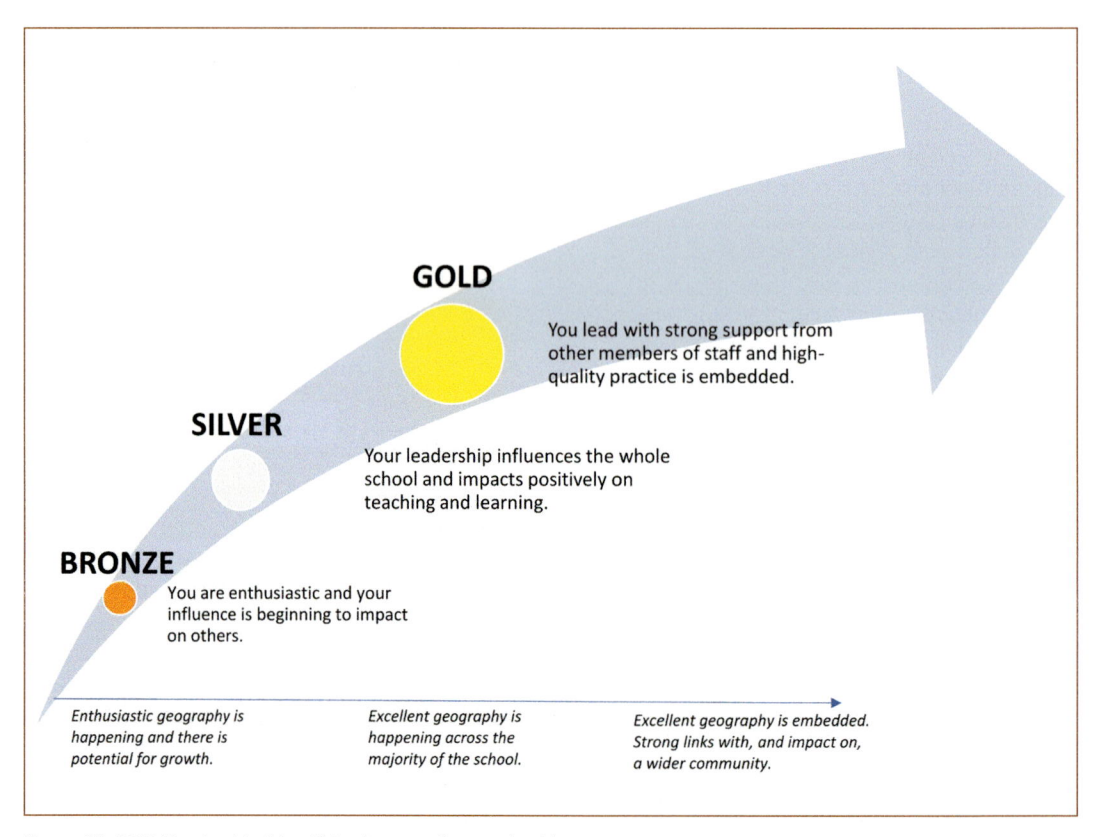

Excellent geography is embedded. Strong links with, and impact on, a wider community.

Figure 27: PGQM leadership, identifying bronze, silver and gold.

There is clear scope for developing pupils' geography in all three areas of Ofsted's quality education and this in turn can help schools to become at least good and hopefully outstanding in relation to this.

Intent: There is a significant emphasis on widening the curriculum and making it more ambitious, providing opportunities to acquire the knowledge and cultural capital that pupils need in order to thrive in their lives. It is difficult to imagine a better, more appropriate, subject than geography for doing just that. Primary geography is an ideal umbrella subject for providing a meaningful, integrated curriculum that pupils can engage with and that will give them some of the life skills and knowledge they are going to need for the future.

Implementation: Teaching and assessing a rich, coherent and inclusive curriculum will be an essential part of the implementation of quality learning and teachers will need a good knowledge of the subject and the areas that they teach. Being engaged with curriculum and professional development will be crucial for all class teachers as well as subject leaders. Reading, adapting and using information such as that provided in *Primary Geography* and engaging with the subject association is one excellent way of keeping abreast of the subject's content and pedagogy. It will also help you to tackle areas of the subject without excessive additional workload that you might not be so comfortable with but clearly do need to teach, and once you do, we can guarantee you will grow to love!

Impact: Pupils should be able to develop comprehensive knowledge and adaptable skills in all areas of the curriculum. Primary geography, through its effective teaching and learning approaches such as enquiry and critical thinking, will help them to do that and enable them to progress in their learning. They can then adapt and build on this, developing their curiosity and embedding their passion for asking questions, seeking answers and reaching informed decisions; in short preparing them for a fulfilled and happy life.

Figure 28: Ofsted's quality education – intent, implementation and impact. Source: Rawlinson and Willy, 2019.

To access further support and resources from the *Leading Primary Geography* web page, see page 164

References

Biesta, G., Allan, J. and Edwards, R. (2011) 'The Theory Question in Research Capacity Building in Education: Towards an Agenda for Research and Practice', *British Journal of Educational Studies*, 59, 3, pp. 225–39.

Bruner, J. (1960) *The Process of Education*. Harvard, MA: The President and Fellows of Harvard College.

Falcon, K. (2019) Presentation to Charney Manor primary geography conference, 01/02/2019.

Geographical Association (2014) *Assessment without levels – practical steps to support progression and attainment in geography*. Available at: https://bit.ly/2IR3TF0 (last accessed 12/6/19).

Mackintosh, M. (2008) 'The Process of Progress', *Primary Geography*, 65, pp. 5–14.

Newman, L. and Leggett, N. (2019) 'Practitioner research: with intent', *European early childhood education research journal*, 27, 1, pp. 120–37.

Ofsted (2011) Geography: *Learning to make a world of difference*. London: Office for Standards in Education, Children's Services and Skills.

Ofsted (2018) *HMCI commentary: curriculum and the new education inspection framework*. Available at: https://bit.ly/2NQnQiI (last accessed 12/6/2019).

Rawlinson, S. and Willy, T. (2019) 'Editorial', *Primary Geography*, 99, pp. 4–5.

Tuan, Y.F. (1977) *Space and Place: The perspective of experience*. Minneapolis, MN: University of Minnesota Press.

Wiliam, D. (2011) *Embedded Formative Assessment*. Cheltenham, VIC: Hawker Brownlow Education Pty Ltd.

Index

A

action plans 115, 123, 128–9, 135, 136–7
action research 151–2
additional educational needs and disabilities (AEND) 141
aerial photographs 34, 106, 142
Ancient Egypt *see* Egypt
art and design 94–6
artefacts
  CPD 154
  criteria for 120
  fieldwork 108
  managing transition 147–8
aspirations 9, 14, 37, 61, 130
assemblies 80, 135
assessment 135–9
  and classroom leadership 114–18
  formative 141, 143
  and planning 138
  self and peer 143–6
  summative 141–2, 148
atlases 119

B

badges and certificates 135
beaches 86
Beck, Harry 95
blogs 135
books, fiction/non-fiction 79, 119
British Council Connecting Classrooms Programme 47, 51
buddies 144, 146, 148

C

Cambridge Primary Review 69
Catling, S. 56, 58–9, 64
certificates and badges 135
charts *see* graphicacy
children's rights 63
citizenship 89–91, 109–10
classroom observation 118, 146, 147, 150
climate change 18, 25, 87
coastal areas 86
collaboration 61
  class links 121
  and communication 37
  and CPD 155
  leadership 114–18
community engagement 87, 88, 108, 109–11, 114, 121, 125, 152
compass skills 38–9, 119
computers *see* ICT; websites
concepts 18–19, 22–3, 100, 130–1
continuity and change 91
core knowledge 21, 74–5, 133
CPD (continuing professional development) 60, 149–56
creativity 60, 63
  cross-curricular 72, 80
  and curriculum content 60
  and graphicacy 35
  local studies 61
  and residential fieldwork 40
  sound maps 31, 96
  and topic work 99, 102
  see also play
critical thinking 47–8, 50–1, 106, 108–9, 121, 133
cross-curricular links 61, 63, 68–97, 131–2
cultural issues 23, 88, 92, 102
curriculum
  changes in 56–7, 128–35
  as content and process 56
  curriculum making 44, 57–8, 139
  definitions 56
  planning 58, 126–8, 135
  see also assessment; National Curriculum

D

data
  analysis and pattern seeking 80–1

measuring and collecting 37, 108–10
presentation 83
qualitative/quantitative 37
  see also graphicacy
debate 48–50
decision making
  environmental geography 108–9
  pupils' role in 63–4
dialogue 114–18
digital maps 34, 106, 119–20
displays 125, 135
  graphicacy 35–6
  news items and issues 121, 122
  pupil responses 118
  see also images; photographs
distant places
  school linking 72–3, 121
  topic work 99, 105–6
diversity 23, 88, 102, 147
drama and role play 79, 93, 94, 96

E

Egypt 75, 101–2
emotional learning 34, 35, 37, 60, 89, 133
emotional resilience 149
empathy 96, 99
empowerment 11, 14, 23–5
  curriculum making 58
  debate as 49
  environmental action 87
energy 76
English 77–80
enquiry skills/approach 46–7
  classroom-based 79
  and CPD 155
  cross-curricular links 83, 84–6, 91–2
  enquiry-based learning 62–3
  topic work 98
environment 18, 23
environmental geography 25–7, 52, 87, 107–8
  see also sustainability
ethical and moral questions 89–91
  see also citizenship; sustainability
evaluation 47–8

curriculum 123, 126, 128–9
everyday geography 58–60
evidence-informed teaching 151
expertise 75, 100, 122, 153–4
EYFS (Early Years Foundation Stage) 8, 18, 68, 86

F

Fairtrade 81, 82
Falcon, K. 149
familiar places 24, 103, 104
  see also local area; school and grounds
fieldwork 35–9
  cross-curricular links 84
  evaluation 40
  and soundscapes 31, 96
  virtual 40
  whole-school focus 155
figures see graphicacy
floating and sinking 86
food and food production 108–9
foundation subjects, integrating geography 88–97
fracking 46, 49

G

games
  literacy 34, 35
  maps for 119
  outdoors 38
  see also play
Geographical Association 76, 139, 149–50, 165
  see also Primary Geography Quality Mark
geographical thinking 14, 22–5
geography subject leaders 13–14, 58, 112–57
  assessment 135–9
  curriculum planning and change 56–7, 126–35
  leadership strategies 114–18, 122–56
  resources 119–22
  vision and policy statements 123–7
GIS (Geographic Information System) 34
globes 119
Google Earth and Google Maps 34, 99
governors 114–15, 117, 146
graphicacy 35–6, 83, 94
Greenwood, R. 98

H

Head teachers and senior management 114
health/well-being 37
history 56, 91–4, 120
human geography 19, 36, 108
humanities, and critical thinking 47

I

ICT 104, 127
　digital maps 34, 99, 106, 119–20
images
　criteria for 120
　local area 90, 142
　　see also photographs
inspection see Ofsted
interconnections and interdependence 19, 23, 25, 87, 98, 106, 107
internet 119
　see also websites

J

jobs, awareness of 104
journeys 95, 104
　see also fieldwork; maps and mapwork

K

key concepts 17–27
key skills 29–40
KWHL grids 77
KWL grids 63–4

L

land use 90, 93
language see literacy and numeracy; speaking and writing
learning progression 69, 75, 100, 110, 120, 129, 135, 140–1
　framework 61, 139
　monitoring 141–7
　questions for 35
learning walls 45
lesson observations 118, 146, 147, 150
literacy and numeracy 69, 77–83
　see also speaking and writing

literature, children's, fiction/non-fiction 78–9
Liverpool case study 69, 71
local area 44
　case studies 69–71, 86, 90, 95, 105, 110
　cross-curricular links 61
　fieldwork 104–5
　land use and settlement 90
　settlement and processes 100
　sustainability 52
　topic work 99
　topical debate 50
local businesses, fieldwork 120
locality studies 44–5

M

Mackintosh, M. 95, 143
maps and mapwork 30–6, 39, 88, 90
　as art 95
　digital 34, 106, 119–20
　distant places 107–8
　local area 33
　managing transition 147–8
　recording progress 142–3
　topics 100
mathematics 80–3
modelling strategies 141
models, building 94
motivation 37, 60, 64, 77
music 31, 96

N

National Curriculum 36–7, 128
　changes in 56–7, 128–35
　maps and mapwork 119–20
navigation skills 38–9
news media, current 45, 61, 102, 121, 134
non-fiction genres 79–80, 119
Northern Ireland, curriculum 56–7, 128

O

Ofsted 68, 69, 72, 128, 150, 156–7
online materials see ICT; websites
oral activities 77–80
Ordnance Survey maps 119

orienteering 38–9
outdoor experiences 35–9
   see also fieldwork

P

parents 117, 146, 148
patterns and processes 23, 30, 82
   climate 24, 107
   language 34–5
   science and geography 84–5
   see also settlement
peer assessment 143–6
personal, social, health and economic (PSHE) education 70, 89, 103
personal experiences and links 120–1
personalising your teaching 61–5
photographs 90, 120, 142, 143, 144
physical geography, topic work 86–7, 107–8
place 23, 69, 131, 133–4
   and emotions 89
   and school links 72
planning 14, 58
   dialogue 114–18
   and pupil voice 63–4
   reflection on 44
   sustainability 52
   for topics 101–2
   see also assessment; curriculum
play 12, 34, 94
   see also games
portfolios of pupils' work 142, 148
powerful ideas 69
powerful knowledge 59–60
Primary Geography (journal) 135, 149–50, 151, 154
Primary Geography Quality Mark (PGQM) 123, 135, 146, 150–1
   for quality assurance 155–6
prior knowledge 44, 64, 133–4
problem solving 47
procedural knowledge 22
professional development 60, 149–56
progression *see* learning progression
propositional knowledge 21
pupil voice 63–4, 117–18

Q

quality assurance 155–6
questions 24, 45–6, 48
   distant places topic work 106
   fieldwork 37
   and KWL grids 64
   topic work 98
quizzes 121–2

R

rainforests 74–5
reading *see* literacy and numeracy
recordings, video and audio 144
reflection 44, 46, 59, 64, 146, 152
   see also evaluation
religious education (RE) 88–9
resources 151
   essential 119–22
   issues-based topics 108–10
   place-based 106
responsibility and independence 37
rights and responsibilities 15, 63, 91
risk assessments, fieldwork 40
rivers 20, 25, 34, 86, 93, 105
road safety 70
role play and drama 79, 93, 94, 96
Royal Geographical Society 153

S

scale 23, 91, 98, 131
schemes of work 130
school and grounds
   fieldwork 39, 79
   integrating mathematics 82
   topic work 102–3
school community 11
school travel plan 70, 75
science 83–7
Scotland, curriculum 37, 128
seaside *see* coastal areas
secondary school, links and transition 72, 147–9
self-assessment 143–5
senior staff 114

sensory learning 37, 88
settlement 90, 91, 93, 100, 107
signs and symbols 31–3, 34, 142
sketches 37, 95, 110
    see also graphicacy
skills progression 29–40, 99–100
    see also maps and mapwork; weather and climate
social justice 78, 106
social media
  and CPD 155
  and critical thinking 47
  resources 108, 121
software
  digital maps 34, 119–20
  fieldwork 40
sound maps 31, 96
space 23, 98, 131
spatial awareness 102
    see also maps and mapwork
speaking and listening 77–8
    see also drama and role play
speaking and writing 49–50, 77–81
  fieldwork 70, 90
  procedural writing 99
  and subject knowledge 69
  topics 104, 105
    see also vocabulary
stories, cross-curricular links 78–9
subject association support 152–3, 165
subject knowledge, and cross-curricular links 68–9
substantive knowledge 21
sustainability 23, 51–2, 106

T

tables see graphicacy
tally charts 36
teachers
  own subject knowledge 60
  supporting 12–14
  and topic work 99–100
teaching approaches 43–53
  personalising 61–5
teaching assistants 143–4
terminology see vocabulary
tests 141
thematic studies
  cross-curricular links 72, 73–4
    see also specific themes
themes, thematic knowledge 21, 52
topic work 10, 24, 61–2, 98–111, 130
  advantages to pupils of 98
  advantages to teachers of 99–100
  cross-curricular links 63
  drawbacks of 100
  pupil voice 63–4
    see also specific topic headings
tourism and travel 21, 48–9
trade
  ethical and moral questions 89
  Fairtrade 81, 82
trainee teachers 12–14
transition 147–9
travel buddies 73
treasure trails 39

U

United Nations Convention on the Rights of the Child 63

V

value of geography 10–12, 18–19
video and audio recordings 144
vision statements 123–5
vocabulary 34–5, 88, 133, 143–4
volcanoes 107–8
Vygotsky, L. 94

W

Wales, curriculum 37, 56, 128
weather and climate 20, 74, 134
  impacts 25
  measuring 38, 39, 85, 86–7
websites
  Geographical Association 76, 135, 139, 150, 165
  geography blogs 135
  maps 34

for research 85
   Royal Geographical Society 153
   school 108, 117, 126, 135
word glossaries 35
work, the world of 104
writing, procedural 99
   see also speaking and writing

Accessing your online content

To keep you abreast of the more dynamic aspects of primary geography education, we have tried to ensure that the content of this book remains as timeless as possible and have created a password-protected web page where you can find ongoing support, resources and guidance to supplement your geography teaching in the most suitable format over the years to come.

You will find a wealth of support:

- Links will take you direct to information on the GA and other websites to keep you up to date on all things geographical – from curriculum change to CPD opportunities
- Templates and tables that you can use in school will be available to download
- Extended versions of the case studies that illustrate the book will be available to download
- Further reading lists will direct you to further information.

To access the web page, you will need to key in the following URL into the address bar in your browser: www.geography.org.uk/LPG (see Step 1 below). Please note that you cannot get to this page through searching or via the GA website.

You will be asked to enter a password. The unique password for this book is TADT19. Click on the Submit button.

To discover yet more ways in which the Geographical Association can support you, see page 165.

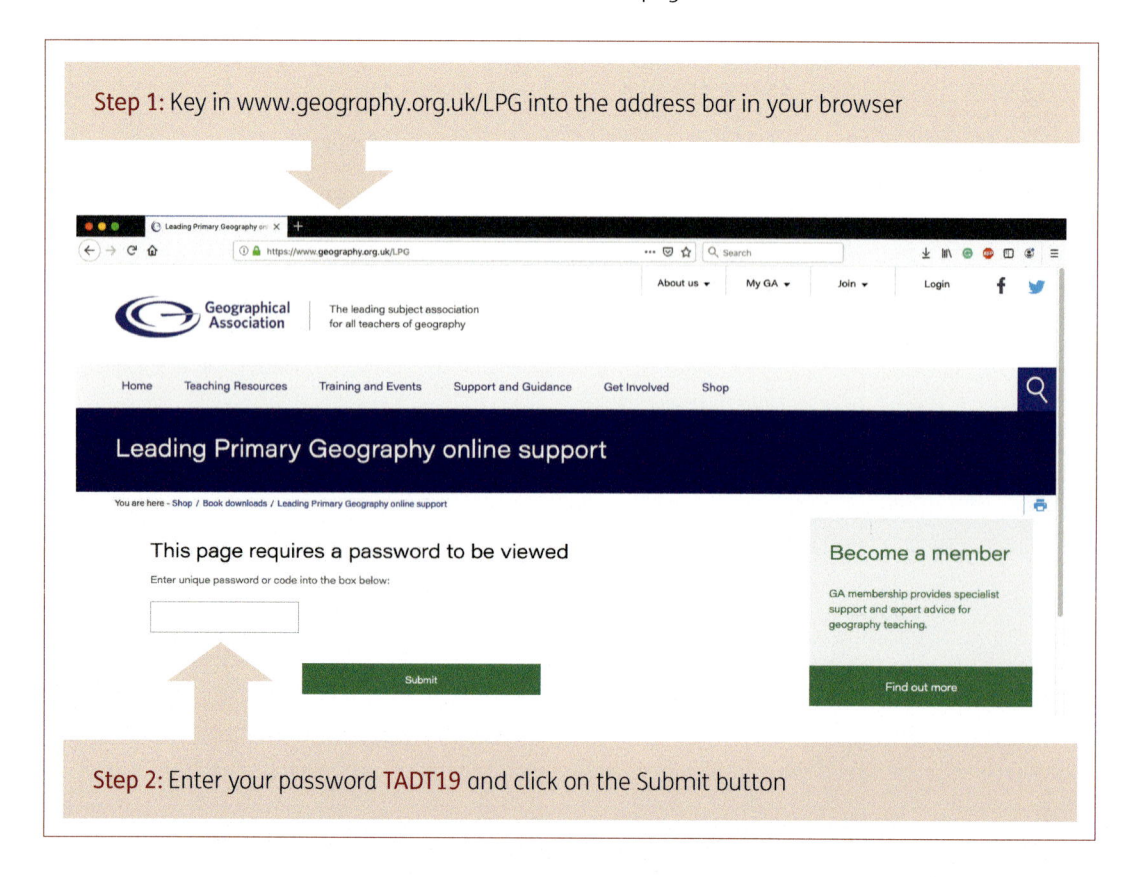

Step 1: Key in www.geography.org.uk/LPG into the address bar in your browser

Step 2: Enter your password TADT19 and click on the Submit button

Your Geographical Association

Geographical Association membership offers you support, guidance and expert advice for teaching geography. Whatever your needs, we are here to meet them with:

- online access to teaching materials and topical resources
- journals packed with practical teaching ideas and professional advice
- latest news about geography, geography teaching and the curriculum
- online and face-to-face networking
- primary update email every half term full of news and ideas
- discounts on attendance fees for the GA Annual Conference
- discounts on our range of in-school and external CPD training courses
- substantial discounts on our extensive range of publications and resources
- discounted bespoke consultancy
- access to the Primary Geography Quality Mark
- funding opportunities for fieldwork, study tours and international linking
- a trusted voice to represent the views of geography teachers and demonstrate the value of geographical education more widely with government and other bodies.

What our members say

'Being a member of the GA means that I am, and genuinely feel, part of a community of like-minded individuals, dedicated to furthering an understanding of the value and importance of geography.'

Justin Woolliscroft

'The GA has underpinned my career in geography education from the beginning. The GA conference, time and time again, has provided opportunities to learn and grow as a geography teacher.'

Grace Healy

'The GA means to me a great community of committed and inspiring geographers and educators who continually inspire and surprise me.'

Juanita Shepherd

To learn more about the GA, or to join thousands of others in our subject community, visit: **www.geography.org.uk**

Contributors

Editor

Tessa Willy is currently co-lead for the primary PGCE programme at UCL-Institute of Education and prior to that was Associate Professor of Teacher Education at Kingston University and a senior lecturer in primary geography at the University of Roehampton. She spent the first years of her career as a primary school teacher in a variety of different settings across the UK and as a secondary school geography teacher in the UK as well as in Malawi. Her areas of particular interest are in issues around the ethics of geography, notably climate change, sustainability, social justice and global citizenship. She is a member of the *Primary Geography* Editorial Board and a member of the GA's Early Years and Primary Phase Committee and Publications Board.

Authors

Steve Rawlinson trained as a physical geographer and developed a more holistic view of the subject while studying for his Master's degree at Aberystwyth. Having gone on to teach every age range from little ones to those entering their third age, he nurtured a passion for fieldwork and outdoor education. As President of the GA 2015–16 his theme of Making Geographical Connections sought to celebrate and explore the links that give geography its dynamism and relevance to the lives of all geography students, whatever their age and ambition. He continues to indulge his passion for the subject as part of the Wildthink moot and as Chair of the *Primary Geography* Editorial Board.

Simon Catling is Emeritus Professor of Primary Education at Oxford Brookes University. He was President of the Geographical Association 1992–93 and remains involved as a member of the GA's Early Years and Primary Phase Committee. He has written widely on primary geography for children (e.g. *Mapstart*), for teachers, including many articles in *Primary Geography* since its inception, and *Understanding and Teaching Primary Geography* (with Tessa Willy, 2018), and for teacher educators and researchers (e.g. *Research and Debate in Primary Geography*, 2015). He has run in-service courses and lectured nationally and internationally for many years. He collects map postcards.

Stephen Pickering is the Course Leader for Primary and Outdoor Education and Senior Lecturer at the University of Worcester. He is a member of the *Primary Geography* Editorial Board and a consultant for the Geographical Association, and has written widely for the Geographical Association as well as being editor of *Teaching Outdoors Creatively* (2017) and contributing chapters for *Teaching Geography Creatively* (2013, 2nd ed 2017) and *Learning to Teach in the Primary School* (2018). Stephen is a qualified Forest School leader and Earth Education leader. His research interests include learning and teaching outdoors, the global dimension, literature as a vehicle for learning, and all things geographical!

Richard Hatwood is an Inclusion Officer at Denbighshire County Council and Consultant to the Geographical Association. He qualified at Bangor University in 2010 with a degree in Primary Education. After graduating, Richard taught at a Junior School in St Asaph for eight years and was the Humanities Subject Leader. He supported the development of, and piloted, the Welsh Primary Geography Quality Mark and is currently a member of the National Moderation Panel. In addition, Richard is a member of the *Primary Geography* Journal Editorial Board and a Trustee of the Geographical Association.

Richard Greenwood is a Senior Lecturer in Primary Education at Stranmillis University College in Belfast. Since 1990 he has taught on the B.Ed. Primary programme as well as the PGCE (Early Years) and Master's modules. His main areas of interest are the teaching of geography in primary schools, outdoor learning, ICT and preparation of students for school placements. He has published and presented at conferences on thematic approaches to teaching in primary schools. Recent work has included papers on cross-curricular approaches, 'playful' approaches to outdoor learning, and the use of KWL grids as an example of pupil involvement in planning.

Leszek Iwaskow taught for 22 years, in both primary and secondary schools. He was a chief examiner for GCSE geography and worked with QCA on both curriculum and examination specification revue. As a local government adviser he had responsibility for the full range of humanities and special responsibility for school improvement and supporting schools causing concern. He was an HMI and National Adviser for Geography from 2001 until retirement in 2016, during which he also worked with DfE, including on various National Curriculum revisions. Leszek currently supports a number of schools as an educational consultant and provides support and advice on geography nationally as a consultant for the Geographical Association.

Julia Tanner is an education consultant, specialising in primary humanities and children's emotional wellbeing and mental health. She is editor of *The Everyday Guide to Primary Geography* series, and a member of the GA's Early Years and Primary Phase Committee and Publications Board.

Ben Ballin is a consultant to the GA, a member of the *Primary Geography* Editorial Board and leads primary geography networks for Shropshire and Staffordshire. Among his many publications and articles on geography, sustainability and global learning, he authored the GA *SuperSchemes: Investigating World Trade*. With Alf Wilkinson, he writes teaching materials and leads training on integrated approaches to geography and history. A former special school teacher in Kenya, Ben is a fellow of the National Association for Environmental Education (UK), a co-opted trustee for the teachers' network Tide~ global learning, and a consultant to Big Brum Theatre in Education.

Susan Pike is a Lecturer in Geography Education at the DCU Institute of Education, Ireland. Susan is Senior Vice President (2019–20) of the Geographical Association, and a member of the GA's Early Years and Primary Phase Committee. She is an active member of a number of DCU centres, including the Centre for Human Rights and Citizenship, Disadvantage Centre and Water Institute. Susan's research interests span education in schools, teacher education and communities, specifically learning in geography, environmental education.

Paula Owens has been a primary class teacher, a geography subject leader, a deputy and acting Head teacher. She piloted the PGQM, with her school achieving Gold in 2006. As an independent consultant, Paula works with LESSCO2 schools, the RGS, OS Digimap for Schools, BBC CBeebies, and the GA, where she was Primary Curriculum Leader for ten years. Paula is a member of the GA's *Primary Geography* Editorial Board and Early Years and Primary Phase Committee, a Visiting Senior Research Fellow at Canterbury Christ Church University and part of the Meaningful Maps research team.